G000129756

Part 1

Introduction

Shakespeare's Life

"He was not of an age, but for all time"   (Ben Jonson)

Birth and Parentage

"Sweet Swan of Avon"   (Ben Jonson)

William Shakespeare was born in 1564 in Stratford-upon-Avon. He was the third and eldest surviving child of John Shakespeare and Mary Arden. He had three younger brothers and two sisters. John Shakespeare was a glove-maker by trade and also a successful general agricultural merchant. He rose high in the municipal life of Stratford and was elected a constable, became a chamberlain, an alderman and a bailif.

There is no record of William Shakespeare's schooling. It is assumed that he attended the grammar school like the sons of other important townsmen in Stratford. However, John Shakespeare fell into debt, his wife's estate was mortgaged and William was taken out of school to work. There is practically no information about William Shakespeare's life during the five years after he left school.

Marriage and Early Career

"For a good poet's made, as well as born"   (Ben Jonson)

In 1582, at the age of eighteen, William Shakespeare married Ann Hathaway who was eight years older than him. His daughter Susanna was born six months later and twins Judith and Hamnet were born in 1585. The period 1585–1592 is known as the "lost years". Little is known about his departure from Stratford-upon-Avon. There is a popular legend that he had to leave because he had made a powerful enemy of Sir Thomas Lucy of Charlecote for poaching from his land. There are other claims that he became a school master. One way or another the next six years of his life are unrecorded, but in 1592 he already had a reputation as an actor and playwright in London. Robert Greene referred to him in his work *Groatsworth of Witte*, as *"...bought with a Million of Repetance (Repetition)..."* as *"...an upstart Crow..."* who *"...supposes he is as well able to bombast out a blanke verse as the best of you: and being an absolute Johannes fac totum, is in his owne conceit the onely Shakes-scene in a countrey"*. It is thought that Shakespeare began his career as a writer by adapting and re-writing plays by other authors.

Player and Playwright

"Soul of the age, The applause, delight, the wonder of our stage"   *(Ben Jonson)*

Shakespeare wrote several historical plays and comedies between 1588 and 1594. *Romeo and Juliet* in 1594 was his first tragedy. In 1594 he joined the Lord Chamberlain's Company of actors. In 1599 the Lord Chamberlain's Company moved to the Globe Theatre which was owned by the actors and in which Shakespeare had a one-tenth share. By 1598 he was recognized as the greatest English dramatist. In 1603, his company became the King's Majesty Players, known as The King's Men, and came under royal patronage.

Between 1601 and 1608 Shakespeare wrote his greatest tragedies as well as several comedies. In a period of just over twenty years he wrote thirty-seven plays as well as many sonnets and poems. One of his patrons was the Earl of Southhampton to whom many of his sonnets are addressed.

Death

"We wonder'd, SHAKESPEARE, that thou went'st so soon
From the world's stage to the grave's tiring-room"   *(I.M.)*

The Tempest was the last play Shakespeare wrote in 1611 and sometime after that he retired to Stratford-upon-Avon. He died five years later, at the age of fifty-two, on April 23rd, 1616.

The Folio

"SHAKESPEARE, at length thy pious fellows give
The world thy works"   *(L. Digges)*

Shakespeare's plays were collected by two of his fellow actors, John Heminge and Henry Condell, and in 1623 the first Folio edition of Shakespeare's work contained plays which had never been printed before. The other nineteen had already appeared separately as quarto volumes. No play in Shakespeare's handwriting is known to exist and it does not appear as if he himself supervised the publication of his plays. Like the quartos, the Folio is full of printers' and other mistakes and for centuries editors have wrangled over the correct interpretation of the quartos and Folio texts. However, in the words of Ben Jonson, Shakespeare is:

"...alive still, while thy book doth live,
And we have wits to read, and praise to give."

*Quotations from Ben Jonson, I.M. and L. Digges taken from the Prefatory Verses from the First Folio.

The Elizabethan Theatre

The stage conditions for which a play was written could affect the methods employed in the play. Shakespeare's plays were designed for performance in the Elizabethan theatre. One source of information regarding the structure of Elizabethan theatres is the copy made by De Witt's friend of his drawing in 1596 of the Swan Theatre. A second source is the contract for the Fortune Theatre which gave exact specifications for the theatre which, although square in shape, was to be modelled on the Globe.

The theatres of Shakespeare's day were high, either round, octagonal or square in shape and the stage could be seen from all sides. The interior of the theatre was generally circular and exposed to the open sky. In this open pit audiences had to stand. Three tiers of galleries were around the inside wall with seats for those prepared to pay more and this was roofed. The stage projected out into the pit. Above the stage, against the back wall, the middle gallery served as a kind of balcony overlooking the stage. A canopy stretched forward high above the stage supported by pillars. These pillars divided the stage into two parts – the front part projecting into the pit. At the back of the second part of the stage was a recess known as the *"rere"* or *"inner"* stage. On either side of this inner stage were dressing rooms. Thus there were four distinct parts to the stage which could be utilized – the front stage, the middle stage where most of the action took place, the rear stage and the upper stage. In *Macbeth*, the upper stage was probably used for Duncan's chamber and for the hanging out of the banners in Act 5, Scene V. Curtains were sometimes drawn across the inner stage to separate it but there was no drop curtain.

The construction of the plays was influenced by the stage arrangements. Because the actors were surrounded by the audience this facilitated frequent asides and soliloquies. The actor simply came forward to the front of the stage, out of earshot of the other characters, and revealed what was going on in his mind to the audience. Macbeth speaks some of his soliloquies for the benefit of the audience; in others he speaks to himself rather than the audience. There were few props and no elaborate scenery. This gave the playwright greater freedom in the number of scenes he could introduce, unhampered by any inconvenience of changing scenery. There are eight scenes in the final act of *Macbeth*. Many of the scenes are very short and occur in quick succession because there are no interruptions or delays. Information as to where things were happening, the time of year, time of day, the weather, had to be given verbally. Scenery was conveyed through language. The scene of Macbeth's castle is suggested through the words of Duncan:

> *"This castle hath a pleasant seat; the air*
> *Nimbly and sweetly recommends itself*
> *Unto our gentle senses."*   *(Act 1, Scene VI)*

This descriptive poetry serves a dramatic purpose.

The chorus in *King Henry V* called the stage "*an unworthy scaffold*" and advised the audience:

> *"Piece out our imperfections with your thoughts...*
> *Think when we talk of horses that you see them*
> *Printing their proud hoofs i' the receiving earth;*
> *For 'tis your thoughts that now must deck our kings,*
> *Carry them here and there, jumping o'er times,*
> *Turning the accomplishment of many years*
> *Into an hour-glass:"*

Here Shakespeare directly tells the audience to use their imagination and he thereby dispenses with the dramatic limitations of the stage.

Nevertheless, although there were few props, there was plenty of spectacle onstage. In *Macbeth,* the stage directions call for "*drum and colours*". The plays took place in the afternoon and so the action was presumed to be taking place in daytime unless night was mentioned directly. Reference was made to torches, candles, as in *Macbeth,* to emphasise the darkness.

In Elizabethan drama the emphasis was placed on the delivery of the speeches rather than on staging techniques. Stage management intruded very little on the play.

Elizabethan English

There are many points of difference in grammar, syntax and meaning between Elizabethan English and modern English usage. What may now be considered as bad grammar was the accepted form of the language in Shakespeare's time. It was characteristic of Elizabethan writers to use one part of speech in the place of another. Adjectives could be used as nouns, *"The blanket of the dark"*; as adverbs, *"Things bad begun make strong themselves by ill"* and it was quite common for adjectives to follow the noun, *"I have seen hours dreadful and things strange"*. Likewise adverbs tended to be placed where they gave most emphasis, *"No more that Thane of Cawdor shall deceive"*. A noun could be used as an adverb, *"We doubt it nothing"*, as an adjective, *"you secret, black, and mid-night hags!"* or as a verb *"to dew the sovereign flower"*. Shakespeare frequently used abstract nouns in the plural, *"Revenges burn in them"*. The Elizabethans tended to drop the endings of the past participle, *"I have spoke"*. Shall and should were frequently used instead of will and would giving a different meaning to the sentence, *"they should find/What 'twere to kill a father; so should Fleance"*. Here should does not mean ought but would.

In order to give greater emphasis a double comparative, considered quite incorrect in modern speech, was used in Elizabethan English, *"others that lesser hate him"*. Likewise double negatives reinforced meaning, *"Tongue nor heart/Cannot conceive nor name thee."* Other grammatical discrepancies include the use of which for who, *"I have known those which have walked in their sleep"*, the use of who for abstract nouns, *"My thought, whose murder yet is but fantastical,"* and the use of his for its, *"Treason has done his worst"*.

The Elizabethan use of prepositions can cause some confusion to the modern reader – *"of (with) kerns and gallowglasses so supplied"*, *"tugg'd with (by) fortune"*, *"from (on account of) broad words"*, *"Forced (reinforced) with (by) those that should be ours"*. Difficulties in syntax are mostly due to the Elizabethan tendency to leave out articles, conjunctions, relative pronouns and even verbs. *"As if it yelled out like (a) syllable of dolour"*, *"never/Shall (the) sun that morrow see"*. The conjunction if is often omitted, *"go not my horse the better, I/I must become a borrower of the night"*. So is often omitted, *"The victory fell on us.... That now/Sweno, the Norway's king, craves composition;"*. Sometimes the omission of a relative pronoun makes very little difference *"There's one did laugh in his sleep"*, but sometimes it distorts the meaning, *"And the very ports (on which) they blow"*. Verbs are sometimes omitted but mostly in the imperative mood *"Therefore to horse"*.

Students of Shakespeare should not be put off by the unfamiliarity of syntax. It is simply a different arrangement of words and usually the meaning is quite clear.

Tragedy

Most discussions of tragedy start from Aristotle's assumption that the best tragedy concerns a man who does a deed of horror in ignorance. Macbeth indeed performs a deed of horror, but not in ignorance. He clearly foresees the consequences of his act.

No one tragedy fits perfectly any one definition of it, but the conventions of tragedy require certain tragic elements. A play is not a tragedy simply because it depicts death or suffering. Aristotle considered tragedy to be the fall of princes. Generally, Shakespeare's tragic hero is a man of high degree. Macbeth is a thane and becomes a king. In Greek and Classical tragedy, Fate is usually the cause of the catastrophe and the play portrays the hero's struggle against Fate. Since Fate is preordained, it was a useless struggle ending in the inevitable destruction of the tragic hero. In Classical tragedy the tragic hero is constrained by the gods, by circumstances beyond his control, to act in a certain way. Although Shakespeare introduces a supernatural element into his tragedies, the supernatural is not made responsible for the hero's actions and Macbeth is prepared to even challenge destiny:

> *"...come, Fate into the list,*
> *And champion me to th' utterance!"*   *(Act 3, Scene I)*

In Shakespearian tragedy evil is the cause of the catastrophe. Shakespeare conceived of tragedy as the struggle between good and evil in the world. The tragic hero illustrates the fickleness of fortune, but the hero's own actions and character are responsible for his destruction. There is a feeling of a presiding ultimate power for good and the tragedy always ends on a note of reconciliation.

Generally Shakespeare's heroes possess definite characteristics. The Shakespearian tragic hero is always a man of exceptional nature, a great man with a more powerful consciousness, deeper emotions and a more splendid imagination than ordinary men. He is a sensitive being with a spiritual bias. He has a divided soul, he is torn by an internal struggle. However, the tragic hero in Shakespeare's tragedies has some weakness, some flaw which contributes to his downfall. Aristotle called this internal weakness of the hero the *"hamertia"*, the tragic flaw, an essential element in tragedy. Macbeth's tragic flaw is his ambition. He succumbs to this powerful failing in his nature and is destroyed by it. His ambition pushes him into a sequence of actions which inevitably leads to his death. Macbeth attempts the impossible, to usurp the lawful king, and because the means he employs are evil and against the natural law, the inevitable consequences of his action work themselves out and the result is tragedy.

Aristotle's criterion of good tragedy was that the spectator should experience *"catharsis"*, that is, pity and terror for the tragic hero. According to him catharsis elevated the mind and purified the emotions. The sensitive, conscience-stricken, tortured Macbeth inspires pity, and the tyrannical Macbeth, *"in blood stepp'd in so far"*, inspires terror. A problem arises in Macbeth because the spectator must desire the defeat of Macbeth and yet his suffering compels sympathy. However Shakespeare carefully balances sympathy for Macbeth with the recognition of the desirability of the destruction of evil and the triumph of good.

Tragedy shows man in unsuccessful conflict with circumstances. Although modern tragedy is very different from Classical tragedy or Shakespearian tragedy, the element of conflict is still the essence of tragedy.

Preface

This book consists of three parts.

Part 1 begins with background information and includes a brief outline of Shakespeare's life, a note on Elizabethan theatre and Shakespearian English. This section also includes an outline of the principle elements of tragedy so that the student may appreciate *Macbeth* in the wider context of tragedy as a dramatic genre.

Part 2 is a scene by scene study of the text itself. Each scene contains annotations on the difficult vocabulary, expressions or lines, plus notes on the dramatic significance of the scene and a commentary on the characters. Questions are suggested as aids to study to reinforce the student's understanding and appreciation of each scene. At the end of each act there is a suggested revision scheme. The strands of the plot are drawn together in a very brief summary, essential points before proceeding to the next scene are highlighted and there is an assignment which demands a step by step revision of the main points of the plot. This ensures that the student has a clear grasp of one act before going on to the next.

Part 3 is designed for further study after the play has become familiar to the student. It deals with such aspects as Theme, Language, and offers a further study of Macbeth and Lady Macbeth. Extra questions and essays are given after this section to encourage students to a more in-depth study of the play as a whole.

A glossary of dramatic terms is included so the students may become familiar with the important terms of criticism in the study of drama. For Higher Level students who may be interested in more extensive reading, the suggested reading list is a helpful guide.

This book is dedicated to the memory of my father, Matthew Deegan, who loved Shakespeare.

Anne Deegan

Part 2

Text and Scene Analysis

Characters

Duncan	King of Scotland
Malcolm }	his sons
Donalbain	
Macbeth }	Generals of the King's army
Banquo	
Macduff	
Lennox	
Ross	
Menteith	Noblemen of Scotland
Angus	
Caithness	
Fleance	Son to Banquo
Siward	Earl of Northumberland, General of the English forces
Young Siward	his son
Seyton	an officer attending on Macbeth
A Boy	Son to Macduff
A Sergeant	
A Porter	
An Old Man	
An English Doctor	
A Scottish Doctor	
Three Murderers	
Lady Macbeth	
Lady Macduff	
A Gentlewoman	attending on Lady Macbeth
Three Witches	
Hecate	
Apparitions	
Lords, Gentlemen, Officers, Soldiers, Attendants, and Messengers	

Act 1
Scene I

A desert heath.

(Sense of Forboding)

Thunder and lightning. Enter three witches.

1st Witch	When shall we three meet again
	In thunder, lightning, or in rain?
2nd Witch	When the hurlyburly's¹ done,
	When the battle's lost and won.
3rd Witch	That will be ere² the set of sun.
1st Witch	Where the place?
2nd Witch	Upon the heath.
3rd Witch	There to meet with Macbeth.
1st Witch	I come, Graymalkin!³
2nd Witch	Paddock⁴ calls.
3rd Witch	Anon.⁵
All	Fair is foul, and foul is fair:
	Hover through the fog and filthy air.

pathetic fallacy: where nature is used by an author to convey a mood

storm

noise and confusion

10

¹noise and confusion
²before
³grey cat; a supposed Satanic spirit in animal form
⁴toad; another witches' spirit
⁵coming at once

before
hill
supernatural
at once
(L)

[Exeunt.

Scene Analysis

There is a sense of upheaval at the outset of the play. The witches have prophetic powers

Scene 1 is short and spectacular and establishes the threatening and ominous atmosphere of the play. Against the background of thunder and lightning, fog and filthy air, three witches who refer to a *"battle lost and won"* plan to meet later on the heath to greet Macbeth.

Shakespeare was writing for an audience that believed in the formidable powers of witchcraft. Disturbances in the heavens were considered to indicate upheaval and strife and the presence of evil. The question of the first witch:

> *"When shall we three meet again*
> *In thunder, lightning, or in rain?"*

establishes the extent of the witches' powers. They can control the elements at will. The witches speak in riddles:

> *"When the hurlyburly's done,*
> *When the battle's lost and won."*

and there is evidence of their prophetic powers in the third witch's statement:

> *"That will be ere the set of sun."*

The witches here predetermine their meeting with Macbeth. The short scene ends with the ominous chant:

> *"Fair is foul, and foul is fair:*
> *Hover through the fog and filthy air."*

This sets the key note of the play – the confusion between good and evil, appearance and reality and the complete reversal of values. Thus the themes of the play are given dramatic expression through the ambiguous incantation of the witches. The scene also arouses interest in Macbeth, suspense about the battle and doubt about the intentions of the witches.

CHARACTERS
THE WITCHES

The witches are servants of evil. The grey cat to which the first witch calls was commonly thought to be a spirit of Satan in the shape of a cat. The second witch is attended by a toad, also associated with witchcraft. The rhyme in which they speak gives a sense of incantation. Their chant is a calling upon evil to reverse the concepts of good and bad. The witches, the thunder and lightning, the reference to the *"hurlyburly"*, the calling out to *Graymalkin* and *Paddock,* create a sinister atmosphere.

EXERCISES

1. Discuss the effect of the appearance of the witches in the opening scene.
2. What do you understand by the riddle *"Fair is foul, and foul is fair"*?
3. *Scene 1* is very short. Would it have made any difference if it had been omitted altogether?

Scene II

A Camp near Forres.
Alarum[1] within.

Enter King Duncan, Malcolm, Donalbain, Lennox, with Attendants, meeting a bleeding Sergeant.

Duncan	What bloody[2] man is that? He can report, As seemeth by his plight[3], of the revolt The newest state[4].
Malcolm	This is the sergeant Who like a good and hardy soldier fought 'Gainst my captivity.[5] Hail, brave friend! Say to the King the knowledge of the broil[6] As thou didst leave it.
Sergeant	Doubtful it stood, As two spent[7] swimmers that do cling together And choke their art.[8] The merciless Macdonwald –

Margin notes:
[1] trumpet blast
[2] covered in blood
[3] condition
[4] latest news
[5] to prevent my captivity
[6] brawl, i.e. battle
[7] exhausted
[8] hinder their skill

Worthy to be a rebel, for to that   *10*
The multiplying villanies of nature[9]
Do swarm upon him — from the Western Isles
Of kerns and gallowglasses[10] is supplied;
And Fortune, on his damned quarrel smiling,
Show'd like a rebel's whore;[11] but all's too weak,
For brave Macbeth, — well he deserves that
    name, —
Disdaining Fortune, with his brandish'd[12] steel,
Which smok'd with bloody execution[13],
Like valour's minion,[14] carv'd out his passage
Till he fac'd the slave;   *20*
Which ne'er shook hands, nor bade farewell to
    him,
Till he unseam'd him from the nave to the
    chaps[15],
And fix'd his head upon our battlements.

Duncan O valiant cousin! worthy gentleman!

Sergeant As whence the sun 'gins[16] his reflection
Shipwracking storms and direful[17] thunders
    break,
So from that spring whence comfort seem'd to
    come
Discomfort swells. Mark, King of Scotland, mark:
No sooner justice had with valour arm'd
Compell'd these skipping kerns to trust their
    heels,   *30*
But the Norweyan lord,[18] surveying vantage,[19]
With furbish'd arms[20] and new supplies of men
Began a fresh assault .

Duncan   Dismay'd not this
Our captains, Macbeth and Banquo?

Sergeant   Yes;
As sparrows eagles, or the hare the lion.
If I say sooth,[21] I must report they were
As cannons overcharg'd with double cracks;[22]
So they doubly redoubled strokes upon the foe:
Except[23] they meant to bathe in reeking wounds,
Or memorize another Golgotha,[24]   *40*
I cannot tell —
But I am faint, my gashes cry for help.

Duncan So well thy words become thee as thy wounds;
They smack of honour both. Go, get him
    surgeons.

[*Exit Sergeant, attended.*

---

[9] the increasing evils of his nature

[10] light and heavy armed Irish footsoldiers

[11] fortune prostituted herself for Macdonwald

[12] flourished
[13] steamed with the blood of killed enemies
[14] courage's favoured one

[15] cut open from his navel to his jaws

[16] begins
[17] terrible

[18] Norwegian lord
[19] seeing his advantage
[20] unused

[21] truth
[22] double charges of powder

[23] whether
[24] as memorable as Golgotha – 'place of the skull' in the scriptures

Enter Ross.

	Who comes here?
Malcolm	The worthy Thane²⁵ of Ross.
Lennox	What a haste looks through his eyes!
	So should he look that seems²⁶ to speak things
	strange.
Ross	God save the King!
Duncan	Whence cam'st thou, worthy Thane?
Ross	From Fife, great King;
	Where the Norweyan banners flout the sky 50
	And fan our people cold.
	Norway himself, with terrible numbers,
	Assisted by that most disloyal traitor,
	The Thane of Cawdor, began a dismal conflict;
	Till that Bellona' s bridegroom,²⁷ lapp'd in
	proof,²⁸
	Confronted him with self-comparisons,²⁹
	Point against point, rebellious arm 'gainst arm,
	Curbing his lavish³⁰ spirit: and, to conclude,
	The victory fell on us. —
Duncan	Great happiness! 60
Ross	That now
	Sweno, the Norways' king, craves composition;³¹
	Nor would we deign³² him burial of his men
	Till he disbursed,³³ at Saint Colme's Inch,³⁴
	Ten thousand dollars³⁵ to our general use.
Duncan	No more that Thane of Cawdor shall deceive
	Our bosom interest.³⁶ Go pronounce his present
	death,
	And with his former title greet Macbeth.
Ross	I'll see it done.
Duncan	What he hath lost, noble Macbeth hath won.
	[Exeunt.

Margin notes:

²⁵ Scottish title (= Earl)

²⁶ who looks as if about to

²⁷ Macbeth is seen as the bridegroom of the Roman goddess of war
²⁸ clad in armour tested for strength
²⁹ an equal match
³⁰ wild

³¹ peace terms
³² condescend
³³ paid
³⁴ a small island on which there is an abbey dedicated to St. Columbcille
³⁵ a silver coin used in the reign of Elizabeth I
³⁶ intimate friendship

Scene Analysis

The disturbed atmosphere of the first scene continues in the second scene where we have a description of battle, bloodshed and treachery.

A sergeant, wounded and bleeding, gives an account of the battle referred to briefly in the first scene. In the light of the evil threat of *Scene I*, suspense is sharpened by the dramatic entry of a "*bloody man*". This is the first of many references to blood throughout the play and indeed the sergeant's description of the battle is very violent.

This is the sergeant
Who like a good and hardy soldier fought
'Gainst my captivity.

(Malcolm, Act 1, Scene II)

Three separate battles are referred to in this scene. Macdonwald with rebel forces has fought against the king, a local lord of Norway has attacked near Forres and King Sweno, king of Denmark and Norway, has taken advantage of the internal conflict to invade the country. This foreign invasion is due to the treachery of the Thane of Cawdor. The speech of the sergeant testifies to Macbeth's fearlessness and success in battle. Macbeth is presented as the saviour of the realm. With vigour and violence he has defeated all three attackers.

Duncan echoes the witches' phrase "*lost and won*" when he says:

> *"What he hath lost, noble Macbeth hath won."*

This makes us wonder again about the witches' involvement with Macbeth.

CHARACTERS
DUNCAN
Duncan seems somewhat ineffective as a king. When we first meet him, he is not with his army but awaiting a report on the outcome of the battle. It seems that Duncan is unable to control the insurrections breaking out in his kingdom. Certainly the rebellions are evidence that he rules a troubled land. He is generous in his praise of the bravery of Macbeth:

> *"O valiant cousin! worthy gentleman!"*

MALCOLM
Malcolm, eldest son of Duncan, must be introduced at this early stage of the play as he has a crucial part in the plot. We learn a little about his character at this point.

His first speech suggests a generous nature as he introduces to his father (the king) the sergeant who bravely defended him. He greets him:

> *"Hail, brave friend!"*

and praises this man:

> *"Who like a good and hardy soldier fought*
> *'Gainst my captivity."*

THE SERGEANT
He is described by Malcolm as:

> *"a good and hardy soldier"*

He gives a graphic description of the battle and seems to relish the *"bloody execution"*. He does not confine himself to informing the king of the outcome of the battle but comments freely on the participants. Macdonwald is, in his opinion, *"Worthy to be a rebel"* and brave Macbeth:

> *"...well he deserves that name"*

His speech is bombastic and he makes much use of simile for added effect. Fortune *"Show'd like a rebel's whore"*. He conveys the shock of the second battle by stating:

> *"As whence the sun 'gins his reflection*
> *Shipwracking storms and direful thunders break,*
> *So from that spring whence comfort seem'd to come*
> *Discomfort swells."*

Having received the praise of his king, he leaves to obtain help for his wounds.

ROSS, ANGUS & LENNOX

Their characters are not developed in this scene, they are simply introduced. They represent those who are loyal to their king and country. Malcolm greets Ross as *"The worthy Thane of Ross"* and it is Ross who continues the account of the battle. He is one of the chief news bearers and commentators on the action in the play. Ross is charged by the king to pronounce the death of the Thane of Cawdor and to greet Macbeth with the title.

MACBETH

Our first impression of Macbeth is of a loyal, brave and much respected soldier:

> *"...brave Macbeth"*
> *"...Bellona's bridegroom"*
> *"...noble Macbeth"*

He is the commander of Duncan's forces and fights his way fearlessly to victory. He is presented to us as a man of great daring and courage.

EXERCISES

1. What do we learn of the state of Scotland from the second scene of the play?

2. Is the description of the battles dramatically effective?

3. What are your impressions of Macbeth from the descriptions given in this scene?

4. Explain in your own words:

> *"As whence the sun 'gins his reflection*
> *Shipwracking storms and direful thunders break,*
> *So from that spring whence comfort seem'd to come*
> *Discomfort swells."*

Scene III

A Heath.

Thunder. Enter the three Witches.

1st Witch	Where hast thou been, sister?
2nd Witch	Killing swine. Pigs
3rd Witch	Sister, where thou?
1st Witch	A sailor's wife had chestnuts in her lap,
	And munch'd, and munch'd, and munch'd:
	'Give me,' quoth I:
	'Aroint thee[1], witch!' the rump-fed ronyon[2] cries.
	Her husband's to Aleppo[3] gone, master o' th'
	Tiger:
	But in a sieve I'll thither sail,
	And, like[4] a rat without a tail,
	I'll do, I'll do, and I'll do.
2nd Witch	I'll give thee a wind.
1st Witch	Th'art kind.
3rd Witch	And I another.
1st Witch	I myself have all the other;
	And the very ports[5] they blow,
	All the quarters that they know
	I' th' shipman's card.[6]
	I'll drain him dry as hay:
	Sleep shall neither night nor day
	Hang upon his pent-house lid;[7]
	He shall live a man forbid.[8]
	Weary se'n nights, nine times nine
	Shall he dwindle, peak[9] and pine:
	Though his bark[10] cannot be lost,
	Yet it shall be tempest-tost.
	Look what I have.
2nd Witch	Show me, show me.
1st Witch	Here I have a pilot's thumb,
	Wrack'd as homeward he did come.
	[Drum within.
3rd Witch	A drum! A drum!
	Macbeth doth come.
All	The Weird Sisters, hand in hand,
	Posters[11] of the sea and land,
	Thus do go about, about:
	Thrice[12] to thine, and thrice to mine,
	And thrice again, to make up nine.
	Peace! the charm's wound up.[13]

Line numbers: 10, 20, 30

[1] be off
[2] scabby creature fed on rump meat
[3] old city of Northern Syria
[4] in the form of

[5] The witch can make the ports inaccessible by controlling the winds
[6] directions on sailor's compass card

[7] compares the eyelid to the sloping roof of a penthouse probably because his eyelid is drooping in weariness
[8] cursed
[9] waste away
[10] three masted ship

[11] travelling post haste

[12] they circle three times for each of them

[13] completed

Theatrical device to linking Macbeth to the witches

Enter Macbeth and Banquo.

cannot see the witches

Macbeth	So foul and fair a day I have not seen.
Banquo	How far is't call'd to Forres? What are these, *40*

Saw the witches first

So wither'd, and so wild in their attire,
That look not like th' inhabitants o' th' earth,
And yet are on't? Live you? or are you aught[14]

not to be trusted

[14]anything

That man may question? You seem to
  understand me,
By each at once her choppy[15] finger laying
Upon her skinny lips: you should be women,
And yet your beards forbid me to interpret
That you are so.

[15]chapped

Macbeth	Speak, if you can: what are you?
1st Witch	All hail, Macbeth! Hail to thee, Thane of Glamis! *50*
2nd Witch	All hail, Macbeth! Hail to thee, Thane of Cawdor!
3rd Witch	All hail, Macbeth! that shalt be king hereafter.
Banquo	Good sir, why do you start, and seem to fear

Things that do sound so fair? I' the name of
  truth,
Are ye fantastical,[16] or that indeed
Which outwardly ye show? My noble partner
You greet with present grace[17] and great
  prediction
Of noble having[18] and of royal hope,[19]
That he seems rapt withal:[20] to me you speak
      not.
If you can look into the seeds of time,[21]   *60*
And say which grain will grow and which will not,
Speak then to me, who neither beg nor fear
Your favours nor your hate.

[16]imaginary (a product of fantasy)

[17]Macbeth already holds the title of Thane of Glamis
[18]having the title of Thane of Cawdor
[19]hope of royalty
[20]completely absorbed
[21]the future

1st Witch	Hail!
2nd Witch	Hail!
3rd Witch	Hail!
1st Witch	Lesser than Macbeth, and greater.
2nd Witch	Not so happy, yet much happier.
3rd Witch	Thou shalt get[22] kings, though thou be none: So, all hail, Macbeth and Banquo! *70*
1st Witch	Banquo and Macbeth, all hail!
Macbeth	Stay, you imperfect[23] speakers, tell me more:

you will be the father of kings

[22]be the father of

[23]vague
[24]Macbeth's father

By Sinel's[24] death I know I am Thane of Glamis;
But how of Cawdor? The Thane of Cawdor lives,
A prosperous gentleman; and to be king
Stands not within the prospect of belief
No more than to be Cawdor. Say, from whence

You owe this strange intelligence? or why
Upon this blasted[25] heath you stop our way
With such prophetic greeting? Speak, I charge[26]
   you. — *demanding*   80

                         [Witches vanish.

Banquo   The earth hath bubbles, as the water has,
And these are of them. Whither are they
   vanish'd?

Macbeth   Into the air, and what seem'd corporal[27] melted
As breath into the wind. Would they had stay'd!

Banquo   Were such things here as we do speak about?
Or have we eaten on the insane root[28]
That takes the reason prisoner?

Macbeth   Your children shall be kings.

Banquo   You shall be King.

Macbeth   And Thane of Cawdor too; went it not so?

Banquo   To th' self-same tune and words. Who's here? 90

       Enter Ross and Angus.

Ross   The King hath happily receiv'd, Macbeth,
The news of thy success; and when he reads
Thy personal venture in the rebels' fight,
His wonders and his praises do contend[29]
Which should be thine or his. Silenc'd with that,
In viewing o'er the rest o' the self-same day,
He finds thee in the stout Norweyan ranks,
Nothing afeard of what thyself didst make,
Strange images of death. As thick as hail
Came post with post,[30] and every one did bear 100
Thy praises in his kingdom's great defence,
And pour'd them down before him.

Angus   We are sent
To give thee from our royal master, thanks;
Only to herald[31] thee into his sight,
Not pay thee.

Ross   And, for an earnest[32] of a greater honour,
He bade me, from him, call thee Thane of
   Cawdor:
In which addition,[33] hail, most worthy Thane!
For it is thine.

Banquo   What! can the devil speak true?

Macbeth   The Thane of Cawdor lives: why do you dress
   me   110
In borrow'd robes?

---

25 desolate
26 order
27 bodily
28 the root of the hemlock plant, believed to cause madness if eaten
29 The king is torn between wonder of the deed and praise of Macbeth
30 one messenger after another
31 lead with honour
32 assurance
33 title

Angus	Who was the Thane lives yet;
	But under heavy judgement bears that life
	Which he deserves to lose. Whether he was combin'd[34]
	With those of Norway, or did line[35] the rebel
	With hidden help or vantage, or that with both[36]
	He labour'd in his country's wrack,[37] I know not;
	But treasons capital,[38] confess'd and prov'd,
	Have overthrown him.
Macbeth	Glamis, and Thane of Cawdor:
	[Aside] The greatest is behind.[39] 120
	[To Ross and Angus] Thanks for your pains.
	[To Banquo] Do you not hope your children shall be kings,
	When those that gave the Thane of Cawdor to me
	Promis'd no less to them?
Banquo	[Aside to Macbeth] That, trusted home,[40]
	Might yet enkindle you unto the crown.[41]
	Besides the Thane of Cawdor. But 'tis strange:
	And oftentimes, to win us to our harm,
	The instruments of darkness tell us truths,
	Win us with honest trifles,[42] to betray's 130
	In deepest consequence.[43]
	Cousins, a word, I pray you.
Macbeth	[Aside] Two truths are told,
	As happy prologues[44] to the swelling act[45]
	Of the imperial theme.[46] I thank you, gentlemen.
	[Aside] This supernatural soliciting[47]
	Cannot be ill, cannot be good; if ill,
	Why hath it given me earnest of success,
	Commencing in a truth? I am Thane of Cawdor:
	If good, why do I yield to that suggestion
	Whose horrid image doth unfix my hair 140
	And make my seated heart[48] knock at my ribs,
	Against the use[49] of nature? Present fears
	Are less than horrible imaginings;
	My thought, whose murder yet is but fantastical,
	Shakes so my single state of man that function[50]
	Is smother'd in surmise,[51] and nothing is
	But what is not.[52]
Banquo	Look, how our partner's rapt.
Macbeth	[Aside] If chance will have me King, why, chance may crown me,
	Without my stir. 150

[34] allied
[35] reinforce
[36] Sweno and Macdonwald
[37] ruin
[38] treasons punishable by death

[39] yet to come

[40] if you believe that entirely
[41] urge you to possess

[42] unimportant things
[43] in most important matters

[44] introductions
[45] unfolding
[46] theme of royalty

[47] inviting

[48] firmly placed
[49] custom

[50] action

[51] speculation

[52] nothing exists but his thought which has no reality

	Banquo	New honours come upon him,

[53] new clothes
[54] do not fit

Banquo New honours come upon him,
Like our strange garments,[53] cleave not to their
  mould[54] *Contemplating*
But with the aid of use.

Macbeth [Aside] Come what come may,

[55] Even on the roughest day things will run their course
[56] we await your pleasure
[57] occupied

Time and the hour runs through the roughest day.[55]

Banquo Worthy Macbeth, we stay upon your leisure.[56]

Macbeth Give me your favour: my dull brain was wrought[57]
With things forgotten. Kind gentlemen, your
  pains

[58] in the brain, the book of memory

Are register'd where every day I turn[58]
The leaf to read them. Let us toward the King.
[Aside to Banquo] Think upon what hath

[59] meantime

  chanc'd; and, at more time,[59]
The interim having weigh'd it, let us speak   *160*
Our free hearts each to other.

Banquo [Aside to Macbeth] Very gladly.

Macbeth [Aside to Banquo] Till then, enough. Come,
  friends.

[Exeunt].

Scene Analysis

Scene III connects the witches – the power of evil – with Macbeth. The witches meet again in thunder on the heath.

One has been killing swine, another promises vengeance on the sailor's wife who refused her chestnuts, and has the thumb of a pilot who was shipwrecked on his way home to prove it. The ominous incantation:

> *"I'll do, I'll do, and I'll do."*

leaves us in no doubt of her malicious intentions. She threatens that the sailor will be deprived of sleep – the first reference in the play to sleep which is essential to man's wellbeing. As a result of lack of sleep the sailor will *"dwindle, peak and pine"*. Later Macbeth thinks that he has in fact murdered sleep and his punishment is given expression in the voice that he imagined crying out *"Sleep no more!"*. Lady Macbeth's sleep is also troubled and, in *"slumbery agitation"*, she re-enacts the horror of the murder.

As Macbeth approaches, the witches speak of *"the charm"* being *"wound up"*, suggesting that a plot has been hatched. As Macbeth enters he unconsciously echoes the words of the witches when he says to Banquo:

> *"So foul and fair a day I have not seen"*.

All hail, Macbeth! that shalt be king hereafter. (3rd Witch, Act 1, Scene III)

This points to Macbeth's identification with the evil world of the witches. It is Macbeth who asks them to speak. Each of the witches greets him in turn, the first by his own title *"Thane of Glamis"*; the second addresses him as *"Thane of Cawdor"* and the third as *"King hereafter"*. Banquo cannot understand why Macbeth should start:

> *"...and seem to fear*
> *Things that do sound so fair?"*

We know that the second prophesy has already been fulfilled, but Macbeth does not, so why in-deed should he start fearfully? Is he already afraid of his guilty thoughts? His silence is surely significant:

> *"...he seems rapt withal"*

Banquo addresses the witches with perfect composure:

> *"Speak then to me, who neither beg nor fear*
> *Your favours nor your hate".*

The witches answer him in riddles:

> *"Lesser than Macbeth, and greater."*
> *"Not so happy, yet much happier."*

Macbeth wishes to know:

> *"...from whence*
> *You owe this strange intelligence?"*

but the witches vanish.

At the very moment that Macbeth and Banquo are discussing what they have seen and heard, Ross and Angus arrive with the news for Macbeth that he has been made Thane of Cawdor. Banquo associates this news with the devil:

> *"What! can the devil speak true?"*

Macbeth seeks clarification:

> *"The Thane of Cawdor lives: why do you dress me*
> *In borrow'd robes?"*

On hearing the explanation:

> *"...treasons capital, confess'd and prov'd,*
> *Have overthrown him."*

he immediately considers it as an indication of the attainment of the third prophesy:

> *"Glamis, and Thane of Cawdor:*
> *The greatest is behind."*

He wonders if Banquo could possibly be thinking along the same lines:

> *"Do you not hope your children shall be kings,*
> *When those that gave the Thane of Cawdor to me*
> *Promis'd no less to them?"*

Banquo's answer is one of the deepest truths of the play:

> *"...oftentimes, to win us to our harm,*
> *The instruments of darkness tell us truths,*
> *Win us with honest trifles, to betray's*
> *In deepest consequence."*

The witches have indeed won Macbeth with the "*honest trifle*" i.e. the title of Thane of Cawdor and they certainly betray Macbeth "*in deepest consequence*".

Macbeth's soliloquy shows that the witches have touched on a deep wish and ambition, "*the imperial theme*". This "aside" marks the beginning of Macbeth's guilt. By his own admission he is yielding:

> *"...to that suggestion*
> *Whose horrid image doth unfix my hair*
> *And make my seated heart knock at my ribs,*
> *Against the use of nature..."*

Already he is struggling to control his treacherous thoughts.

> *"My thought, whose murder yet is but fantastical,*
> *Shakes so my single state of man*
> *That function is smother'd in surmise..."*

Banquo remarks a second time on the fact that Macbeth is so "rapt". He compares his new honours to "strange garments", thus reiterating Macbeth's image of "borrow'd robes". This clothing imagery recurs throughout the play.

Recalled to attention by his friends, Macbeth urges Banquo to:

> *"Think upon what hath chanc'd"*

and proposes that

> *"...having weigh'd it, let us speak*
> *Our free hearts each to other."*

Yet neither Macbeth nor Banquo speak freely to each other after this. Macbeth disguises his ambition and Banquo disguises his suspicions.

CHARACTERS
THE WITCHES
The witches are unearthly. They:

> "...look not like th' inhabitants o' the earth,
> And yet are on't..."

Banquo wonders if they are flesh and blood:

> "Live you?"

They look like women, yet they have beards, rough hands and skinny lips. They look wild and withered. They can kill swine, sail in a sieve, take the form of a rat, control the wind and the ports. Their vindictiveness is vividly conveyed in the first witch's description of what is in store for the master of the ship, the Tiger. She will draw blood and banish sleep from him.

The witches have a malignant effect on all with whom they come into contact. They are *"imperfect speakers"*. They are *"instruments of darkness"* who, once having wound up *"the charm"*, disappear by dissolving into thin air. Macbeth says of them in his letter to Lady Macbeth:

> "...they have more in them than mortal knowledge."

They call themselves *"the Weird Sisters"* and weird is a word which was formerly associated with fate.

MACBETH

In *Scene III we* see something of the temptations, fears and inner struggle of Macbeth. He starts, therefore he recognizes the evil temptation. From the moment the witches greet him, we see ambition at work in Macbeth's mind:

> "The greatest is behind."

> "Two truths are told,
> As happy prologues to the swelling act
> Of the imperial theme."

> "...earnest of success"

> "...chance may crown me,
> Without my stir."

He begs the witches to stay and tell him more:

> "Speak, I charge you."

He accepts their greeting as prophetic, thus acknowledging a belief in *"supernatural solicitings"*. His success makes him very vulnerable. Having established that he is Thane of Cawdor, he immediately thinks of murder. At first it is a *"suggestion"*, *"horrible imaginings"*, to be pushed aside in the hope that he will become king through chance.

Think upon what hath chanc'd;
and, at more time,
The interim having weigh'd it, let us speak
Our free hearts each to other.   (Macbeth, Act 1, Scene III)

Macbeth knows that he is guilty in thought:

> *"This supernatural soliciting*
> *Cannot be ill, cannot be good;"*

Moreover he has consciously formulated his secret ambition:

> *"...chance may crown me"*

The purpose shaping in his mind takes the form of a "*horrid image*" which is so terrible that it shakes his "*single state of man*". He realizes that speculation prevents constructive action:

> *"...Is function, smother'd in surprise"*

a fault that Lady Macbeth accuses him of later. He is so meditative that Banquo remarks:

> *"Look, how our partner's rapt."*

and Macbeth is almost unaware of the presence of Banquo, Ross and Angus. Yet Macbeth is shrewd enough to pretend disinterest in the prophesy of the witches. He constantly diverts his interest to Banquo's destiny:

> *"Your children shall be kings".*
> *"Do you not hope your children shall be kings...."*

There is no doubt but he wants to talk with Banquo further on the matter, with a view to finding out exactly what he thinks:

> "... and, at more time,
> The interim having weigh'd it, let us speak
> Our free hearts each to other."

BANQUO

In *Scene II* Banquo was described as being equally brave as Macbeth in battle. Banquo's importance as a character lies in the fact that he is exposed to the same temptations as Macbeth. It is Banquo who addresses the witches and challenges them:

> "...are you aught
> That man may question?"

He seems puzzled by Macbeth's reaction:

> "Good sir, why do you start, and seem to fear
> Things that do sound so fair?"

Unlike Macbeth, he is not "*rapt*" but seems calm, purposeful and matter of fact. He actually appears to be more interested in what exactly the witches are and where and how they vanished, than in what they said. He scarcely seems affected by their puzzling prophecies and riddles. He is astute enough to realize the significance of Macbeth's new title:

> "That, trusted home,
> Might yet enkindle you unto the crown..."

Banquo recognizes in the witches "*instruments of darkness*" and warns Macbeth of the dangers of dwelling on the prophecy.

Banquo appears to have little desire to encounter the witches again and although he is amazed at the witches' prophecy he does not entertain any guilty thoughts. His innocence offsets Macbeth's guilt.

ROSS

He announces to Macbeth the new honour that Duncan has conferred upon him:

> "And, for an earnest of a greater honour,
> He bade me, from him, call thee Thane of Cawdor:"

ANGUS

He gives an account of the treachery of the Thane of Cawdor. His account is brief and to the point:

> "Who was the Thane lives yet;
> But under heavy judgement bears that life

Which he deserves to lose. Whether he was combin'd
With those of Norway, or did line the rebel
With hidden help or vantage, or that with both
He labour'd in his country's wrack, I know not;"

EXERCISES

1. Discuss the dramatic effectiveness of the appearance of the witches before the encounter with Macbeth and Banquo.
2. Is there any significance in Macbeth's statement "*So foul and fair a day I have not seen*"?
3. Describe the meeting of the witches with Macbeth and Banquo.
4. Contrast the behaviour of Macbeth and Banquo in this scene.
5. Trace the changes in Macbeth's mood in this scene.
6. Study Macbeth's speech "*Two truths are told...*" What does this soliloquy reveal about his character?
7. Comment on the three clothing images in this scene.

Scene IV

Forres — A Room in the Palace. ~noble man
Flourish. Enter Duncan, Malcolm, Donalbain, Lennox, and
Attendants. The kings Son
servents

King
Duncan	Is execution done on Cawdor? Are not	[1] those ordered to execute Cawdor
	Those in commission[1] yet return'd?	
Malcolm	My liege,[2]	[2] my lord
	They are not yet come back; but I have spoke	
	With one that saw him die; who did report	
	That very frankly he confess'd his treasons,	
	Implor'd your Highness' pardon and set forth	
	A deep repentance. Nothing in his life	
	Became him[3] like the leaving it; he died	[3] suited him
	As one that had been studied in his death[4]	[4] as one who had rehearsed his manner of death
	To throw away the dearest thing he ow'd, *10*	
	As 'twere a careless trifle.	
Duncan	There's no art	
	To find the mind's construction in the face:[5]	[5] one cannot judge a man's character from his face
	He was a gentleman on whom I built	
	An absolute trust.	

Enter Macbeth, Banquo, Ross and Angus.   [*Macbeth*]
                                                    O worthiest cousin!

The sin of my ingratitude even now
Was heavy on me. Thou art so far before
That swiftest wing of recompense is slow
To overtake thee:[6] Would thou hadst less
    deserv'd
That the proportion both of thanks and
    payment
Might have been mine![7] Only I have left to say,   20
More is thy due than more than all[8] can pay.

Macbeth   The service and the loyalty I owe,
In doing it, pays itself.[9] Your Highness' part
Is to receive our duties; and our duties
Are to your throne and state, children and
    servants;
Which do but what they should by doing
    everything
Safe toward your love and honour.

Duncan   Welcome hither:
I have begun to plant thee,[10] and will labour
To make thee full of growing. Noble Banquo,
That hast no less deserv'd, nor must be known   30
No less to have done so, let me infold thee
And hold thee to my heart.

Banquo   There if I grow,
The harvest is your own.

Duncan   My plenteous joys
Wanton[11] in fulness, seek to hide themselves
In drops of sorrow. Sons, kinsmen, thanes,
And you whose places are the nearest,[12] know
We will establish our estate upon
Our eldest, Malcolm, whom we name hereafter
The Prince of Cumberland;[13] which honour must
Not unaccompanied invest him only,   40
But signs of nobleness, like stars, shall shine
On all deservers. From hence to Inverness,
And bind us further to you.[14]

Macbeth   The rest is labour, which is not us'd for you:[15]
I'll be myself the harbinger,[16] and make joyful
The hearing of my wife with your approach
So, humbly take my leave.

Duncan   My worthy Cawdor!

Macbeth   [*Aside*] The Prince of Cumberland! That is a step,
On which I must fall down, or else o'er-leap,[17]
For in my way it lies. Stars, hide your fires!   50

---

[6] Macbeth's merits are far ahead of the rewards Duncan can give him

[7] that Duncan might have been able to give thanks and payment in the proper proportion to his merits
[8] everything he possesses
[9] serving you is sufficient reward

[10] Duncan has begun to honour Macbeth by making him Thane of Cawdor

[11] unrestrained

[12] nearest in the rank to the king

[13] title of heir to the throne

[14] make his obligation to Macbeth even greater
[15] rest is like labour when not devoted to the king's service
[16] one who announces another's arrival

[17] overcome

Handwritten notes: Duncan saying he can't repay Macbeth; named his successor

	Let not light see my black and deep desires.

Let not light see my black and deep desires.
The eye wink at the hand;[18] yet let that be
Which the eye fears, when it is done, to see. *[Exit.*

Duncan   True, worthy Banquo; he is full so valiant,
And in his commendations I am fed;[19]
It is a banquet to me. Let's after him,
Whose care is gone before to bid us welcome:
It is a peerless kinsman.[20]

[Flourish. Exeunt.

[18] may the eye not look at the hand to purposely avoid seeing

[19] Duncan is full of his praise

[20] a relation without equal: Macbeth was Duncan's first cousin

Scene Analysis

Scene IV highlights the theme of treachery. Duncan talks about the betrayal of the trust of the Thane of Cawdor, but the new Thane of Cawdor also has treachery in his heart. Duncan's comment:

> *"There's no art*
> *To find the mind's construction in the face:"*

is a striking example of dramatic irony in the play. Just as he states the impossibility of judging a man's character from appearance, Macbeth enters. Duncan receives Macbeth with lavish praise and gratitude and Macbeth replies humbly and courteously, revealing nothing of his treacherous thoughts.

Duncan uses the imagery of natural growth which runs through the play and is associated with wholesomeness:

> *"I have begun to plant thee, and will labour*
> *To make thee full of growing."*

Duncan does not realize that by sowing the seeds of Macbeth's greatness he is in fact nurturing ambition.

Then Duncan makes the unexpected announcement that Malcolm is to receive the title of Prince of Cumberland, thus nominating him as heir to the throne. Macbeth is quick to see this as an obstacle to his ambition:

> *"...That is a step*
> *On which I must fall down, or else o'er-leap,*
> *For in my way it lies."*

This is crucial to the development of the action as it is unlikely that Macbeth will be crowned by chance (since the succession is established) and Macbeth now has a motive for murder. Moreover Duncan's decision to visit Macbeth's castle that same evening gives him the opportunity for action.

CHARACTERS

DUNCAN

King Duncan is not a good judge of character. Not only did he trust the Thane of Cawdor who then betrayed this *"absolute trust"*, but at the very moment that he expresses the need of being on guard even with those in whom one has deep trust, he welcomes Macbeth with almost exaggerated gratitude. He is a man of effusive feelings:

> *"O worthiest cousin!*
> *The sin of my ingratitude even now*
> *Was heavy on me. Thou art so far before*
> *That swiftest wing of recompense is slow*
> *To overtake thee..."*

Duncan is generous in his praise of others. He also possesses qualities of innocence, grace and courtesy. His own admission of his inability to judge people is an indication of his trusting nature.

MALCOLM

Malcolm appears to be serious and thoughtful. He seems to be affected by the Thane of Cawdor's manner of death and makes a reflective observation:

Thou art so far before
That swiftest wing of recompense is slow
To overtake thee   *(Duncan, Act 1, Scene IV)*

> *"Nothing in his life*
> *Became him like the leaving it; he died*
> *As one that had been studied in his death*
> *To throw away the dearest thing he ow'd*
> *As 'twere a careless trifle."*

Malcolm has obviously earned the confidence and respect of his father who is prepared to name him as his successor to the throne.

BANQUO

Duncan recognizes that Banquo is no less deserving of praise than Macbeth:

> *"Noble Banquo,*
> *That hast no less deserv'd, nor must be known*
> *No less to have done so...."*

Banquo's simple response to Duncan's praise contrasts with Macbeth's elaborate speech. Banquo develops Duncan's image of planting, replying:

> *"There if I grow,*
> *The harvest is your own."*

Duncan calls him *"worthy Banquo."*

MACBETH

Macbeth acts the part of the perfect, loyal subject and kinsman of the king. The frustration of his hopes spurs his desire. His immediate reaction to the naming of Malcolm as successor to the throne is:

> *"...in my way it lies."*

He recognizes his *"black and deep desires"* for what they are, but wishes to hide them:

> *"Stars, hide your fires!*
> *Let not light see my black and deep desires;"*

Already murder is associated with darkness and there is conflict in his mind between his desire to have the crown and fear of the means by which he is to achieve this desire. He asks the eye to disregard what the hand does in an attempt to disassociate his will from the action of the hands:

> *"The eye wink at the hand"*

He knows in advance that:

> *" ...the eye fears, when it is done, to see."*

He repeats Duncan's image of the stars to "*shine/On all deservers*". But Macbeth does not want the stars to shine. He takes his leave of the king to arrive in Inverness before Duncan.

EXERCISES

1. What aspects of Duncan's character are highlighted in this scene?
2. What effect on Macbeth has Duncan's proclamation of Malcolm as heir to the throne?
3. Comment on the following quotation:

> "The eye wink at the hand; yet let that be
> Which the eye fears, when it is done, to see."

Scene V

Inverness – Macbeth's Castle

Enter Lady Macbeth, reading a letter.

Lady Macbeth   'They met me in the day of success; and I have
learned by the perfectest report, they have
more in them than mortal¹ knowledge. When I
burned in desire to question them further, they
made themselves air, into which they vanished.
Whiles I stood rapt in the wonder of it, came
missives² from the King, who all-hailed me,
'Thane of Cawdor;' by which title, before, these
weird sisters saluted me, and referred me to the
coming on of time, with,
'Hail, king that shalt be!' This have I thought
  good to   *10*
deliver thee, my dearest partner of greatness,
that thou mightest not lose the dues of
rejoicing³ by being ignorant of what greatness is
promised thee. Lay it to thy heart, and farewell.'

Glamis thou art, and Cawdor; and shalt be
What thou art promis'd. Yet do I fear thy nature;
It is too full o' the milk of human kindness⁴
To catch the nearest way.⁵ Thou wouldst be great,
Art not without ambition, but without
The illness⁶ should attend it; what thou   *20*
  wouldst highly,
That thou wouldst holily;⁷ wouldst not play false
And yet wouldst wrongly win: thou'dst have,
  great Glamis,

¹human

²messengers

³the rejoicing that is Lady
  Macbeth's right

⁴gentleness of human
  nature
⁵to use the quickest
  method
⁶evil

⁷whereas Macbeth very
  much wants the crown, he
  wants to remain innocent

Soliloquy

That which cries, 'Thus thou must do, if thou
  have it';
And that which rather thou dost fear to do
Than wishest should be undone. Hie thee hither,
That I may pour my spirits in thine ear,
And chastise[8] with the valour of my tongue   [8] suppress
All that impedes[9] thee from the golden round,[10]   [9] prevents
                                      [10] the crown
Which fate and metaphysical[11] aid doth seem   30   [11] supernatural
To have thee crown'd withal.[12]   [12] with

Enter a Messenger.

           What is your tidings?[13]   [13] news

Messenger   The King comes here to-night.
Lady Macbeth   Thou'rt mad to say it.
Is not thy master with him? who, were't so,
Would have inform'd for preparation.
Messenger   So please you, it is true: our Thane is coming;
One of my fellows had the speed of him,[14]   [14] came ahead of him
Who, almost dead for breath, had scarcely more
Than would make up his message.
Lady Macbeth   Give him tending;[15]   [15] look after him
He brings great news.   *[Exit Messenger.*
           The raven[16] himself is hoarse   [16] A bird of ill-omen
That croaks the fatal entrance of Duncan   40
Under my battlements. Come, you spirits
That tend on mortal thoughts![17] Unsex me here,   [17] mortal – human & deadly
And fill me, from the crown to the toe, top-full
Of direst cruelty. Make thick my blood,
Stop up the access and passage to remorse,
That no compunctious visitings of nature[18]   [18] natural scruples
Shake my fell[19] purpose, nor keep peace between   [19] cruel
The effect and it! Come to my woman's breasts,
And take my milk for gall,[20] you murdering
  ministers,   [20] bitterness
Wherever in your sightless[21] substances   50   [21] invisible
You wait on[22] nature's mischief. Come, thick   [22] assist
  night,
And pall[23] thee in the dunnest[24] smoke of hell,   [23] cloak;
That my keen knife see not the wound it makes,   [24] darkest
Nor heaven peep through the blanket of the
  dark,
To cry 'Hold, hold!'

Enter Macbeth.

Great Glamis! Worthy Cawdor!
Greater than both, by the all-hail hereafter!
Thy letters have transported me beyond
This ignorant present, and I feel now

[25] the present

The future in the instant.[25]

Macbeth   My dearest love,
Duncan comes here to-night.   60

Lady Macbeth   And when goes hence?

Macbeth   To-morrow, as he purposes.

Lady Macbeth   O! never
Shall sun that morrow see!
Your face, my thane, is as a book where men
May read strange matters. To beguile the
        time,[26]

[26] to deceive the world

Look like the time; bear welcome in your eye,
Your hand, your tongue: look like the innocent
        flower,
But be the serpent under't. He that's coming

[27] looked after – there is the
double meaning of
murdered in this context
[28] management

Must be provided for,[27] and you shall put
This night's great business into my dispatch;[28]
Which shall to all our nights and days to come   70

[29] royal power

Give solely sovereign sway[29] and masterdom.

Macbeth   We will speak further.

[30] appear to have a clear
conscience
[31] to show disturbance is
cowardice

Lady Macbeth   Only look up clear;[30]
To alter favour ever is to fear.[31]
Leave all the rest to me.   [*Exeunt.*

(handwritten annotations: "Duncan won't leave alive", "I will organise this murder", and letter "L")

Scene Analysis

The news of his meeting with the witches and their prediction of his new title is of such significance to Macbeth that he sends a letter in advance of his arrival to Lady Macbeth. It is clear from the letter that Macbeth is in no doubt that the third prophecy will be fulfilled:

> *"This I have thought good to deliver thee, my dearest partner of greatness,*
> *that thou mightest not lose the dues of rejoicing,*
> *by being ignorant of what greatness is promised thee."*

Lady Macbeth reads the letter and thinks about her husband's character. When the messenger comes she is jolted and exclaims "*Thou'rt mad to say it.*" She realizes instantly the opportunity handed to them:

> *"I feel now*
> *The future in the instant."*

She is quite determined to have the strength to realize her ambition and calls on unseen powers to aid her in her determination.

Macbeth greets his wife non-committedly. It is Lady Macbeth who emphatically proclaims that Duncan must die. Macbeth neither agrees nor protests. All he says is:

> *"We will speak further."*

CHARACTERS
LADY MACBETH
The most evident qualities of character in Lady Macbeth at the beginning of the play are her singleness of purpose and her strength of will. She immediately grasps the significance of the witches' prophecy:

> *"Glamis thou art, and Cawdor; and shalt be*
> *What thou art promis'd."*

Without hesitation she decides on the murder of Duncan:

> *"He brings great news. –*
>   *The raven himself is hoarse*
> *That croaks the fatal entrance of Duncan*
> *Under my battlements."*

There are no moral or political considerations. Without conscience to deter her, Lady Macbeth can envisage the murder of Duncan quite simply in terms of a deed which must be done. Duncan's visit to their castle is their chance "*to catch the nearest way.*" Having seen clearly what must be done, Lady Macbeth knows that she will need strength of purpose to see it through and so she calls on

> *"...spirits*
> *That tend on mortal thoughts"*

to possess her body and soul. She does not want a woman's physical or emotional weakness to hinder her and she goes so far as to ask:

> *"...Unsex me here,*
> *And fill me, from the crown to the toe, top-full*
> *Of direst cruelty."*

It is a harsh and shocking prayer which denies her nature as a woman. She does not want to experience any tender feeling lest her purpose be shaken:

> *"Stop up the access and passage to remorse,*
> *That no compunctious visitings of nature*
> *Shake my fell purpose, nor keep peace between*
> *The effect and it!"*

This have I thought good to deliver thee, my dearest partner of greatness
(Lady Macbeth, Act 1, Scene V)

Like Macbeth, she calls on the night to hide her deed, beneath *"the blanket of the dark"*. She actually envisages herself committing the murder:

> *"And pall thee in the dunnest smoke of hell,*
> *That my keen knife see not the wound it makes..."*

She undertakes the organization of Duncan's murder:

> *"...you shall put*
> *This night's great business into my dispatch."*
> *"Leave all the rest to me."*

Macbeth calls her *"my dearest partner of greatness"*. She understands her husband's character but, in her opinion, Macbeth's good points are weaknesses. She knows her own strength of character and determines to drive away all his scruples and:

> *"...chastise with the valour of my tongue*
> *All that impedes thee from the golden round,"*

Her advice to Macbeth shows her self-control, her ability to disguise her true feelings:

> *"...look like the innocent flower,*
> *But be the serpent under't."*

MACBETH

Lady Macbeth gives us an insight into Macbeth's character. She points out the contradictions in his mind, which prepares us for his later vacillations. She knows Macbeth's ambitions, weakness and hesitancy. She knows that he is ambitious but not unscrupulous:

> *"...thou wouldst be great,*
> *Art not without ambition, but without*
> *The illness should attend it..."*

She knows he desires the crown but would like to remain innocent while attaining it:

> *"...what thou wouldst highly,*
> *That thou wouldst holily; wouldst not play false,*
> *And yet wouldst wrongly win;"*

His nature according to her is *"too full o' the milk of human kindness"*. This aspect of his character is in stark contrast to the presentation of Macbeth in *Scene II* as the merciless warrior. Macbeth's virtues, his kindness, essential goodness and openness are viewed negatively by Lady Macbeth who sees those qualities as obstacles to power. It is these very qualities which ensure our sympathy for Macbeth and make him the essential tragic hero.

...you shall put
This night's great business into my dispatch

(Lady Macbeth, Act 1, Scene V)

EXERCISES

1. What effect has Macbeth's letter on Lady Macbeth?
2. What do we learn of Macbeth's character from Lady Macbeth? Is her interpretation consistent with what we have seen of Macbeth so far in the play?
3. Describe Lady Macbeth.
4. How would you describe the relationship between Macbeth and Lady Macbeth?

Scene VI

The Same – Before the Castle.

Hautboys¹ and torches. Enter Duncan, Malcolm, Donalbain, Banquo, Lennox, Macduff, Ross, Angus, and Attendants.

¹ oboe players

[handwritten: King] [handwritten: King sons] [handwritten: Macbeths best friend]

Duncan	This castle hath a pleasant seat;² the air Nimbly³ and sweetly recommends itself Unto our gentle senses.
Banquo	This guest of summer, The temple-haunting⁴ martlet,⁵ does approve By his lov'd mansionry⁶ that the heaven's breath Smells wooingly⁷ here; no jutty,⁸ frieze,⁹ Buttress,¹⁰ nor coign of vantage,¹¹ but this bird Hath made his pendent¹² bed and procreant cradle:¹³ Where they most breed and haunt,¹⁴ I have observ'd The air is delicate.¹⁵

² situation
³ there is a gentle wind

⁴ lives around the temples
⁵ a kind of swallow called a martin becauses the bird crosses France around St. Martin's day
⁶ nest
⁷ invitingly
⁸ part that juts out
⁹ ornamental sculptured band
¹⁰ support
¹¹ convenient corner
¹² hanging
¹³ nest where the young are hatched
¹⁴ frequent
¹⁵ mild

[line number] 10

[handwritten: admiring the castle]

Enter Lady Macbeth.

Duncan	See, see, our honour'd hostess! The love that follows us sometime is our trouble, Which still we thank as love.¹⁶ Herein I teach you How you shall bid¹⁷ God 'eyld¹⁸ us for your pains, And thank us for your trouble.
Lady Macbeth	All our service, In every point twice done, and then done double, Were poor and single¹⁹ business, to contend²⁰ Against those honours deep and broad wherewith Your Majesty loads our house: for those of old, And the late dignities heap'd up to them,

¹⁶ his subjects' love is sometimes trouble, yet he is grateful to them for that love
¹⁷ pray
¹⁸ yield
¹⁹ simple
²⁰ compete

[handwritten: Thanks for having us]

[handwritten: least we can do]

[21] the hermit lived in solitude and prayed so Lady Macbeth is telling Duncan that they will pray for him
[22] followed him closely
[23] official who went ahead of the king to secure his lodgings
[24] helped

[25] accountable
[26] present their account
[27] always return what are your own possessions

Duncan   We rest your hermits.[21]   20
          Where's the Thane of Cawdor?
We cours'd him at the heels,[22] and had a purpose
To be his purveyor;[23] but he rides well,
And his great love, sharp as his spur, hath holp[24] him
To his home before us. Fair and noble hostess,
We are your guest to-night.

(handwritten: "where is Macbeth")

Lady Macbeth   Your servants ever
Have theirs, themselves, and what is theirs, in compt,[25]
To make their audit[26] at your Highness' pleasure,
Still to return your own.[27]

Duncan   Give me your hand;
Conduct me to mine host: we love him highly,
And shall continue our graces towards him.   30
By your leave, hostess.
                                        [*Exeunt.*

(handwritten: Makes his fatal advancement into his doom)

Scene Analysis

Scene VI, a scene of pastoral tranquillity which marks Duncan's *"fatal entrance"*, is in marked contrast to the scene of murder and darkness which follows. Duncan remarks on the pleasant location of the castle and Banquo replies with a beautiful description:

> *"This guest of summer,*
> *The temple-haunting martlet, does approve*
> *By his lov'd mansionry that the heaven's breath*
> *Smells wooingly here:"*

The beauty invoked by the language of the scene is particularly effective after *"the dunnest smoke of hell"* referred to by Lady Macbeth in the previous scene. The description of Macbeth's castle evokes details which oppose the images of Lady Macbeth. She speaks of the raven as croaking *"the fatal entrance"*, Banquo speaks of the martlet as a *"guest of summer"*. Lady Macbeth has called on the *"dunnest smoke of hell"* but Banquo remarks that *"the heaven's breath/Smells wooingly here."* The martlet has made the castle its procreant cradle but Lady Macbeth has just denied procreation. The beauty of this scene sharpens our awareness of the darkness within the castle.

Lady Macbeth welcomes Duncan with assurances of her loyalty and expressions of gratitude for the honours bestowed on them. Macbeth on the other hand does not come to greet him.

CHARACTERS

DUNCAN

Our last glimpse of Duncan takes place in an atmosphere of beauty and peace. He greets
Lady Macbeth with elaborate courtesy, confessing that the love of his subjects is sometimes
tiresomely attentive. Yet he acknowledges it as love, never doubts in fact that it is love,
whereas in this case it is hypocrisy. His visit, he points out, though inconvenient, springs
from his loving regard.

BANQUO

In this scene Banquo utters some of the most beautiful lines in the play. It is perhaps an
indication of his innocence that he can indulge in such poetic sentiments with Duncan
whereas Macbeth is presumably too uneasy in the presence of the king to even receive him.

LADY MACBETH

Lady Macbeth is able to follow the advice she gave Macbeth to *"look up clear"*. Without
any qualms she receives Duncan, heaping courtesies and gratitude on his head:

> *"All our service,*
> *In every point twice done, and then done double,*
> *Were poor and single business, to contend*
> *Against those honours deep and broad wherewith*
> *Your Majesty loads our house:"*

Her show of welcome is indicative of her self-possession.

EXERCISES

1. Write a brief note to illustrate the irony of this scene.
2. (a) Comment on the role of Lady Macbeth in this scene.
   (b) Is there any significance in the absence of Macbeth?

Scene VII   Duncan is
                 Macbeths cousin

The Same — A Room in the Castle.

Hautboys and torches. Enter, and pass over the stage, a Sewer[1],
and divers Servants with dishes and service. Then, enter Macbeth.

[1] person who set the table and looked after the guests

murder
↓

Macbeth	If it were done when 'tis done, then 'twere well
	It were done quickly; if the assassination
If I coud be	Could trammel up[2] the consequence and catch
gaurenteed I	With his surcease,[3] success; that but[4] this blow
coud get	Might be the be-all and the end-all here,
away with	But here, upon this bank and shoal of time,[5]
murder than	

[2] catch in a net; prevent all consequences
[3] death
[4] if only
[5] this life

I would kill. Sometimes one woong move
Could change our lives.

⁶risk the next life

⁷presents

⁸powers
⁹uncorrupted

¹⁰his death

¹¹the winds

¹²Shakespeare uses the metaphor of a horseman who jumping too eagerly into the saddle falls on the other side

¹³acquired

¹⁴splendour

We'd jump the life to come.⁶ But in these cases
We still have judgement here; that we but teach
Bloody instructions, which, being taught, return
To plague the inventor; this even-handed justice   10
Commends⁷ the ingredients of our poison'd chalice
To our own lips. He's here in double trust:
First, as I am his kinsman and his subject,
Strong both against the deed; then, as his host,
Who should against his murderer shut the door,
Not bear the knife himself. Besides, this Duncan
Hath borne his faculties⁸ so meek, hath been
So clear⁹ in his great office, that his virtues
Will plead like angels trumpet-tongu'd against
The deep damnation of his taking-off;¹⁰   20
And pity, like a naked new-born babe,
Striding the blast, or heaven's cherubin, hors'd
Upon the sightless couriers¹¹ of the air,
Shall blow the horrid deed in every eye,
That tears shall drown the wind. I have no spur
To prick the sides of my intent, but only
Vaulting ambition, which o'er-leaps itself,
And falls on the other.¹² –

Enter Lady Macbeth.

How now! what news?

Lady Macbeth   He has almost supp'd: why have you left the chamber?
Macbeth   Hath he ask'd for me?   30
Lady Macbeth   Know you not he has?
Macbeth   We will proceed no further in this business:
He hath honour'd me of late; and I have bought¹³
Golden opinions from all sorts of people,
Which would be worn now in their newest gloss,¹⁴
Not cast aside so soon.
Lady Macbeth   Was the hope drunk,
Wherein you dress'd yourself? Hath it slept since,
And wakes it now, to look so green and pale
At what it did so freely? From this time
Such I account thy love. Art thou afeard
To be the same in thine own act and valour   40
As thou art in desire? Wouldst thou have that
Which thou esteem'st the ornament of life,
And live a coward in thine own esteem,

[Handwritten note: Problem is he is killing off a good king who Scotland adores.]

[Handwritten note: She is furious with Macbeth]

Macbeth

Letting 'I dare not' wait upon 'I would',
Like the poor cat i' the adage?[15]
                        Prithee,[16] peace.
I dare do all that may become a man;
Who dares do more is none.

Lady Macbeth

                What beast was't, then,
That made you break[17] this enterprise to me?
When you durst[18] do it, then you were a man;
And, to be more than what you were, you
    would   50
Be so much more the man. Nor time nor place
Did then adhere,[19] and yet you would make
    both:
They have made themselves, and that their
    fitness now
Does unmake you. I have given suck, and know
How tender 'tis to love the babe that milks me:
I would, while it was smiling in my face,
Have pluck'd my nipple from his boneless gums,
And dash'd the brains out, had I so sworn as you
Have done to this.[20]

Macbeth   If we should fail,—

Lady Macbeth   We fail!
But screw your courage to the sticking-place,[21]   60
And we'll not fail. When Duncan is asleep,
Whereto the rather shall his day's hard journey
Soundly invite him, his two chamberlains
Will I with wine and wassail[22] so convince[23]
That memory, the warder of the brain,
Shall be a fume,[24] and the receipt of reason[25]
A limbeck[26] only; when in swinish sleep
Their drenched natures lie, as in a death,
What cannot you and I perform upon
The unguarded Duncan? what not put upon   70
His spongy officers, who shall bear the guilt
Of our great quell?[27]

Macbeth   Bring forth men-children only;
For thy undaunted[28] mettle[29] should compose
Nothing but males. Will it not be receiv'd,[30]
When we have mark'd with blood those sleepy
    two
Of his own chamber, and us'd their very daggers,
That they have done't?

Lady Macbeth   Who dares receive it other,[31]
As[32] we shall make our griefs and clamour roar
Upon his death?

---

[15] the saying: "The cat would eat fish and would not wet her feet"
[16] I pray you
[17] reveal
[18] dared
[19] suit
[20] Duncan's murder
[21] notch; a violin must be strung to the right pitch
[22] liquor
[23] overcome
[24] vapour
[25] the brain
[26] vessel used for distilling liquids, the drink will affect memory and make the reason full of confused haze
[27] killing
[28] fearless
[29] disposition
[30] accepted
[31] otherwise
[32] seeing that

"what kind of a man are you?"

[33] brace

[34] every organ of the body

[35] deceive the world

Macbeth

> I am settled, and bend up[33]
> Each corporal agent[34] to this terrible feat.   *80*
> Away, and mock the time[35] with fairest show:
> False face must hide what the false heart doth
> know.   *[Exeunt.*

Scene Analysis

Scene VII ends Macbeth's indecision and is the most crucial scene in *Act 1*. Macbeth is obviously uneasy in the presence of Duncan and he leaves the banquet to ponder over the risks and consequences of his purpose. He considers what may happen after the crime. What he seems most afraid of is revenge and retribution in this life. He considers his duties as a host and relative of Duncan. He recognizes that his crime would be a violation of all the laws of kinship and hospitality. He considers Duncan's success as a king. He realizes that Duncan would be pitied and he himself condemned by the king's subjects who hold him in such high regard. Macbeth identifies Duncan with divine law and understands instinctively that the murder would be sacrilegious, and so associates the murder with damnation. His conscience reminds him that nothing justifies his purpose, it is prompted by his own *"vaulting ambition"* which can only lead to disaster.

Lady Macbeth interrupts his thoughts and when she tells him that the king has asked for him he seems to make up his mind and states firmly, *"We will proceed no further in this business."* He again uses the imagery of clothes:

> *"I have bought*
> *Golden opinions from all sorts of people,*
> *Which would be worn now in their newest gloss,*
> *Not cast aside so soon."*

She charges him with not knowing his own mind, she questions his courage and manhood, she ridicules him with his own imagery of clothes:

> *"Was the hope drunk,*
> *Wherein you dress'd yourself ?"*

She blackmails him:

> *"From this time*
> *Such I account thy love."*

She challenges him:

> *"Wouldst thou have that*
> *Which thou esteem'st the ornament of life,*
> *And live a coward in thine own esteem,"*

She taunts him –

> *"Letting 'I dare not' wait upon 'I would',*
> *Like the poor cat i' the adage?"*

In her attempt to show Macbeth the solemnity of his promise, Lady Macbeth tells him that if she had so sworn she would have killed the baby at her breast rather than break her oath. Her vehemence causes Macbeth to waver and his next question has to do with the consequences rather than the issue of whether or not Duncan should be murdered. Faced with such determination and scorn, when Lady Macbeth points out how easily the murder can be accomplished, he agrees – *"I am settled"*. The fact that he has to:

> *"bend up*
> *Each corporal agent to this terrible feat*

shows the strain of the decision.

CHARACTERS
DUNCAN
Scene VII gives a final insight into the character of Duncan and reveals more fully the characters of Macbeth and Lady Macbeth.

Macbeth cites Duncan's qualities and virtues. As a king Duncan has exercised his power meekly, with humility and gentleness. Moreover his rule has been above reproach:

> *"...this Duncan*
> *Hath borne his faculties so meek, hath been*
> *So clear in his great office, that his virtues*
> *Will plead like angels trumpet-tongu'd against*
> *The deep damnation of his taking off."*

The fact that Duncan was a benign king makes Macbeth's deed even more treacherous.

MACBETH
Lady Macbeth summed up Macbeth's state of mind exactly when she said in *Scene V*:

> *"Thou'dst have, great Glamis,*
>
> *That which cries, 'Thus thou must do, if thou have it,'*
>
> *And that which rather thou dost fear to do*
> *Than wishest should be undone."*

He wishes the action could be over and done with, wishes he could act without having to face the consequences. This speech is a perfect example of prolepsis, where objections to his deed are foreseen. He is not worried about *"the life to come"*, but this life where sometimes:

> *"...this even-handed Justice*
> *Commends the ingredients of our poison'd chalice*
> *To our own lips."*

He is very much concerned here with himself rather than Duncan, with immediate retribution and with his reputation as one who has *"bought/Golden opinions from all sorts of people"*. He moves from the fear of personal retribution to the argument of moral responsibility, his duty as Duncan's kinsman and subject. Then, as the full implications of what he is about to do dawn on him, images take shape in his mind:

> *"And pity, like a naked new-born babe,*
> *Striding the blast, or heaven's cherubim, hors'd*
> *Upon the sightless couriers of the air,*
> *Shall blow the horrid deed in every eye,*
> *That tears shall drown the wind."*

Macbeth has an intense awareness of the enormity of the murder which is given expression through divine metaphors.

It is Macbeth's sense of guilt, not cowardice, which causes him to change his mind many times before the murder is done. What is emphasied throughout *Act I*, is how difficult it is to get him to come to terms with the evil he is contemplating. He starts, he hesitates, he contemplates, he hopes in chance, decides against the murder, but then changes his mind:

> *"...yet let that be*
> *Which the eye fears, when it is done, to see"*

Disturbed by doubts, he again refuses to commit murder:

> *"We will proceed no further in this business."*

It requires all Lady Macbeth's force to win him back to the *"enterprise"*.

Macbeth's vacillation earns our sympathy at this stage of the play.

LADY MACBETH

In *Scene V* Lady Macbeth knew that she would have to *"chastise with the valour of my tongue."* In *Scene VII* she indeed chastises Macbeth with such scorn that his defence against her taunts is hopelessly inadequate. Swayed by the sheer force of her eloquence, the wavering Macbeth is dominated. Her conscience as Duncan's hostess does not assail her and so she does not understand Macbeth's conscience. She misinterprets his conscience and guilt as cowardice and completely distorts what Macbeth says:

> *"I dare do all that may become a man...."*

Her cutting reply is:

> *"When you durst do it, then you were a man;*
> *And, to be more than what you were, you would*
> *Be so much more the man."*

Was the hope drunk,
Wherein you dress'd yourself? (Lady Macbeth, Act 1, Scene VII)

Macbeth has used the image of the helpless newborn babe when thinking about Duncan's virtues, but Lady Macbeth's use of the same image is shocking:

> *"...I have given suck, and know*
> *How tender 'tis to love the babe that milks me:*
> *I would, while it was smiling in my face,*
> *Have pluck'd my nipple from his boneless gums,*
> *And dash'd the brains out, had I so sworn*
> *As you..."*

This same woman who pleaded with the spirits to *"unsex"* her, now flaunts her womanhood in the face of Macbeth's manhood. Macbeth's tribute to her courage ironically refers to her womanly nature:

> *"Bring forth men-children only:*
> *For thy undaunted mettle should compose*
> *Nothing but males."*

Faced with her husband's vacillation, it is Lady Macbeth who plans the murder. The plan is simple: when Duncan is asleep, she will make his two chamberlains drunk, they will remember nothing, and, therefore, will bear the guilt. She ignores the fact of the murder itself, its effect on Macbeth and the inevitable suspicions which must be aroused. Unlike Macbeth, Lady Macbeth shows no scruples before the murder, she entertains no thought of failure. Her *"undaunted mettle"* wins the admiration and confidence of her husband.

EXERCISES

1. Summarize the character of Duncan as portrayed by Shakespeare throughout the first act.
2. Study Macbeth's soliloquy. What do you think of his arguments against the murder of Duncan?
3. Describe the confrontation between Macbeth and Lady Macbeth. How is Macbeth dominated by the stronger will of his wife?
4. Contrast the characters of Macbeth and Lady Macbeth from your study of *Act 1*.

REVISION

> *"Thriftless ambition, that wilt ravin up*
> *Thine own life's means."*   (Ross, Act 2, Scene IV)

Macbeth and Banquo, returning to report to King Duncan after two victorious battles, meet three witches who promise Macbeth that he will become Thane of Cawdor and King of Scotland, and Banquo that his descendants will be kings. As a reward for his victory

Macbeth is given the title of *"Thane of Cawdor"* and he considers the possibility of fulfilling the rest of the prophecy. Lady Macbeth, on receiving the news that Duncan is to spend the night at their castle, determines that the king will be murdered. Duncan is welcomed to the castle. Macbeth's scruples are over-ruled by the sheer force of his wife's arguments and the murder is planned.

POINTS TO NOTE

1. The tempestuous atmosphere of the opening scene indicates the presence of evil.
2. In the speeches of the witches, Macbeth's fate is foreshadowed. Like the sailor, Macbeth will be drained spiritually, and deprived of sleep.
3. In *Act I* Macbeth is respected and honoured.
4. Duncan and Macbeth were cousins, both grandsons of King Malcolm and therefore had equal claim to the throne. Duncan did not have to name his eldest son as his successor.
5. Banquo's mind dwells on the reality or unreality of the witches, but Macbeth is concerned only with the predictions.
6. From as early as *Scene III,* Macbeth is contemplating murder. By the end of *Scene IV,* the suggestion of murder has grown.
7. Lady Macbeth contrasts with Macbeth in that her decision to murder Duncan is unhesitating.
8. Already the forces of good and evil have come into play. The imperial theme is the focus of the action, the theme of appearance and reality has been introduced by Duncan and the complex pattern of imagery has been established. *(See Part 3)*

REVISION ASSIGNMENT

Trace the progress of Macbeth's ambition up to the point where the decision is made to murder Duncan. Pay particular attention to his changes of mood and the influence Lady Macbeth has on his decision.

Act 2
Scene I

Inverness – Court within Macbeth's castle.

Banquo's son

Enter Banquo, and Fleance bearing a torch before him.

Banquo	How goes the night, boy?
Fleance	The moon is down; I have not heard the clock.
Banquo	And she goes down at twelve.
Fleance	I take't, 'tis later, sir.
Banquo	Hold, take my sword. There's husbandry[1] in heaven; all is not well in Scotland
	Their candles[2] are all out. Take thee that too.
	A heavy summons[3] lies like lead[4] upon me,
	And yet I would not sleep. Merciful powers
	Restrain in me the cursed thoughts that nature
	Gives way to in repose!

Enter Macbeth and a Servant with a torch.

	Give me my sword. —
	Who's there? 10
Macbeth	A friend.
Banquo	What, sir! not yet at rest? The king's a-bed:
	He hath been in unusual pleasure, and
	Sent forth great largess[5] to your offices.[6]
	This diamond he greets your wife withal,
	By the name of most kind hostess, and shut up[7]
	In measureless content.[8]
Macbeth	Being unprepar'd,
	Our will became the servant to defect,[9]
	Which else should free have wrought.
Banquo	All's well.
	I dreamt last night of the three Weird Sisters: 20
	To you they have show'd some truth.
Macbeth	I think not of them:
	Yet, when we can entreat an hour to serve,[10]
	We would spend it in some words upon that business,
	If you would grant the time.
Banquo	At your kind'st leisure.
Macbeth	If you shall cleave to my consent,[11] when 'tis,
	It shall make honour for you.
Banquo	So I lose none
	In seeking to augment it, but still keep
	My bosom franchis'd[12] and allegiance clear,
	I shall be counsell'd.

[1] economizing

[2] stars
[3] call to sleep
[4] Morpheus, the god of sleep, was represented with a leaden club

[5] generous gifts
[6] servants quarters

[7] has retired

[8] infinitely happy

[9] their will to serve Duncan was limited by their deficiencies; had they been prepared, they would have served him better

[10] have an hour at our disposal

[11] follow my advice

[12] free

Macbeth	Good repose the while!
Banquo	Thanks, sir: the like to you. 30

[Exeunt Banquo and Fleance.

Macbeth   Go bid thy mistress, when my drink is ready,
She strike upon the bell. Get thee to bed.

Siliqouy   *[Exit Servant.*

Is this a dagger which I see before me,   Ⓛ
The handle toward my hand? Come, let me
   clutch thee:
I have thee not, and yet I see thee still.
Art thou not, fatal vision, sensible
To feeling as to sight? or art thou but
A dagger of the mind, a false creation,
Proceeding from the heat-oppressed[13] brain?   [13] feverish
I see thee yet, in form as palpable   40
As this which now I draw.
Thou marshall'st[14] me the way that I was going;   [14] lead
And such an instrument I was to use.
Mine eyes are made the fools o' the other senses,[15]   [15] either his eyes are deceived by the other senses, or else they are more reliable than all the rest
Or else worth all the rest: I see thee still:,
And on thy blade and dudgeon[16] gouts[17] of blood,   [16] handle
Which was not so before. There's no such thing: [17] drops
It is the bloody business which informs[18]   [18] forms this shape
Thus to mine eyes. Now o'er the one half-world

most famous speech of the play

Ⓛ Nature seems dead, and wicked dreams abuse   50
The curtain'd sleep, witchcraft celebrates
Pale Hecate's[19] offerings; and wither'd murder,   [19] Goddess of the witches
Alarum'd[20] by his sentinel, the wolf,[21]   [20] called to action
Whose howl's his watch, thus with his stealthy   [21] associated with murder
   pace,
With Tarquin's[22] ravishing[23] strides, toward his   [22] Tarquinius Sextus caused the downfall of his father by his rape of Lucretia, the wife of a nobleman, about 500 B.C.
   design
Moves like a ghost. Thou sure and firm-set earth,   [23] violating
Hear not my steps, which way they walk, for fear   [24] chatter
Thy very stones prate[24] of my whereabout,
And take the present horror from the time,
Which now suits with it. Whiles I threat,
   he lives: 60
Words to the heat of deeds too cold breath
   gives.

[A bell rings.

Lady Macbeth signals the time for the murder has come

I go, and it is done; the bell invites me.
Hear it not, Duncan; for it is a knell[25]   [25] funeral bell
That summons thee to heaven or to hell.

This bell will summon Duncan to his death

Scene Analysis

Scene I is set in the castle courtyard. There is an atmosphere of uneasiness as Banquo and Fleance remark on the total darkness of the night:

> *"The moon is down..."*
> > *"There's husbandry in heaven,*
> *Their candles are all out."*

Banquo fears *"the cursed thoughts"* that arise in sleep. He is very much on edge and calls for his sword on hearing the approach of footsteps.

In the conversation between Macbeth and Banquo we learn that Duncan has gone to bed content with his visit, having generously sent gifts to the servants' quarters and a diamond to Lady Macbeth. Banquo raises the subject of the witches, telling Macbeth that he dreamt of them and remarks on the truth of one of the prophecies. Macbeth immediately lies, saying, *"I think not of them..."*, but he asks for a talk about them another time. His remark to Banquo is quite obscure:

> *"If you shall cleave to my consent, when 'tis,*
> *It shall make honour for you."*

Does he simply mean Banquo to follow his advice or is he in fact asking for his support?

When Macbeth is alone, waiting for the signal of the bell, a vision of a dagger covered in blood appears to him. It is an hallucination caused by his horror at what he is about to do. The dramatic effect of the scene just before Duncan's murder is extremely effective. Macbeth's mood of expectant horror is conveyed vividly by his vision of the bloody dagger. The darkness, the eerie sense of all the world asleep, Macbeth's fear of the sound of his own footsteps – all heighten the tension and suspense.

CHARACTERS

BANQUO

Already the character of Banquo has undergone some change. In this scene Banquo is troubled and edgy. The darkness of the night seems to oppress him. Like Macbeth, Banquo no longer sleeps the sleep of the innocent. He has obviously been struggling with temptation. He prays to be freed of the evil thoughts which visit him in his sleep:

> *"...merciful powers*
> *Restrain in me the cursed thoughts that nature*
> *Gives way to in repose!"*

The Banquo who seemed unmoved by the presence and prophecies of the witches is now uneasy about them. He tells Macbeth:

> *"I dreamt last night of the three Weird Sisters."*

Moreover he is obviously thinking of the implications of the prophecy:

> *"To you they have show'd some truth."*

However Banquo openly admits his temptations whereas Macbeth pretends not to think of them; Banquo fights the temptation, Macbeth succumbs to it.

Macbeth does not give Banquo the opportunity to discuss the matter, yet Banquo was with him when he encountered the witches, shares the secret prophecies with him, and knows of their partial fulfilment. Like Macbeth he must be thinking of the third prophecy and then the prophecy to himself. Macbeth makes a rather ambiguous statement to Banquo.

> *"If you shall cleave to my consent, when 'tis,*
> *It shall make honour for you,"*

It would appear that Macbeth is asking Banquo to follow his advice or stand by him and if so, he will be rewarded. Banquo's answer shows that he suspects a treasonable proposal but that he has no intention of accepting it:

> *"So I lose none*
> *In seeking to augment it, but still keep*
> *My bosom franchis'd and allegiance clear*
> *I shall be counsell'd."*

Banquo is essentially honourable and wishes to keep his conscience clear and his loyalty intact.

We see in this scene that Banquo is subject to the same pressure from evil influences as Macbeth, but that he resists.

MACBETH

Macbeth is self-possessed in his encounter with Banquo and avoids discussing with him the subject of the witches. He is shrewd enough to realize that it is important to keep Banquo on his side and vaguely promises him:

> *"It shall make honour for you."*

When he is alone, he is overwrought and his fears take visible shape in the vision of the dagger. Macbeth's struggle with his conscience is embodied in his highly emotional state. It is, he knows, a *"fatal vision."*

> *"It is the bloody business which informs*
> *Thus to mine eyes."*

Art thou not, fatal vision, sensible
To feeling as to sight?   (Macbeth, Act 2, Scene 1)

Macbeth's sensivity to the horror of the deed is conveyed in his poetic speech. He imagines half the world in darkness experiencing wicked dreams, he hears the cry of the wolf and he visualizes *"wither'd murder"* moving like a ghost. In the silence of the night he guiltily fears every sound, even his own footsteps. He is aware that this dark and silent hour suits the horrible deed. There is a conflict between words and actions:

"Words to the heat of deeds too cold breath gives."

Almost trance-like he obeys the summons of t[...]
and agonizing:

"I go, and it is done; the bell invites me."

> The murder of Duncan takes place off stage. Major catalyst te[...] of the play. Cowardly act. This points to a notion of cowardice and deceit that pervades the narrat[...] of the play.

EXERCISES

1. What light does this scene throw on Banq[...]
2. Study Macbeth's soliloquy: – how would y[...]
3. Discuss the dramatic effectiveness of the v[...]

plot developments

Scene II

The Same.

Enter Lady Macbeth.

Lady Macbeth	That which hath made them drunk hath made me bold, *corageous*
	What hath quench'd them hath given me fire. Hark! Peace!
	It was the owl[1] that shriek'd, the fatal bellman,[2]
	Which gives the stern'st good-night.[3] He is about it: *The murder is happening*
	The doors are open, and the surfeited[4] grooms
	Do mock their charge with snores: I have drugg'd their possets,[5]
	That death and nature do contend about them,
	Whether they live or die.
Macbeth	*[Within]* Who's there? what, ho!
Lady Macbeth	Alack! I am afraid they have awak'd,
	And 'tis not done; the attempt and not the deed
	Confounds[6] us. Hark! I laid their daggers ready;
	He could not miss them. Had he not resembled
	My father as he slept, I had done't. My husband!

[1] considered a bird of ill-omen
[2] It was a custom for a night watchman to ring a bell outside a condemned person's cell the night before his execution
[3] death
[4] drunken
[5] bedtime drink made of hot milk, ale, wine, spice, eggs and sugar

10

[6] ruins

Lady Macbeth doesn't trust Macbeth.

REGICIDE -killing a King

Duncan is dead

Macbeth	I have done the deed. Didst thou not hear a noise?

Paranoia

Lady Macbeth	I heard the owl scream and the crickets cry. Did not you speak?
Macbeth	When?
Lady Macbeth	Now.
Macbeth	As I descended?
Lady Macbeth	Ay.
Macbeth	Hark! Who lies i' the second chamber?

bloody

Lady Macbeth	Donalbain.
Macbeth	This is a sorry sight. *[Looking at his hands.]* 20
Lady Macbeth	A foolish thought to say a sorry sight.
Macbeth	There's one did laugh in's sleep, and one cried 'Murder!' That they did wake each other: I stood and heard them;

[7] prepared themselves

But they did say their prayers, and address'd[7] them
Again to sleep.

Lady Macbeth	There are two lodg'd together.
Macbeth	One cried 'God bless us!' and 'Amen' the other: As they had seen me with these hangman's hands. Listening their fear, I could not say 'Amen', When they did say 'God bless us!'
Lady Macbeth	Consider it not so deeply. 30
Macbeth	But wherefore could not I pronounce 'Amen?' I had most need of blessing, and 'Amen' Stuck in my throat.
Lady Macbeth	(L) These deeds must not be thought After these ways; so, it will make us mad.

Foreshadowing
Lady macbeth
decent into
madness

Macbeth	Methought I heard a voice cry 'Sleep no more! Macbeth does murder sleep,' the innocent sleep,

[8] skein of thread or yarn

Sleep that knits up the ravell'd sleave[8] of care,
The death of each day's life, sore labour's bath,

[9] the main course of a meal

Balm of hurt minds, great nature's second course,[9]
Chief nourisher in life's feast, —   40

Lady Macbeth	What do you mean?
Macbeth	Still it cried, 'Sleep no more!' to all the house: 'Glamis hath murder'd sleep, and therefore Cawdor Shall sleep no more, Macbeth shall sleep no more!'

Lady Macbeth	Who was it that thus cried? Why, worthy Thane,
	You do unbend your noble strength to think
	So brainsickly of things. Go get some water,
	And wash this filthy witness from your hand.
	Why did you bring these daggers from the place?
	They must lie there: go carry them, and smear
	The sleepy grooms with blood. 50

Macbeth   I'll go no more:
I am afraid to think what I have done;
Look on't again I dare not.

Lady Macbeth   Infirm[10] of purpose!
Give me the daggers. The sleeping and the dead
Are but as pictures; 'tis the eye of childhood
That fears a painted devil. If he do bleed,
I'll gild[11] the faces of the grooms withal;
For it must seem their guilt.

[Exit.

[Knocking within.

Macbeth   Whence is that knocking?
How is't with me, when every noise appals me?
What hands are here! Ha! they pluck out mine eyes.
Will all great Neptune's[12] ocean wash this blood   60
Clean from my hand? No, this my hand will rather
The multitudinous[13] seas incarnardine,[14]
Making the green one red.

Re-enter Lady Macbeth.

Lady Macbeth   My hands are of your colour, but I shame
To wear a heart so white. *[Knocking within.]* I hear a knocking
At the south entry; retire we to our chamber;
A little water clears us of this deed;
How easy is it, then! Your constancy
Hath left you unattended.[15] *[Knocking within.]*
Hark! more knocking.   70
Get on your night-gown, lest occasion call us
And show us to be watchers. Be not lost
So poorly in your thoughts.

Macbeth   To know my deed 'twere best not know
myself.[16]   *[Knocking within.*
Wake Duncan with thy knocking! I would thou
couldst!   *[Exeunt.*

[10] weak

[11] cover with a thin layer or gold, i.e. blood (pun on gild and guilt)

[12] Roman god of the sea

[13] numerous
[14] dye red

[15] deserted

[16] it is better to be lost in thought than look his deed in the face

will I ever be free

Scene Analysis

Lady Macbeth awaits Macbeth's return from Duncan's chamber. Her nervousness is obvious as she hears the cry of the owl and associates it with *"the fatal bellman"*. The sound of Macbeth's calling *"Who's there?"* heightens the tension. Macbeth returns and strain, fear and tension is shown in their tense exchange of fearful questions and abrupt answers.

> *"Did not you speak?*
> *When?*
> *Now.*
> *As I descended?*
> *Ay."*

Macbeth suddenly notices the blood on his hands and becomes obsessed with the voices he thought he heard. He relives the moment of panic in the chamber when the grooms almost woke up. His speech about sleep shows an acute awareness of the goodness and innocence he has destroyed. Because he has destroyed peaceful sleep his punishment is:

> *"Sleep no more!"*

While Macbeth is tortured by his conscience and the dawning horror of the murder just committed, Lady Macbeth asks matter-of-factly:

> *"Who was it that thus cried?"*

While Macbeth is concerned with the imaginative implications of murdering *"the innocent sleep"*, Lady Macbeth is very much concerned with the reality. She reprimands him:

> *"Why, worthy Thane,*
> *You do unbend your noble strength to think*
> *So brainsickly of things."*

She orders him:

> *"Go get some water,*
> *And wash this filthy witness from your hand."*

She questions him:

> *"Why did you bring these daggers from the place?"*

Gripped by revulsion, Macbeth cannot bring himself to go back with the daggers which he has mistakenly carried away from the scene of the crime. Angrily, Lady Macbeth dismisses his fears:

> *"The sleeping and the dead*
> *Are but as pictures; 'tis the eye of childhood*
> *That fears a painted devil."*

Will all great Neptune's ocean wash this blood
Clean from my hand?
(Macbeth, Act 2, Scene II)

Not only is she prepared to return to Duncan's chambers to leave back the daggers, she decides:

> *"If he do bleed,*
> *I'll gild the faces of the grooms withal;"*

While she is gone, a knocking at the gate is heard and Macbeth reacts in panic:

> *"Whence is that knocking?*
> *How is't with me, when every noise appals me?"*

While Lady Macbeth is in the very act of smearing the grooms with Duncan's blood, Macbeth is staring helplessly at the blood on his hands. His terrible sense of guilt is conveyed in the image of his bloody hands turning the green ocean red and he wonders:

> *"Will all great Neptune's ocean wash this blood*
> *Clean from my hand?"*

Contrary to her husband Lady Macbeth believes:

> *"A little water clears us of this deed;"*

and she orders Macbeth to retire to his room and put on a nightgown to avoid suspicion.

CHARACTERS
LADY MACBETH

Lady Macbeth shows remarkable composure in preparing for Duncan's murder. She has organized everything as she said she would. She drugs the grooms and lays out the daggers in readiness. However, the effort it must cost her is indicated by the fact that she has to nerve herself with some of the drink given to the grooms, in order to give herself courage. The softer side of her nature is shown in her acknowledgement that she could not kill Duncan herself because he resembled her father. The lady who claimed that she could kill her own baby is not without heart after all. Yet she scornfully dismisses Macbeth's qualms of conscience:

> *"A foolish thought to say a sorry sight."*

She is totally practical, concentrating on immediate considerations. The daggers must be returned, all traces of blood must be removed from her hands and those of her husband and they must return to their chambers before whoever is knocking at the south entry discovers that they are still up. She fears Macbeth's thoughts:

> *"Consider it not so deeply."*

She does not understand his poetic image of sleep, asking:

> *"What do you mean?"*

My hands are of your colour, but I shame
To wear a heart so white.   (Lady Macbeth, Act 2, Scene II)

She may not understand his thought but she does understand that:

"These deeds must not be thought
After these ways; so, it will make us mad."

She shows immense self-control when she realizes that Macbeth has carried away the daggers. Lady Macbeth could not kill Duncan because of his resemblance to her father, yet she has to return to the chamber and actually smear Duncan's blood on the faces of the grooms. Macbeth himself does not dare to *"Look on't again"*, so Lady Macbeth rises to the occasion. She pays a very high price for this act, which she forces herself to do because of her husband's total loss of self-control:

"Yet who would have thought the old man to have had so much blood in him?"

she asks poignantly in the sleep-walking scene.

Lady Macbeth has to calm Macbeth's excited state and so she is cool and practical. She is not horrified at the blood, she is not startled at the knocking. Yet the events of the night imprint themselves forever on her memory and she relives the horror nightly, until she is finally driven to erase the memory once and for all by taking her own life.

MACBETH

Macbeth is in a trance-like state after the murder. As he recounts the terrible deed to Lady Macbeth, he becomes overwrought by the evidence of his guilt. His bloody hands, *"a sorry sight"*, are to him *"these hangman's hands"*. He is deeply troubled at not being able to answer *"Amen"* to the cry of one of the half-waking grooms. His conscience is embodied in the voice he imagines calling out:

> *"Glamis hath murder'd sleep, and therefore Cawdor*
> *Shall sleep no more, Macbeth shall sleep no more!"*

Duncan is natural and healing sleep personified and Macbeth has therefore murdered sleep itself. His thoughts about sleep show a deep sense of guilt, regret and recognition that his life has changed irrevocably. He does not want to know himself as a murderer:

> *"To know my deed 'twere best not know myself."*

In the grip of his conscience Macbeth cannot think rationally or act practically. His mistake in carrying away the daggers shows a serious loss in self-control at the time of the murder. His point blank refusal to return them shows a total loss of nerve:

> *"I'll go no more:*
> *I am afraid to think what I have done;*
> *Look on't again I dare not."*

He is, at this point, totally incapable of thought or action so that it is with some justification that Lady Macbeth remarks:

> *"Your constancy*
> *Hath left you unattended."*

Macbeth is obsessed with the horror of the murder and seems oblivious of the danger of immediate discovery. Aware of the knocking, he is troubled but irresolute. It is Lady Macbeth who urges him to the practicalities of washing his hands and putting on a nightgown. While she is facing reality, he is wishing the deed undone:

> *"Wake Duncan with thy knocking! I would thou couldst."*

EXERCISES

1. Is the murder scene dramatically successful?
2. Give an account of the conversation between Macbeth and Lady Macbeth after the murder.
3. Show how there is a clear contrast between the characters of Macbeth and Lady Macbeth in this scene.
4. Discuss the effect of the knocking on the gate on (a) Macbeth; (b) Lady Macbeth; (c) the audience.
5. Comment on the effectiveness of the imagery of sleep and blood in this scene.

Scene III

Scene of comic relief

The Same.

Knocking within. Enter a porter.

Porter Here's a knocking indeed! If a man were porter of hell-gate he should have old turning the key.[1] *[Knocking within.]* Knock, knock, knock! Who's there, i' the name of Beelzebub?[2] Here's a farmer that hanged himself on the expectation of plenty:[3] come in time; have napkins[4] enough about you; here you'll sweat for't. *[Knocking within.]* Knock, knock! Who's there, i' the other devil's name! Faith, here's an equivocator,[5] that could swear in both the scales against either   10 scale;[6] who committed treason enough for God's sake, yet could not equivocate to heaven: O! come in, equivocator. *[Knocking within.]* Knock, knock, knock! Who's there? Faith, here's an English tailor come hither for stealing out of a French hose:[7] come in, tailor; here you may roast your goose.[8] *[Knocking within.]* Knock, knock; never at quiet! What are you? But this place is too cold for hell. I'll devil-porter it no further: I had thought to have let in some of all   20 professions that go the primrose way[9] to the everlasting bonfire. *[Knocking within.]* Anon, anon! I pray you, remember the porter. *[Opens the gate.]*

Enter Macduff and Lennox.

Macduff Was it so late, friend, ere you went to bed, That you do lie so late?

Porter Faith, sir, we were carousing[10] till the second cock;[11] and drink, sir, is a great provoker of three things.

Macduff What three things does drink especially provoke?

Porter Marry,[12] sir, nose-painting, sleep, and   30 urine. Lechery,[13] sir, it provokes, and unprovokes; it provokes the desire, but it takes away the performance. Therefore much drink may be said to be an equivo-cator with lechery; it makes him; and it mars him; it sets him on, and it takes him

[1] he would have to turn the key very often

[2] the Prince of the devils

[3] expecting an abundant crop which would bring down the price of corn
[4] hankerchiefs
[5] one who uses ambiguous words: a topical point at the time. Garnet (also called Farmer) was hanged on 3rd May 1 606 for his part in the Gunpowder plot. At his trial, he defended himself by equivocation
[6] justice was represented as a lady holding a scales
[7] wide breeches. The tailor cheated by skimping
[8] a tailor's iron

[9] the easy way

[10] drinking heavily
[11] about 3 a.m.

[12] by Mary

[13] lust

off; it persuades him, and disheartens him;
makes him stand to, and not stand to; in
conclusion, equivocates him in a sleep, and,
giving him the lie,[14] leaves him.   40

Macduff   I believe drink gave thee the lie[15] last night.
Porter   That it did, sir, i' the very throat o' me: but I
                requited[16] him for his lie; and, I think, being
                too strong for him, though he took up my legs
                sometime, yet I made a shift to cast him.[17]
Macduff   Is thy master stirring?

Enter Macbeth.

Our knocking has awak'd him; here he comes.
Lennox   Good morrow, noble sir.
Macbeth   Good morrow, both.
Macduff   Is the King stirring, worthy Thane?
Macbeth   Not yet.
Macduff   He did command me to call timely[18] on him: 50
                I have almost slipp'd the hour.
Macbeth   I'll bring you to him.
Macduff   I know this is a joyful trouble to you;
                But yet 'tis one.
Macbeth   The labour we delight in physics[19] pain.
                This is the door.
Macduff   I'll make so bold to call,
                For 'tis my limited service.[20]
                                                        [*Exit.*

macduff goes to find the king

Lennox   Goes the King hence to-day?
Macbeth   He does: he did appoint so.
Lennox   The night has been unruly:[21] where we lay,
                Our chimneys were blown down; and, as they say,
                                                               60

Pathetic fallacy

Lamentings heard i' the air; strange screams of
  death,
And prophesying with accents terrible
Of dire combustion[22] and confus'd events
New hatch'd to the woeful time.[23] The obscure
  bird[24]
Clamour'd the livelong night: some say the
  earth
Was feverous and did shake.
Macbeth   'Twas a rough night.
Lennox   My young remembrance cannot parallel
                A fellow to it.[25]

[14] making him dream
[15] made you drunk
[16] repaid
[17] the porter describes his struggle against drunkeness as a wrestling match
[18] early
[19] cures
[20] appointed duty
[21] wild
[22] terrible tumult
[23] produced by a sorrowful state of affairs
[24] the owl; the night bird
[25] remember a night equal to this one.

Re-enter Macduff.

Macduff	O horror! horror! horror! Tongue nor heart
	Cannot conceive nor name thee! 70
Macbeth & Lennox	What's the matter?
Macduff	Confusion now hath made his masterpiece!
	Most sacrilegious[26] murder hath broke ope
	The Lord's anointed temple, and stole thence
	The life o' the building!
Macbeth	What is't you say? the life?
Lennox	Mean you his Majesty?
Macduff	Approach the chamber, and destroy your sight
	With a new Gorgon:[27] Do not bid me speak;
	See, and then speak yourselves.

[*Exeunt Macbeth and Lennox.*

Awake! awake!
Ring the alarum-bell. Murder and treason!
Banquo and Donalbain! Malcolm! awake! 80
Shake off this downy sleep,[28] death's
  counterfeit,[29]
And look on death itself! Up, up, and see
The great doom's image![30] Malcolm! Banquo!
As from your graves rise up, and walk like
  sprites,[31]
To countenance[32] this horror! Ring the bell.

[*Bell rings.*

Enter Lady Macbeth.

Lady Macbeth	What's the business,
	That such a hideous trumpet calls to parley[33]
	The sleepers of the house? Speak, speak!
Macduff	O gentle lady!
	'Tis not for you to hear what I can speak;
	The repetition in a woman's ear 90
	Would murder as it fell.

Enter Banquo.

O Banquo! Banquo!
Our royal master's murder'd!

Lady Macbeth	Woe, alas!
	What! in our house?
Banquo	Too cruel any where.
	Dear Duff, I prithee, contradict thyself,
	And say it is not so.

26 Kings were themselves considered divine because they represented God

27 in classical mythology the snake-haired monster Medusa turned any onlooker into stone

28 placid sleep

29 image

30 the picture of the last judgement

31 spirits

32 face

33 discussion

Re-enter Macbeth and Lennox, with Ross.

I cant live

³⁴happening	**Macbeth**

Macbeth
Had I but died an hour before this chance³⁴
I had liv'd a blessed time; for, from this instant,
There's nothing serious in mortality,³⁵

³⁵human life

All is but toys; renown and grace is dead,

³⁶dregs
³⁷world

The wine of life is drawn, and the mere lees³⁶   *100*
Is left this vault³⁷ to brag of.

Enter Malcolm and Donalbain.

Donalbain   What is amiss?
Macbeth   You are, and do not know't.
The spring, the head, the fountain of your
        blood,
Is stopp'd; the very source of it is stopp'd.

Macduff   Your royal father's murder'd.
Malcolm   O! by whom?

Servants

Lennox   Those of his chamber, as it seem'd, had done't:

³⁸marked distinctly

Their hands and faces were all badg'd³⁸ with
        blood;
So were their daggers, which unwip'd we found
Upon their pillows: they star'd, and were
        distracted;
No man's life was to be trusted with them.   *110*

Macbeth   O! yet I do repent me of my fury,
That I did kill them.

Macduff   Wherefore did you so?

³⁹bewildered
⁴⁰moderate

Macbeth   Who can be wise, amaz'd,³⁹ temperate⁴⁰ and
        furious,
Loyal and neutral, in a moment? No man:

⁴¹haste
⁴²because of his violent love
   for Duncan he did not
   pause to listen to reason
⁴³streaked

The expedition⁴¹ of my violent love
Outran the pauser,⁴² reason. Here lay Duncan,
His silver skin lac'd⁴³ with his golden blood;
And his gash'd stabs look'd like a breach in
        nature
For ruin's wasteful entrance: there, the
        murderers,
Steep'd in the colours of their trade, their
        daggers   *120*

⁴⁴cover

Unmannerly breech'd⁴⁴ with gore; who could
        refrain,
That had a heart to love, and in that heart
Courage to make his love known?

Lady Macbeth → Faints   Help me hence, ho!
Macduff   Look to the lady.

Malcolm	*[Aside to Donalbain]* Why do we hold our tongues,
	That most may claim this argument for ours?[45]
Donalbain	*[Aside to Malcolm]* What should be spoken
	Here, where our fate, hid in an auger-hole,[46]
	May rush and seize us? Let's away:
	Our tears are not yet brew'd. 130
Malcolm	*[Aside to Donalbain]* Nor our strong sorrow
	Upon the foot of motion.[47]
Banquo	Look to the lady:

[Lady Macbeth is carried out.

vow revenge

> And when we have our naked frailties hid,[48]
> That suffer in exposure, let us meet,
> And question this most bloody piece of work,
> To know it further. Fears and scruples shake us:
> In the great hand of God I stand, and thence
> Against the undivulg'd[49] pretence I fight
> Of treasonous malice.

Macduff	And so do I. 140
All	So all.
Macbeth	Let's briefly put on manly readiness,
	And meet i' the hall together.
All	Well contented.[50]

[Exeunt all but Malcolm & Donalbain.

Malcolm	What will you do? Let's not consort[51] with
	them:
	To show an unfelt sorrow is an office[52]
	Which the false man does easy. I'll to England.
Donalbain	To Ireland, I; our separated fortune

our lives are in danger

> Shall keep us both the safer: where we are,
> There's daggers in men's smiles: the near in
>   blood, (L)
> The nearer bloody.[53]

Malcolm	This murderous shaft[54] that's shot

I will flee to London

I will flee to Ireland

> Hath not yet lighted, and our safest way
> Is to avoid the aim: therefore, to horse,   150
> And let us not be dainty[55] of leave-taking,
> But shift away:[56] there's warrant in that theft[57]
> Which steals itself when there's no mercy left.

[Exeunt.

Side notes:

[45] That have the most claim to make ourselves heard

[46] hole bored in wood with an auger, a tool for boring holes in wood, i.e. an unsuspected place

[47] ready to act

[48] when we have dressed ourselves

[49] hidden plot

[50] agreed

[51] keep company

[52] task

[53] the most closely related to Duncan are most likely the murderers

[54] arrow

[55] particular

[56] slip away unnoticed

[57] there's justification for stealing away

Scene Analysis

The porter who finally appears to answer the knocking at the gate imagines that he is a porter of hell, a very obvious symbol for the castle which has become a hell. The grim humour of the porter, interspersed with the continuous knocking, gives intense dramatic impact to this scene of the murder. Although the porter cannot just be considered as comic relief, there is a certain release of tension at this point. The porter's speech touches on themes which run through the play. His reference to Garnet, the equivocator, reinforces the theme of equivocation. His reference to treason reminds us of Macbeth's crime. His antitheses and riddles call to mind the riddles and antitheses of the witches.

Macbeth calmly greets Macduff and Lennox, not even flinching when Macduff asks *"Is the King stirring?"* While Macduff goes to awaken the king, Lennox speaks of unnatural happenings during the night, reflecting in natural and supernatural terms the disorder of Macbeth's deed:

> *"...prophesying with accents terrible*
> *Of dire combustion and confus'd events*
> *New hatch'd to the woeful time."*

Macduff's horrified reaction to the murder of Duncan brings home the awful reality of what Macbeth has done. His words ring out:

> *"O horror! horror! horror! Tongue nor heart*
> *Cannot conceive nor name thee!"*

Macbeth does not betray himself, asking

> *"What's the matter?"*
> *"What is't you say? the life?"*

Macbeth now has sufficient self-control to be able to go to Duncan's chamber with Lennox. Lady Macbeth puts on a good act of not knowing anything:

> *"What's the business,*
> *That such a hideous trumpet calls to parley*
> *The sleepers of the house? Speak, speak!"*

Macduff's words to her are ironic in the extreme:

> *"O gentle lady!*
> *'Tis not for you to hear what I can speak;*
> *The repetition in a woman's ear*
> *Would murder as it fell."*

Macbeth's words, when he returns, are on the surface hypocritical, but there is an underlying sense of truth in the sentiments expressed. Macbeth is pretending innocence so the words are a lie and yet they reveal the truth of the consequences of the deed. However, as he tries to explain to Macduff why he murdered the grooms, his speech is somewhat suspect because of the exaggerated degree of stress and over-emphasis on the blood:

> *"Here lay Duncan,*
> *His silver skin lac'd with his golden blood;*
> *And his gash'd stabs look'd like a breach in nature*
> *For ruin's wasteful entrance: there, the murderers,*
> *Steep'd in the colours of their trade, their daggers*
> *Unmannerly breech'd with gore."*

At this moment Lady Macbeth faints. There has been much critical speculation as to whether Lady Macbeth really faints due to the strain, or only pretends to faint in order to divert attention from her husband. It makes little difference which conclusion one comes to – the dramatic effect is the same – Lady Macbeth draws attention to herself and a very critical moment passes.

Banquo takes charge of affairs and declares that he intends to investigate the crime. Malcolm makes no attempt to assert his claim to the throne. Donalbain suggests flight and he agrees.

CHARACTERS
THE PORTER
Because the porter is drunk he is somewhat comic. He is an ordinary man, coarsely humorous and quite saucy. As he goes through the pantomime of admitting various people into hell, he provides a commentary on human weakness, deception, equivocation and hints at subsequent retribution. He exchanges pleasantries with Macduff, joking about the effects of drink. His struggle to stay sober is comically described as a wrestling match with drink which he claims he won. The porter quietly disappears as soon as Macbeth enters to greet Macduff and Lennox.

MACDUFF
Macduff is entrusted with rousing the king for an early departure from Inverness and thus has a special relationship with Duncan. He is overcome with the horror of finding Duncan murdered. He is so upset that he is unable to describe the tragedy.

> *"...Do not bid me speak;*
> *See, and then speak yourselves."*

Macduff raises the alarm but shows the utmost solicitude to Lady Macbeth. It is Macduff who questions Macbeth about his admission of killing the grooms:

> *"Wherefore did you so?"*

He immediately aligns himself with Banquo in his fight against *"treasonous malice"*. We are prepared for Macduff's future leadership because of his closeness to the king and his obvious integrity of character.

LENNOX

With Macduff, Lennox is one of the first to discover the murder of King Duncan. While Macduff goes to call the king, Lennox talks to Macbeth, commenting on the *"unruly"* night:

> *"My young remembrance cannot parallel*
> *A fellow to it."*

Lennox accompanies Macbeth to view the scene of the murder and it is he who describes the apparent guilt of the grooms:

> *"Those of his chamber, as it seem'd, had done't:*
> *Their hands and faces were all badg'd with blood;*
> *So were their daggers, which unwip'd we found*
> *Upon their pillows: they star'd and were distracted;*
> *o man's life was to be trusted with them."*

BANQUO

Banquo is noticeably silent in comparison to Macduff. In the light of his conversation with Macbeth in *Scene I,* there is little doubt that Banquo must suspect the truth on learning of Duncan's murder. It is Banquo who proposes to the others that they meet to discuss and investigate the murder, and he makes a very positive declaration of his integrity of purpose:

> *"...let us meet,*
> *And question this most bloody piece of work,*
> *To know it further. Fears and scruples shake us:*
> *In the great hand of God I stand, and thence*
> *Against the undivulg'd pretence I fight*
> *Of treasonous malice."*

MALCOLM

Malcolm takes no part in the discussion after the murder. He does not make his father's mistake of trusting everybody. He does not know if any of the thanes can be trusted. Malcolm is not deceived by expressions of mourning and realizes how easy hypocrisy is:

> *"To show an unfelt sorrow is an office*
> *Which the false man does easy."*

Malcolm keeps his head in the moment of crisis. Although he has the greatest claim to make himself heard, he shrewdly judges the situation:

> *"This murderous shaft that's shot*
> *Hath not yet lighted, and our safest way*
> *Is to avoid the aim:"*

Malcolm's resoluteness at this point is an indication of his future role as the lawful king of Scotland.

DONALBAIN

Like his brother, Donalbain remains remarkably calm during this scene. With great insight he realizes they are trapped and that it would be better to get away. His sorrow and that of his brother will be expressed at another time, in another place, privately. Donalbain is prepared to go his own way for their mutual safety. With cynical wisdom he realizes:

> *"There's daggers in men's smiles".*

MACBETH

Macbeth appears composed as he greets Macduff and Lennox. However he speaks little, answering their questions briefly. He makes good pretence of not knowing to what Macduff is referring:

> *"What is't you say? the life?"*

Yet again he loses all self-control, murdering the grooms which was not part of the original plan. In comparison to Banquo and Macduff who do not give such easy expression to their very real sorrow, Macbeth's lamentation seems contrived. He searches for metaphors to express his grief:

> *"All is but toys; reknown and grace is dead,*
> *The wine of life is drawn, and the mere lees*
> *Is left this vault to brag of."*

Yet the sentiments expressed are actually ironically sincere when applied to himself:

> *"Had I but died an hour before this chance*
> *I had liv'd a blessed time; for, from this instant,*
> *There's nothing serious in mortality..."*

If indeed he had died he would have been saved from damnation. The image of divine order which he has destroyed is not so much a sign of his hypocrisy, as of his judgement of the deed. His answer to Macduff's question as to why he murdered the grooms has a ring of truth about it, despite its obvious intention to cover up:

> *"Who can be wise, amaz'd, temperate and furious,*
> *Loyal and neutral, in a moment? No man:*
> *The expedition of my violent love*
> *Outran the pauser, reason."*

Macbeth has indeed allowed his feelings to overcome his reason, but he hypocritically attributes it to *"The expedition of my violent love"*. His description of his feelings on beholding Duncan's body becomes somewhat excessive:

> *"...Here lay Duncan,*
> *His silver skin lac'd with his golden blood"*

His description of the bloody scene is so overdone that it causes Lady Macbeth to faint.

Macbeth puts on a good show of being of one mind with the other thanes to *"question this most bloody piece of work"*. He appears to be the one giving the orders, taking the initiative:

> *"Let's briefly put on manly readiness,*
> *meet i' the hall together."*

LADY MACBETH

Lady Macbeth has little to say in this scene. She acts surprised on hearing all the commotion. Her reaction to the news:

> *"Woe, alas!*
> *What! in our house?"*

seems somewhat inadequate and Banquo seems to feel this as he replies:

> *"Too cruel any where"*

After Macbeth makes his speech justifying the killing of the grooms, she calls out for help and faints. Lady Macbeth must have been shocked at hearing Macbeth say that he had murdered the grooms. Moreover, Macbeth's rather gory description must undoubtedly have brought back to mind her traumatic memory of smearing the grooms with Duncan's blood. She may have fainted from a combination of shock and squeamishness. Alternatively, she may have felt that Macbeth was saying too much, was in danger of revealing his involvement with the crime, and deliberately diverted attention. Either way, she saved the situation by interrupting the conversation of the thanes.

EXERCISES

1. What dramatic relevance has the porter scene in the context of the play?
2. Would you consider that the porter scene provides comic relief?
3. (a) Do you think that Macbeth acts well when the murder is discovered?
   (b) Compare the way he acts before and after the murder.
4. (a) Does Lady Macbeth act as well as one might expect in this scene?
   (b) Do you think that she really faints or pretends to faint?
5. Consider how each of the characters who enter after the ringing of the alarum bell reacts to the murder of Duncan.

The Same — Outside the Castle.

Enter Ross and an Old Man. → Representitve of the people of scotland

Old Man	Threescore and ten[1] I can remember well;
	Within the volume of which time I have seen
	Hours dreadful and things strange, but this sore night
	Hath trifled former knowings.[2]
Ross	Ah! good father,
	Thou seest, the heavens, as troubled with man's act,
	Threaten his bloody stage:[3] by the clock 'tis day,
	And yet dark night strangles the travelling lamp.[4]
	Is't night's predominance, or the day's shame,
	That darkness does the face of earth entomb,
	When living light should kiss it?
Old Man	'Tis unnatural,
	Even like the deed that's done. On Tuesday last,
	A falcon, towering in her pride of place[5]
	Was by a mousing[6] owl hawk'd[7] at and kill'd.
Ross	And Duncan's horses,— a thing most strange and certain, —
	Beauteous and swift, the minions[8] of their race,
	Turn'd wild in nature, broke their stalls, flung out,
	Contending[9] 'gainst obedience, as they would
	Make war with mankind.
Old Man	'Tis said they eat each other.
Ross	They did so; to the amazement of mine eyes,
	That look'd upon't. Here comes the good Macduff.

Enter Macduff.

	How goes the world, sir, now?
Macduff	Why, see you not?
Ross	Is't known who did this more than bloody deed?
Macduff	Those that Macbeth hath slain.
Ross	Alas, the day!
	What good could they pretend?
Macduff	They were suborn'd.[10]
	Malcolm and Donalbain, the King's two sons,
	Are stol'n away and fled, which puts upon them
	Suspicion of the deed.

Side notes:

[1] 3 X 20 + 10 = 70

[2] turned previous experiences into mere trifles

[3] the earth
[4] the sun

[5] falconry terms: Towering = circling higher; pride of place = highest soaring point
[6] searching for mice
[7] attacked as if by a howk
[8] most favoured

[9] rebelling

[10] bribed

Handwritten annotations:
First indication Scotland is in Chaos

scotland is in Chaos

¹¹gree   ill!
¹²swall

30

¹³the kings of Scotland were
crowned on the famous
stone of Scone

	king	
Macduff		To be invested.
Ross		Where is Duncan's body?
Macduff		Carried to Colmekill;¹⁴

¹⁴the island of St. Columba
(Iona) where the Scottish
kings were buried

The sacred storehouse of his predecessors
And guardian of their bones.

Ross		*suspicious of Macbeth* Will you to Scone?
Macduff		No, cousin, I'll to Fife.
Ross		Well, I will thither.
Macduff		Well, may you see things well done there:
adieu!

Lest our old robes sit easier than our new!

| Ross | | Farewell, father. |
| Old Man | | God's benison¹⁵ go with you; and with those *40* |

¹⁵blessing

That would make good of bad, and friends of
foes!

[Exeunt.

Scene Analysis

In this scene an anonymous old man, representing the ordinary people of Scotland, discusses the murder of Duncan with Ross. They enumerate the unnatural events which seem supernaturally significant in the light of the crime. Nature is disturbed, the natural order of things reversed. A falcon was killed by an owl, Duncan's beautiful horses turn wild and eat each other, it is dark even though it is daytime. The old man relates *"this sore night"* to Duncan's murder:

> " 'Tis unnatural,
> *Even like the deed that's done."*

Macduff arrives and informs them of the council meeting that morning. We are told that Macbeth has already been named king, that Duncan's two sons have fled the country and have been accused of the crime. Macduff refuses to go to the coronation with Ross and fears that conditions in Scotland will be worse under the new king. The old man gives them his blessing along with those:

> *"That would make good of bad, and friends of foes!"*

again drawing attention to the opposition of good and bad in the play. *Scene IV is* short but very important. It tells us of the success of Macbeth's schemes and gives an indication of the future importance of Macduff as a character.

CHARACTERS

ROSS

Ross, as so many times in the play, has almost the effect of a chorus. He comments on the night's dreadful omens saying:

> *"Thou seest, the heavens as troubled with man's act,*
> *Threaten his bloody stage:"*

He confirms the rumour that Duncan's horses ate each other:

> *"They did so; to the amazement of mine eyes,*
> *That look'd upon 't."*

Ross is puzzled as to why Malcolm and Donalbain should have murdered their father:

> *"What good could they pretend?"*

Yet he immediately accepts that *"thriftless ambition"* prompted their treachery. Ross seems to have no qualms about going to Scone for Macbeth's coronation.

MACDUFF

Macduff seems very curt with Ross in this scene. In reply to Ross's question;

> *"How goes the world, sir, now?"*

he replies gruffly:

> *"Why, see you not?"*

His intention to go home to Fife instead of attending the coronation at Scone indicates his suspicions about Macbeth. He uses the now familiar imagery of clothes to express his unease about the future:

> *"Lest our old robes sit easier than our new!"*

He shows himself to be a man of principle by his refusal to acknowledge the kingship of a man he does not trust.

EXERCISES

1. How does this short scene advance the plot?
2. What is the symbolic significance of all the unusual happenings commented on by the old man and Ross?
3. Discuss the importance of the fact that Macduff does not go to Scone.

REVISION

> "Most sacrilegious murder hath broke ope
> The Lord's anointed temple..."   (Macduff, Act 2, Scene III)

After Duncan retires for the night Macbeth awaits his wife's signal to commit the murder. He meets Banquo and Fleance in the courtyard. Nervous and considerably overwrought, Macbeth thinks he sees a dagger which leads him to Duncan's chamber. The way has been prepared by Lady Macbeth and Macbeth murders the sleeping king. Totally unnerved by the experience, he takes the daggers away with him and refuses to return to the scene of the murder. Scornful of his ineffectiveness, Lady Macbeth replaces the daggers herself. A loud knocking at the gate is heard and the porter lets in Macduff and Lennox who discover the murder. In the confusion Malcolm and Donalbain make their escape and are believed guilty of the murder.

POINTS TO NOTE

1. *Scene I* introduces Fleance, through whom Banquo is to be the father of kings.
2. The scene of the murder does not present the actual deed; it emphasizes the effect of the deed on Macbeth's mind.
3. Lady Macbeth's strength of character comes to the fore in the face of her husband's weakness and panic.
4. In his preoccupation with *"murdering sleep"*, Macbeth strikes a keynote of the play and anticipates the place that loss of sleep will have in the later part of the play.
5. Lady Macbeth ironically foreshadows her own end when she says: *"These deeds must not be thought/After these ways; so, it will make us mad."*
6. Already Macbeth's scrupulous hesitations at the thought of the murder have left him after the murder of Duncan, and he kills the guards without any qualms.
7. The escape of Malcolm and Donalbain completes Macbeth's victory, but ultimately leads to his defeat.
8. It was the general belief of the time that all nature was outraged by the perpetration of a crime against a lawful ruler. The unnatural events reported on the night of the murder suggest the repercussions of the murder and an end to normal living until order is restored.

REVISION ASSIGNMENT

Describe Macbeth before, during and after the murder of Duncan. Assess the role played by Lady Macbeth in the murder.

Act 3
Scene 1

Forres — A Room in the Palace.

Enter Banquo. Banquo is alone on stage

Banquo	Thou hast it now: King, Cawdor, Glamis, all,
	As the weird women promis'd; and, I fear,
	Thou play'dst most foully for't; yet it was said
	It should not stand[1] in thy posterity,[2]
	But that myself should be the root and father
	Of many kings. If there come truth from
	them,—
	As upon thee, Macbeth, their speeches shine,—
	Why, by the verities[3] on thee made good,
	May they not be my oracles as well,
	And set me up in hope? But, hush! no more. *10*

[1] remain
[2] descendants

[3] truth

*Sennet[4] sounded. Enter Macbeth, as King; Lady Macbeth,
as Queen; Lennox, Ross, Lords, Ladies, and Attendants*

[4] trumpet signal

Macbeth has organised a feast in Banquos honour.

Macbeth	Here's our chief guest.
Lady Macbeth	If he had been forgotten,
	It had been as a gap in our great feast,
	And all-thing[5] unbecoming.
Macbeth	To-night we hold a solemn supper, sir,
	And I'll request your presence.
Banquo	Let your Highness
	Command upon me; to the which my duties
	Are with a most indissoluble tie
	For ever knit.
Macbeth	Ride you this afternoon?
Banquo	Ay, my good lord.
Macbeth	We should have else desir'd your good
	advice – *20*
	Which still[6] hath been both grave and
	prosperous[7]–
	In this day's council; but we'll take to-morrow.
	Is't far you ride?
Banquo	As far, my lord, as will fill up the time
	'Twixt[8] this and supper. Go not my horse the better,
	I must become a borrower of the night
	For a dark hour or twain.[9]
Macbeth	(L) Fail not our feast.

[5] entirely

[6] always
[7] profitable

[8] between

[9] if his horse does not go faster than usual he will not be back until an hour or two after nightfall

	Banquo	My lord, I will not.
[10] lodged	**Macbeth**	We hear our bloody cousins are bestow'd[10]
	Patracider —	In England and in Ireland, not confessing *30*
	kill your	Their cruel parricide, filling their hearers
	father	With strange invention; but of that to-morrow,
[11] in addition		When therewithal[11] we shall have cause of state[12]
[12] state affairs		Craving us jointly.[13] Hie you to horse; adieu
[13] needing the attention of us both		Till you return at night. Goes Fleance with you?
[14] we must go	**Banquo**	Ay, my good lord: our time does call upon's.[14]
	Macbeth	I wish your horses swift and sure of foot;
		And so I do commend you to their backs.
		Farewell.

[Exit Banquo.

Let every man be master of his time   *40*
Till seven at night; to make society
The sweeter welcome, we will keep ourself
Till supper-time alone; while then, God be with
    you!

[Exeunt all but Macbeth & an Attendant.

[15] sir(speaking to a servant)		Sirrah,[15] a word with you. Attend those men our
[16] are they awaiting orders?		pleasure?[16]
	Attendant	They are, my lord, without the palace gate.
	Macbeth	Bring them before us.

King   *[Exit Attendant.*

To be thus is nothing;
But to be safely thus. Our fears in Banquo
Stick deep, and in his royalty of nature
Reigns that which would be fear'd. 'Tis much he
    dares,
And to that dauntless temper[17] of his mind,   *50*
He hath a wisdom that doth guide his valour
To act in safety. There is none but he
Whose being I do fear; and under him
My Genius[18] is rebuk'd,[19] as it is said
Mark Antony's was by Caesar. He chid[20] the
    Sisters
When first they put the name of King upon me,
And bade[21] them speak to him; then, prophet-
    like,
They hail'd him father to a line of kings.
Upon my head they plac'd a fruitless crown,[22]   *useless*
And put a barren sceptre in my gripe,[23]   *60*
Thence to be wrench'd with an unlineal hand,[24]
No son of mine succeeding. If't be so,
For Banquo's issue[25] have I fil'd[26] my mind;

[17] quality

[18] guardian spirit
[19] fearful
[20] chided, scolded

Solliloquy

[21] ordered

[22] Macbeth has no son to
    succeed him to the throne
[23] grip
[24] someone not belonging to
    Macbeth's line
[25] children
[26] defiled, dirtied

Soliloquy

For them the gracious Duncan have I murder'd;
Put rancours²⁷ in the vessel of my peace²⁸
Only for them; and mine eternal jewel²⁹
Given to the common enemy of man,³⁰
To make them kings, the seed of Banquo kings!
Rather than so, come, Fate, into the list,³¹
And champion me to th' utterance.³² Who's
    there?   70

²⁷ bitterness
²⁸ my heart
²⁹ immortal soul
³⁰ the devil

³¹ let fate fight against me
³² challenge to the death

Re-enter Attendant, with two Murderers.

Now go to the door, and stay there till we call.
                        [Exit Attendant.
Was it not yesterday we spoke together?

1st Murderer It was, so please your Highness.
Macbeth   Well then, now
Have you consider'd of my speeches? <u>Know</u>
That it was he, in the times past, which held you
So under fortune,³³ which you thought had been
Our innocent self. This I made good³⁴ to you
In our last conference, pass'd in probation³⁵ with
    you,
How you were borne in hand,³⁶ how cross'd, the
    instruments,³⁷
Who wrought³⁸ with them, and all things else
    that might   80
To half a soul³⁹ and to a notion craz'd⁴⁰
Say 'Thus did Banquo.'

³³ beneath true worth
³⁴ explained
³⁵ passed in detail

³⁶ deceived
³⁷ means

³⁸ worked

³⁹ a half-wit
⁴⁰ a crazy mind

Macbeth is bad mouthing Banquo

He's giving the murderers motivation for murder. Banquo was bad mouthing them to the king.

1st Murderer   You made it known to us.
Macbeth I did so; and went further, which is now
Our point of second meeting. Do you find
Your patience so predominant in your nature
That you can let this go? Are you so gospell'd⁴¹
To pray for this good man and for his issue,
Whose heavy hand hath bow'd you to the grave
And beggar'd yours⁴² for ever?

⁴¹ pious

⁴² made your children poor

1st Murderer   We are men, my liege.
Macbeth Ay, in the catalogue ye go for men;   90
As hounds and greyhounds, mongrels, spaniels,
    curs.
Shoughs,⁴³ water-rugs,⁴⁴ and demi-wolves, are
    clept⁴⁵
All by the name of dogs. The valu'd file⁴⁶
Distinguishes the swift, the slow, the subtle,
The house-keeper,⁴⁷ the hunter, every one
According to the gift which bounteous⁴⁸ nature

⁴³ shaggy-haired dogs
⁴⁴ dogs used to water
⁴⁵ called
⁴⁶ list of the value of each

⁴⁷ watch dog
⁴⁸ liberal

Animal imagery — Possible part of an exam question

[49] enclosed, included
[50] special distinction
[51] apart from the list

as long as Banquo lives Macbeth is in danger

[52] removes
[53] fastens
[54] as long as Banquo lives he is in danger

[55] blows
[56] angered

[57] pulled by misfortune

[58] enmity
[59] threatens
[60] heart

Macbeth refuses to murder Banquo himself

[61] justify it

[62] various

[63] the exact time

[64] at some distance
[65] understood
[66] clear of suspicion
[67] uneveness
[68] flaws

[69] important

Hath in him clos'd;[49] whereby he does receive
Particular addition,[50] from the bill[51]
That writes them all alike: and so of men.
Now, if you have a station in the file,   100
Not i' the worst rank of manhood, say 't;
And I will put that business in your bosoms,
Whose execution takes your enemy off,[52]
Grapples[53] you to the heart and love of us,
Who wear our health but sickly in his life,[54]
Which in his death were perfect.

2nd Murderer   I am one, my liege,
Whom the vile blows and buffets[55] of the world
Have so incens'd[56] that I am reckless what
I do to spite the world.

1st Murderer   And I another,
So weary with disasters, tugg'd with fortune,[57]   110
That I would set my life on any chance,
To mend't or be rid on't.

Macbeth   Both of you
Know Banquo was your enemy.

2nd Murderer   True, my lord.
Macbeth
So is he mine; and in such bloody distance[58]
That every minute of his being thrusts[59]
Against my near'st of life;[60] and though I could
With bare-fac'd power sweep him from my sight
And bid my will avouch it,[61] yet I must not,
For certain friends that are both his and mine,
Whose loves I may not drop, but wail his fall   120
Whom I myself struck down. And thence it is
That I to your assistance do make love,
Masking the business from the common eye
For sundry[62] weighty reasons.

2nd Murderer   We shall, my lord,
Perform what you command us.

1st Murderer   Though our lives –
Macbeth
Your spirits shine through you. Within this hour
  at most,
I will advise you where to plant yourselves,
Acquaint you with the perfect spy o' the time,[63]
The moment on't; for't must be done to-night,
And something[64] from the palace; always   130
  thought[65]
That I require a clearness:[66] and with him–
To leave no rubs[67] nor botches[68] in the work–
Fleance his son, that keeps him company,
Whose absence is no less material[69] to me
Than is his father's, must embrace the fate

Fleance too must die

Of that dark hour. Resolve yourselves apart;[70]
I'll come to you anon.

[70]make up your minds in my absence

2nd Murderer   We are resolv'd, my lord.
Macbeth   I'll call upon you straight: abide within.

[*Exeunt Murderers.*

 It is concluded: Banquo, thy soul's flight,
If it find heaven, must find it out to-night.   *140*

[*Exit.*

Scene Analysis

In this scene Banquo's thoughts are on Macbeth, the witches and his own future. He strongly suspects that Macbeth is guilty:

> *"...and, I fear,*
> *Thou play'dst most foully for't;"*

The predictions for Macbeth have all come true and he realizes that there is a good chance of them coming true for him also:

> *"If there come truth from them, –*
> *As upon thee, Macbeth, their speeches shine, –*
> *Why, by the verities on thee made good,*
> *May they not be my oracles as well,*
> *And set me up in hope?"*

Macbeth treats Banquo with great deference, requesting his presence as the chief guest at the *"solemn supper"*. Like Banquo, Macbeth's thoughts are on the second half of the prophesies. He fears Banquo and is embittered that he only has *"a fruitless crown"* and a *"barren sceptre"* while Banquo has the promise of succession. He determines to change his destiny. However he does not want to kill Banquo himself and hires two murderers.

CHARACTERS
THE MURDERERS

The murderers are dour and curt. Macbeth has obviously attempted to persuade them to the murder of Banquo by listing for them their grievances against Banquo:

> *"This I made good to you*
> *In our last conference, pass'd in probation with you,*
> *How you were borne in hand, how cross'd, the instruments,*
> *Who wrought with them, and all things else that might*
> *To half a soul and to a notion craz'd Say 'Thus did Banquo'."*

They kill Banquo out of spite but their spite is not even directed at Banquo in particular. For the second murderer, killing Banquo will spite mankind in general:

> *"I am one, my liege,*
> *Whom the vile blows and buffets of the world*
> *Have so incens'd that I am reckless what*
> *I do to spite the world."*

Because they have nothing to lose they are prepared to do anything:

> *"And I another,*
> *So weary with disasters, tugg'd with fortune,*
> *That I would set my life on any chance,*
> *To mend 't or be rid on't."*

They are hardened, without feeling and perfect tools in the hands of Macbeth.

BANQUO

Despite Banquo's promise to question *"this bloody piece of work"*, he has obviously acquiesced in the official theory that Malcolm bribed the grooms to murder Duncan. Banquo knows Macbeth to be guilty and his silence and inactivity imply that he is now concerned for his own prospects. Banquo has succumbed to temptation, accepting Macbeth's success as a good omen for his own hopes. Banquo seems to pledge his loyalty to Macbeth when he says:

> *"Let your Highness*
> *Command upon me; to the which my duties*
> *Are with a most indissoluble tie*
> *For ever knit."*

He seems to acknowledge the fact that knowledge of the crime is a bond between them. After the coronation Banquo keeps a guilty secret and he is now associated with the evil of Macbeth and the witches. Even before Duncan's murder Banquo has an undefined sense of guilt:

> *"A heavy summons lies like lead upon me,*
> *And yet I would not sleep."*   (Act 2, Scene 1)

He is already experiencing what the Macbeths experience later – the guilty do not find repose in sleep. Macbeth admires Banquo and gives us an insight into his character:

> *"and in his royalty of nature*
> *Reigns that which would be feared: 'tis much he dares,*
> *And to that dauntless temper of his mind,*
> *He hath a wisdom that doth guide his valour*
> *To act in safety."*

Banquo is not afraid of Macbeth but he is cautious. He is honest by nature, but not as honest as Macduff who has enough integrity to refuse all invitations from a man of whom he is suspicious. Banquo's interest as a character is as a foil to Macbeth. The witches appear to both of them, the prophesies relate to both of them, both are exposed to temptation. Macbeth is guilty of acting to fulfil the prophesies. Banquo could not even contemplate treachery. He brushes aside his own thoughts for fear they lead him to guilt *"But hush! no more."* Banquo's guilt lies in the fact that he does not act. By not acting, by not investigating the crime as he promised, he is hoping for his share of the oracle. It is a guilty hope. When we last see Banquo in *Act 3,* he is not the honest Banquo of *Act I.*

LADY MACBETH

Lady Macbeth appears very briefly and merely reinforces Macbeth's extreme politeness to Banquo. She realizes that Banquo's loyalty is all important and defers to him as the *"chief guest":*

> *"If he had been forgotten*
> *It had been as a gap in our great feast,*
> *And all-thing unbecoming."*

MACBETH

The achievement of power has not brought contentment to Macbeth. He is very much aware that the murder has *"fil'd my mind"* and *"put rancours in the vessel of my peace"*. He is aware that he has forfeited his soul to the devil. He is suspicious, insecure and obsessed with the future:

> *"To be thus is nothing;*
> *But to be safely thus. Our fears in Banquo*
> *Stick deep..."*

Even though he admires Banquo's good qualities he resents them:

> *"...and under him*
> *My Genius is rebuk'd, as it is said*
> *Mark Antony's was by Caesar."*

From his jealousy of Banquo he thinks of the witches' prophesies in relation to Banquo and bitterly realizes:

> *"For Banquo's issue have I fil'd my mind;*
> *For them the gracious Duncan have I murder'd;"*

The change in Macbeth since Duncan's murder is striking. He does not consult his wife about the murder of Banquo. Banquo's murder is characterized not by doubts and hesitancies but by lies and hypocrisy. After flattering Banquo that his good advice would be desirable in council, he casually asks, *"Is't far you ride?"* He asks if Fleance is to accompany him as if it is of no interest, *"Goes Fleance with you?"* While appearing to graciously extend an invitation to Banquo, he cunningly extracts the information which will bring about Banquo's death. He has become a master at deception.

He tries to keep himself clear of guilt this time by getting others to commit the murder for him. Macbeth is very insulting to the murderers with his retort that you can divide men up like dogs. He is sarcastic:

> *"...Are you so gospell'd*
> *To pray for this good man and for his issue,*
> *Whose heavy hand hath bow'd you to the grave*
> *And beggar'd yours for ever?"*

He taunts them to prove themselves men by murdering Banquo. He is unnecessarily aggressive with the murderers, dismissing their right to have any feelings about murder. Once the murderers have decided to do the deed he flatters them:

> "Your spirits shine through you."

Already Macbeth has assumed the qualities of a tyrant:

> *"...and though I could*
> *With bare-fac'd power sweep him from my sight*
> *And bid my will avouch it, yet I must not,"*

EXERCISES

1. (a) What evidence is there in this scene that Banquo suspects Macbeth?
   (b) Why did he not act against Macbeth?
2. (a) Why does Macbeth distrust Banquo?
   (b) Do you think his fears are justified?
3. Discuss the changes in the relationship of Macbeth and Banquo since the beginning of the play.
4. How has Macbeth's state of mind changed since the last act?
5. Describe Macbeth's interview with the murderers.

Scene II

The Same — Another Room in The Palace.

Enter Lady Macbeth and a Servant.

Lady Macbeth   Is Banquo gone from court?
Servant   Ay, madam, but returns again to-night.
Lady Macbeth   Say to the King I would attend his leisure
For a few words.
Servant   Madam, I will.

                                                        [Exit.

Lady Macbeth (L)   Nought's had, all's spent,[1]   *All is lost*
Where our desire is got without content:
'Tis safer to be that which we destroy
Than by destruction dwell in doubtful joy.

Enter Macbeth.

How now, my lord! Why do you keep alone,
Of sorriest fancies your companions making,   10
Using those thoughts which should indeed have
   died
With them they think on? Things without all
   remedy
Should be without regard:[2] What's done is done.
Macbeth   We have scotch'd[3] the snake, not kill'd it:
She'll close[4] and be herself, whilst our poor malice
Remains in danger of her former tooth.
But let the frame of things disjoint',[5] both the
   worlds[6] suffer,
Ere we will eat our meal in fear, and sleep
In the affliction of these terrible dreams
That shake us nightly. Better be with the dead, 20
Whom we, to gain our peace, have sent to
   peace,
Than on the torture of the mind to lie
In restless ecstasy. Duncan is in his grave;
After life's fitful fever he sleeps well;
Treason has done his worst: nor steel, nor poison,
Malice domestic,[7] foreign levy,[8] nothing
Can touch him further.
Lady Macbeth   Come on;
Gentle my lord, sleek o'er[9] your rugged[10] looks;
Be bright and jovial among your guests to-night.
Macbeth   So shall I, love; and so, I pray, be you.   30

[1] nothing is gained; all is
   lost

[2] ignored
[3] slashed
[4] heal

[5] the universal order
[6] heaven and earth

[7] civil war
[8] tax

[9] smooth over
[10] furrowed

*macbeths guilty
conscience*

Lady M. is not consulted about the murders of Banquo and Fleance

¹¹give him the highest rank

¹²while unsafe we must sink our honour in flattery

¹³visor covering the face

Let your remembrance apply to Banquo;
Present him eminence,¹¹ both with eye and tongue:
Unsafe the while, that we
Must lave our honours in these flattering streams,¹²
And make our faces vizards¹³ to our hearts,
Disguising what they are.

                        You must leave this.

Lady Macbeth

Macbeth

O! full of scorpions is my mind, dear wife;
Thou know'st that Banquo, and his Fleance, lives.

¹⁴their right to live, given them by nature, is not eternal

¹⁵merry

¹⁶flight around the cloisters

¹⁷borne on its scaly wings

¹⁸curfew

Lady Macbeth

Macbeth

But in them nature's copy's not eterne.¹⁴
There's comfort yet; they are assailable;   40
Then be thou jocund.¹⁵ Ere the bat hath flown
His cloister'd¹⁶ flight, ere to black Hecate's
    summons
The shard-borne¹⁷ beetle with his drowsy hums
Hath rung night's yawning peal,¹⁸ there shall be
    done
A deed of dreadful note.

Lady Macbeth

Macbeth

                     What's to be done?
Be innocent of the knowledge, dearest chuck,

¹⁹blinding

²⁰blindfold

Till thou applaud the deed. Come, seeling¹⁹ night,
Scarf up²⁰ the tender eye of pitiful day,
And with thy bloody and invisible hand

²¹the bond of nature

Cancel and tear to pieces that great bond²¹   50
Which keeps me pale! Light thickens, and the crow
Makes wing to the rooky wood;
Good things of day begin to droop and drowse,
Whiles night's black agents to their preys do rouse.
Thou marvell'st at my words: but hold thee still;
Things bad begun make strong themselves by ill:
So, prithee, go with me.

                          [Exeunt.

Scene Analysis

In *Scene II* we see that, like her husband, Lady Macbeth has found no satisfaction or peace of mind in gaining the crown, but when he enters she hides her own thoughts. She shows concern at her husband's brooding solitariness:

> *"…Why do you keep alone,*
> *Of sorriest fancies your companions making;"*

Macbeth tells her his fears and torments:

> *"We have scotch'd the snake, not kill'd it:"*

Concerned that he will betray himself by his restlessness and uneasiness at the banquet, Lady Macbeth pleads with him:

> *"Come on;*
> *Gentle my lord, sleek o'er your rugged looks;*
> *Be bright and jovial among your guests to-night."*

CHARACTERS
LADY MACBETH

Lady Macbeth's short soliloquy shows her disillusionment:

> *"Nought's had, all's spent,*
> *Where our desire is got without content:"*

She reveals her true feelings when alone:

> *" 'Tis safer to be that which we destroy*
> *Than by destruction dwell in doubtful joy."*

But she does not betray such thoughts to her husband. She resumes her role of advising and chastising him, but she shows real concern for Macbeth. There is gentleness, love, in her reprimands. She suppresses her own doubts and fears, stating firmly:

> *"...What's done is done."*

and she resumes her role of urging him to greater strength. She realizes that he must not be allowed to dwell on his new role of traitor – *You must leave this.*

Macbeth does not discuss the murder of Banquo and Fleance with her, yet she particularly enquires after Banquo from a servant:

> *"Is Banquo gone from court?"*

Macbeth partly confides in her by stating:

> *"O! full of scorpions is my mind, dear wife;*
> *Thou know'st that Banquo, and his Fleance, lives."*

and she must have an idea of Macbeth's next step when she asks:

> *"What's to be done?"*

It is not clear however if Lady Macbeth is alarmed or whether she would approve of Banquo's murder.

MACBETH

Macbeth's mind is totally preoccupied with Banquo and Fleance:

> *"We have scotch'd the snake, not kill'd it:"*

'Tis safer to be that which we destroy
Than by destruction dwell in doubtful joy.   (Lady Macbeth, Act 3, Scene II)

The consciousness of guilt is very strong in him. He is tortured by conscience, fear and jealousy. He keeps alone. His sleep is haunted by nightmares. He envies Duncan who *"sleeps well"* while he himself sleeps *"In the affiction of these terrible dreams".* He wishes to spare Lady Macbeth guilt or anxiety before Banquo's murder:

> *"Be innocent of the knowledge, dearest chuck,*
> *Till thou applaud the deed."*

He knows Banquo will not appear at the supper, yet he instructs Lady Macbeth:

> *"Let your remembrance apply to Banquo;*
> *Present him eminence, both with eye and tongue:"*

He is learning to *"make our faces vizards to our hearts".*

He is affectionate towards Lady Macbeth, calling her *"love"*, *"dear wife"* and *"dearest chuck"*, but he does not share his innermost thoughts with her.

Just as he called on night to conceal his crime before the murder of Duncan, he utters a similar invocation before the murder of Banquo:

> *"...Come, seeling mght,*
> *Scarf up the tender eye of pitiful day"*

There is the same sense of awe, the same consciousness of nature, the same poetic intensity as before the murder of Duncan. Dark and ominous images predominate:

> *"...Ere the bat hath flown*
> *His closter'd flight, ere to black Hecate's summons*
> *The shard-borne beetle with his drowsy hums*
> *Hath rung night's yawning peal, there shall be done*
> *A deed of dreadful note."*

His invocation to the *"seeling mght" is* rather like Lady Macbeth's invocation to the spirits of evil in *Act 1, Scene V.* Like her, Macbeth is committing himself utterly to evil. He wishes that the pitiful eye might not see the murderer's hand. But there is no hesitation as before the murder of Duncan, no real agonizing. It is expedient that Banquo should be killed, *"they are assailable".* This time Macbeth is clear of purpose, and without the help and knowledge of his wife he devises and directs the murder. He is cooly in command and assures Lady Macbeth:

> "Things bad begun make strong themselves by ill..."

Their roles have reversed. Macbeth now takes the lead and urges Lady Macbeth – *"So, prithee, go with me".*

EXERCISES

1. Compare Lady Macbeth's speech beginning at *"Nought's had,"* and that of Macbeth which immediately follows.
2. Discuss the reversal of the positions of Macbeth and Lady Macbeth from what they were in *Acts 1* and *2*.
3. Examine the attitude of Macbeth and his wife towards one another.
4. Is there any noticable change in Macbeth's character in this scene? Compare his thoughts, emotions and language in this scene with his state of mind before the murder of Duncan.

Scene III

The Same — A Park, with a Road leading to the Palace.

Enter three Murderers.

1st Murderer	But who did bid thee join with us?
3rd Murderer	Macbeth.
2nd Murderer	He needs not our mistrust[1], since he delivers[2]
	Our offices,[3] and what we have to do
	To the direction just.[4]
1st Murderer	Then stand with us.
	The west yet glimmers with some streaks of day:
	Now spurs the lated[5] traveller apace
	To gain the timely inn; and near approaches
	The subject of our watch.
3rd Murderer	Hark! I hear horses.
Banquo	*[Within.]* Give us a light there, ho!
2nd Murderer	Then 'tis he: the rest
	That are within the note of expectation[6] 10
	Already are i' the court.
1st Murderer	His horses go about.
3rd Murderer	Almost a mile; but he does usually,
	So all men do, from hence to the palace gate
	Make it their walk.

Enter Banquo and Fleance, with a torch.

2nd Murderer	A light, a light!
3rd Murderer	'Tis he.
1st Murderer	Stand to't.[7]
Banquo	It will be rain to-night.
1st Murderer	Let it come down.

Side notes:
[1] we need not mistrust him
[2] points out
[3] duties
[4] exactly as ordered
[5] belated, delayed
[6] all those expected as guests
[7] get ready

	[They set upon Banquo.
Banquo	O, treachery! Fly, good Fleance, fly, fly, fly!
	Thou mayst revenge. O slave!
	Banqyou is dead *[Dies. Fleance escapes.*
3rd Murderer	Who did strike out the light?
1 st Murderer	Was't not the way?[8]
3rd Murderer	There's but one down; the son is fled. 20
2nd Murderer	We have lost
	Best half of our affair.
1 st Murderer	Well, let's away!
	And say how much is done.
	[Exeunt.

[8] was that not the arrangement

Scene Analysis

Banquo's murder, like Duncan's, takes place under cover of darkness. A third murderer joins the two lying in wait for Banquo and Fleance, indicating Macbeth's lack of trust. As Banquo and Fleance ride past, they are set upon by the murderers. They kill Banquo, but in the confusion the light is put out with the result that Fleance escapes. The second murderer states:

> *"We have lost*
> *Best half of our affair..."*

and whereas Banquo's death will remove some of Macbeth's fear of discovery, Fleance's flight gives obvious truth to the witches' prophesy.

CHARACTERS

THE MURDERERS

The first murderer is suspicious of the third murderer who joins them but the second murderer accepts that he has come to take charge:

> *"He needs not our mistrust, since he delivers*
> *Our offices, and what we have to do*
> *To the direction just."*

They are prepared and waiting for Banquo and Fleance; they have anticipated their movements correctly:

> *"So all men do, from hence to the palace gate*
> *Make it their walk."*

Yet although there are three of them and they have the advantage, Fleance succeeds in getting away.

BANQUO

Banquo realizes immediately that he is being treacherously attacked and urges Fleance to escape. His last wish is that Fleance may avenge his death:

> *"Fly, good Fleance, fly, fly, fly!*
> *Thou mayst revenge."*

There is a hint here of Macbeth's inevitable downfall.

EXERCISES

1. Discuss the dramatic significance of this short scene.
2. Some critics have claimed that the third murderer is Macbeth himself. Is there any evidence to support this view?

Scene IV

The Same — A Room of State in the Palace.

A Banquet prepared. Enter Macbeth, Lady Macbeth, Ross, Lennox, Lords, and Attendants

[1] ranks	**Macbeth**	You know your own degrees;[1] sit down:
[2] once for all		At first and last[2] the hearty welcome.
	Lords	Thanks to your Majesty.
	Macbeth	Our self will mingle with society
		And play the humble host.
		Our hostess keeps her state, but in best time
		We will require her welcome.
	Lady Macbeth	Pronounce it for me, sir, to all our friends;
		For my heart speaks they are welcome.

Enter First Murderer, to the door.

	Macbeth	See, they encounter thee with their hearts' thanks; *10*
		Both sides are even: here I'll sit i' the midst:
[3] enjoy yourselves freely		Be large in mirth;[3] anon, we'll drink a measure
		The table round. *[Approaching the door.*
		There's blood upon thy face.
	Murderer	'Tis Banquo's, then.
[4] It is better that Banquo's blood is on the murderer's face than in his body	**Macbeth**	'Tis better thee without than he within.[4]
		Is he dispatch'd[5]?
[5] killed	**Murderer**	My lord, his throat is cut; that 1 did for him.
	Macbeth	Thou art the best o' the cut-throats;
		Yet he's good that did the like for Fleance;
[6] without equal		If thou didst it, thou art the nonpareil.[6]

Murderer	Most royal sir, Fleance is 'scaped. 20	
Macbeth	Then comes my fit again: I had else been perfect;	
	Whole as the marble, founded as the rock,	[7] free and unrestrained
	As broad and general[7] as the casing[8] air:	[8] surrounding
	But now I am cabin'd,[9] cribb'd, confin'd, bound in	[9] shut in a small space
	To saucy[10] doubts and fears. But Banquo's safe?	[10] annoying
Murderer	Ay, my good lord; safe in a ditch he bides,	
	With twenty trenched[11] gashes on his head;	[11] deeply cut
	The least a death to nature.[12]	[12] life

(handwritten note left margin:) as long as Fleance lives his throne is not secure

Macbeth   Thanks for that.
There the grown serpent lies: the worm that's fled
Hath nature that in time will venom breed,
No teeth for the present. Get thee gone;   30
        to-morrow
We'll hear ourselves again.

                                    [*Exit Murderer.*

Lady Macbeth   My royal lord,
You do not give the cheer: the feast is sold
That is not often vouch'd, while 'tis a-making,
'Tis given with welcome:[13] to feed were best at home;
From thence, the sauce to meat is ceremony;[14]
Meeting were bare without it.

[13] a feast is like a meal away from home that must be paid for if a host does not welcome his guests
[14] ceremony makes a meal more enjoyable

Macbeth   Sweet remembrancer!
Now good digestion wait on appetite,
And health on both!

Lennox   May it please your Highness sit?

The Ghost of Banquo enters, and sits in Macbeth's place.

Macbeth   Here had we now our country's honour roof'd[15] 40
Were the grac'd person of our Banquo present;
Who may I rather challenge for unkindness
Than pity for mischance!

[15] under one roof

Ross   His absence, sir,
Lays blame upon his promise. Please't your Highness
To grace us with your royal company.

Macbeth   The table's full.
Lennox   Here is a place reserv'd, sir.
Macbeth   Where?
Lennox   Here, my good lord.
What is't that moves your Highness?
Macbeth   Which of you have done this? *blame*
Lords   What, my good lord?

Macbeth	Thou canst not say I did it: never shake *50*
	Thy gory locks at me.
Ross	Gentlemen, rise; his Highness is not well.
Lady Macbeth	Sit, worthy friends: my lord is often thus,
	And hath been from his youth: pray you, keep seat;
	The fit is momentary; upon a thought[16]
	He will again be well. If much you note him
	You shall offend him and extend his passion:
	Feed, and regard him not. Are you a man?
Macbeth	Ay, and a bold one, that dare look on that
	Which might appal the devil. *60*
Lady Macbeth	O proper stuff![17]
	This is the very painting of your fear;
	This is the air-drawn dagger which, you said,
	Led you to Duncan. O! these flaws and starts —
	Impostors to true fear — would well become
	A woman's story[18] at a winter's fire,
	Authoriz'd by her grandam. Shame itself!
	Why do you make such faces? When all's done
	You look but on a stool.
Macbeth	Prithee, see there!
	Behold! look! lo! how say you?
	Why, what care I? If thou canst nod, speak
	too. *70*
	If charnel-houses[19] and our graves must send
	Those that we bury back, our monuments
	Shall be the maws[20] of kites.[21]
	[Ghost disappears.
Lady Macbeth	What! quite unmann'd in folly?
Macbeth	If I stand here, I saw him.
Lady Macbeth	Fie, for shame!
Macbeth	Blood hath been shed ere now, i' the olden time,
	Ere human statute purg'd[22] the gentle weal;[23]
	Ay, and since too, murders have been perform'd
	Too terrible for the ear: the times have been,
	That, when the brains were out, the man would
	die, *80*
	And there an end; but now they rise again,
	With twenty mortal murders on their crowns,
	And push us from our stools: This is more strange
	Than such a murder is.
Lady Macbeth	My worthy lord,
	Your noble friends do lack you.
Macbeth	I do forget.
	Do not muse[24] at me, my most worthy friends;
	I have a strange infirmity, which is nothing

Margin notes:

[16] immediately

[17] nonsense

[18] an old wives' tale

[19] tombs, vaults

[20] stomachs
[21] birds of prey – if bodies leave their graves then they will have to be abandoned to kites whose stomachs will become their monuments

[22] cleaned
[23] welfare

[24] wonder

	To those that know me. Come, love and health
	to all;
	Then, I'll sit down. Give me some wine; fill full.
	I drink to the general joy of the whole table, *90*
	And to our dear friend Banquo, whom we miss;
	Would he were here! To all, and him, we thirst,
	And all to all.
Lords	Our duties, and the pledge.

Fear of the suppernatural

Re-enter Ghost.

Macbeth	Avaunt!²⁵ and quit my sight! Let the earth hide	²⁵go away
	thee!	
	Thy bones are marrowless, thy blood is cold;	
	Thou hast no speculation²⁶ in those eyes	²⁶intelligence
	Which thou dost glare with.	
Lady Macbeth	Think of this, good peers,	
	But as a thing of custom: 'tis no other;	
	Only it spoils the pleasure of the time.	
Macbeth	What man dare, I dare: *100*	
	Approach thou like the rugged Russian bear,	
	The arm'd rhinoceros, or the Hyrcan²⁷ tiger;	²⁷tigers were supposed to be
	Take any shape but that, and my firm nerves	bred in Hycranna, south of
	Shall never tremble: Or be alive again,	the Caspian sea
	And dare me to the desert with thy sword;	
	If trembling I inhabit,²⁸ then protest me	²⁸stay at home
	The baby of a girl. Hence, horrible shadow!	
	Unreal mockery, hence! *[Ghost vanishes.*	
	Why so; being gone,	
	I am a man again. Pray you, sit still.	
Lady Macbeth	You have displac'd the mirth, broke the good	
	meeting, *110*	
	With most admir'd disorder.	
Macbeth	Can such things be	
	And overcome us like a summer's cloud,	
	Without our special wonder? You make me	
	strange	
	Even to the disposition that I owe,²⁹	²⁹they make him feel that
	When now I think you can behold such sights,	he doesn't know his own
	And keep the natural ruby of your cheeks,	state of mind
	When mine are blanch'd³⁰ with fear.	³⁰made white
Ross	What sights, my lord?	
Lady Macbeth	I pray you, speak not; he grows worse and worse;	
	Question enrages him. At once, good-night:	
	Stand not upon the order of your going,³¹ *120*	³¹do not be particular about
	But go at once.	

	Lennox	Good-night; and better health
		Attend his Majesty!
	Lady Macbeth	A kind good-night to all!
		[Exeunt Lords and Attendants.

	Macbeth	It will have blood, they say; blood will have blood:
[32] grave stones	*Disturbance of nature*	Stones[32] have been known to move and trees to speak;
[33] auguries, omens		Augurs[33] and understood relations have
[34] magpies		By maggot-pies[34] and choughs[35] and rooks brought forth
[35] blackbirds		
		The secret'st man of blood. What is the night?
[36] struggling	Lady Macbeth	Almost at odds[36] with morning, which is which.
	Macbeth	How sayst thou, that Macduff denies his person
		At our great bidding? 130
	Lady Macbeth	Did you send to him, sir?
	Macbeth	I hear it by the way; but I will send.
		There's not a one of them but in his house
[37] paid (to send information)		I keep a servant fee'd.[37] I will to-morrow
[38] in good time		And betimes[38] I will to the Weird Sisters:
		More shall they speak; for now I am bent to know,
		By the worst means, the worst. For mine own good
[39] considerations		All causes[39] shall give way: I am in blood
		Stepp'd in so far, that should I wade no more,
		Returning were as tedious as go o'er.
		Strange things I have in head that will to hand,[40]
[40] that must be done		140
[41] examined		Which must be acted ere they may be scann'd.[41]
	Lady Macbeth	You lack the season of all natures, sleep.
[42] self-deception	Macbeth	Come, we'll to sleep. My strange and self-abuse[42]
[43] fear of the beginner		Is the initiate[43] fear that wants hard use:
		We are yet but young in deed. *[Exeunt.*

Scene Analysis

Macbeth's role as gracious host is interrupted by the appearance at the door of the first murderer, who tells him the news of Banquo's death and Fleance's escape. When his wife recalls him to his duties as host, he remarks on Banquo's absence. Ironically, at this moment he sees Banquo's ghost and, oblivious of his guests, he addresses himself to the apparition. Lady Macbeth excuses his conduct, the ghost disappears and Macbeth recovers sufficiently to repeat his wife's explanation of the event:

> *"I have a strange infirmity, which is nothing*
> *To those that know me."*

Our self will mingle with society
And play the humble host.

(Macbeth, Act 3, Scene IV)

He then proposes a toast to the nobles and the absent Banquo. At that, the apparition returns and this time Lady Macbeth has to ask the guests to leave. After the departure of the lords, Macbeth seems to find a new determination and defiance. He decides to visit the witches. This, together with the news of Macduff's challenge, marks a turning point in the play. Macbeth senses the retribution when he states:

> *"It will have blood, they say; blood will have blood:"*

Scene IV is a crucial scene for many reasons. It marks the highest point of Macbeth's power, it marks Macbeth's failure to rule Scotland justly, it marks the change in character from a man of feeling and conscience to an insensitive tyrant. From *Scene IV* onward, Macbeth's fall is rapid. The banquet scene highlights both his social and spiritual ruin.

CHARACTERS
MURDERER

The murderer cleverly tells Macbeth the good news first:

> *"My lord, his throat is cut; that I did for him."*

He breaks the news of Fleance's escape calmly:

> *"Most royal sir,*
> *Fleance is 'scaped."*

He is obviously unaffected by the brutality of the murder he has just committed. He cooly reports that Banquo is *"safe in a ditch"*:

> *"With twenty trenched gashes on his head;*
> *The least a death to nature"*

ROSS AND LENNOX

Ross and Lennox treat Macbeth with great deference. Lennox is very solicitous:

> *"May it please your Highness sit?"*

Ross criticizes Banquo for failing to appear at the banquet:

> *"His absence, sir,*
> *Lays blame upon his promise."*

It is Ross who immediately rises and bids the rest of the lords rise when he realizes *"his Highness is not well"*. He attempts to question Macbeth about the *"sights"* he refers to, but refrains immediately when Lady Macbeth tells them to go. Lennox quietly leaves saying:

> *"Good night; and better health*
> *Attend his Majesty!"*

'Tis better thee without than he within.   (Macbeth, Act 3, Scene IV)

MACBETH

At the beginning of the banquet Macbeth is friendly and welcoming:

> *"Our self will mingle with society*
> *And play the humble host."*

He discreetly slips towards the door to speak with the murderer. Macbeth does not flinch at the sight of blood on the murderer's face saying:

> *"'Tis better thee without than he within."*

He praises the man for Banquo's murder:

> *"Thou art the best o' the cut-throats:"*

He realizes that Fleance's escape has made him again subject to doubts and fears but his initial reaction is one of relief that Banquo is *"safe."*

But the conscience that Macbeth has stifled before Banquo's murder rises to confront him in the image of Banquo's ghost. Macbeth never doubts the reality of the apparition that nobody sees but himself. The murderer's description has imprinted itself in his mind and he sees Banquo *"with twenty mortal murders"*. He struggles to absolve himself from guilt saying:

> *"Thou canst not say I did it:"*

Lady Macbeth immediately recognizes Banquo's ghost as being: *"the very painting of your fear"*. Macbeth himself accepts this logical explanation later on:

> *"...My strange and self-abuse*
> *Is the initiate fear that wants hard use:"*

It is significant that Macbeth is able to banish the ghost from his sight by making a supreme effort at self-control – *"Unreal mockery, hence"*. This is in fact Macbeth's last confrontation with conscience. After the murder of Banquo he becomes a ruthless and open tyrant. He realizes that Macduff is quite openly challenging his authority. He trusts nobody and has a servant paid to spy in every household. Having become desperate, he becomes ruthless:

> *"...I am in blood*
> *Stepp'd in so far, that should I wade no more,*
> *Returning were as tedious as go o'er."*

From now on there will be no conflict between the thought and the act:

> *"Strange things I have in head that will to hand,*
> *Which must be acted ere they may be scann'd."*

LADY MACBETH

In this banquet scene Lady Macbeth appears as the praised and gracious queen. She is the perfect hostess, mindful of her guests, unlike her husband who leaves his guests to consult with the murderer. She reprimands Macbeth for failing in his duties:

> *"My royal lord,*
> *You do not give the cheer: the feast is sold*
> *That is not often vouch'd, while 'tis a-making,*
> *'Tis given with welcome: to feed were best at home;*
> *From thence, the sauce to meat is ceremony;*
> *Meeting were bare without it."*

As Macbeth breaks down on seeing Banquo's ghost, she rises to the occasion and with perfect self-control offers an explanation to the guests:

> *"...my lord is often thus,*
> *And hath been from his youth:"*

Avaunt! and quit my sight! Let the earth hide thee!
(Macbeth, Act 3, Scene IV)

Her sharp reprimands to Macbeth recall her previous efforts to control her husband's flights of fancy and yet again she accuses him of cowardice:

> "O! these flaws and starts –
> Impostors to true fear – would well become
> A woman's story at a winter's fire".

She does her best to save the situation but Macbeth is in the grip of imaginative guilt and she cannot maintain any semblance of normality in front of the lords. She dismisses them quickly and efficiently giving them no time to question or protest:

> "I pray you, speak not, he grows worse and worse;
> Question enrages him. At once, good-night:
> Stand not upon the order of your going,
> But go at once."

After the guests leave she makes no reference to what has happened and seems disinterested in what Macbeth is saying. As he regains his composure and deter-mination she grows noticably quieter. She has had to make an enormous effort to save her husband from complete exposure. She has already carried the burden of preventing Macbeth from betraying himself after Duncan's murder and the strain is beginning to tell.

EXERCISES

1. Give a brief account of the banquet scene.
2. Examine Macbeth's behaviour after the first appearance of the ghost and his behaviour after its second appearance. Is there any difference in his attitude?
3. How does Lady Macbeth behave during the critical moments of the banquet scene?
4. What is the effect of the hallucinations on Macbeth?
5. Do you agree with Lady Macbeth that *"This is the air-drawn dagger, which you said,/Led you to Duncan?* Consider why the dagger and the ghost appear. Do they disappear in the same way?
6. (a) Give an account of the conversation between Macbeth and Lady Macbeth at the end of the banquet.
   (b) Why does Lady Macbeth's mood change when the guests leave and she is alone with Macbeth?
7. Is the aftermath of Banquo's murder in any way comparable with that of Duncan's?
8. *"We are yet but young in deed."* What is the effect of this sentiment of Macbeth with which the scene closes?

Scene V

A Heath.
Thunder. Enter the three Witches, meeting Hecate.

[handwritten: Famous Supernatural being – she is used by shakespear to foreshadows evil.]

1st Witch	Why, how now, Hecate! You look angerly.	
Hecate	Have I not reason, beldams[1] as you are,	[1] ugly old women
[handwritten: mad at the witches]	Saucy[2] and overbold? How did you dare	[2] cheeky
	To trade and traffic with Macbeth	
[handwritten: They have entered into this alliace]	In riddles and affairs of death;	
	And I, the mistress of your charms,	
	The close contriver of all harms,	
	Was never call'd to bear my part,	
	Or show the glory of our art?	
	And, which is worse, all you have done 10	
	Hath been but for a wayward[3] son,	[3] self-willed
	Spiteful and wrathful; who, as others do,	
	Loves for his own ends, not for you.	
	But make amends now: Get you gone,	
	And at the pit of Acheron[4]	[4] the pit of hell
	Meet me i' the morning: thither he	
	Will come to know his destiny:	
	Your vessels and your spells provide,	
	Your charms and every thing beside.	
	I am for the air; this night I'll spend 20	
	Unto a dismal and a fatal end:	
	Great business must be wrought ere noon:	
	Upon the corner of the moon	
	There hangs a vaporous drop profound;[5]	[5] a magic drop used by the witches to give them special powers
	I'll catch it ere it come to ground:	
	And that, distill'd by magic sleights,[6]	[6] tricks
	Shall raise such artificial sprites[7]	[7] spirits crated by magic
	As, by the strength of their illusion,	
[handwritten: when they tell what will happen. He will laugh]	Shall draw him on to his confusion:	
	He shall spurn fate, scorn death, and bear 30	
	His hopes 'bove wisdom, grace, and fear;	
	And you all know security	
	Is mortals' chiefest enemy.	

[Song within.
['Come away, come away,'

Hark! I am call'd, my little spirit, see,   [8] waits
Sits in a foggy cloud, and stays[8] for me.

[Exit.

1st Witch   Come, let's make haste, she'll soon be back again.

[Exeunt.

Scene Analysis

Scene V prepares the way for Macbeth's return to the witches. This time they are with their queen, Hecate, who reprimands them for dealing with Macbeth without her. She bids them meet with her the next day with their spells ready for Macbeth. Hecate sees clearly what Macbeth will do and why:

> *"And that, distill'd by magic sleights*
> *Shall raise such artificial sprites*
> *As, by the strength of their illusion,*
> *Shall draw him on to his confusion:*
> *He shall spurn fate, scorn death, and bear*
> *His hopes 'bove wisdom, grace, and fear..."*

The scene reinforces our impression of evil and raises an ominous expectation about Macbeth's defeat.

CHARACTERS

HECATE

Hecate is angry. She is:

> *"... the mistress of your charms,*
> *The close contriver of all harms"*

and yet she was not consulted in the affair with Macbeth. She considers Macbeth to be an unworthy recipient of their charms:

> *"...a wayward son,*
> *Spiteful and wrathful; who, as others do,*
> *Loves for his own ends, not for you."*

She tells them to meet her at the pit of Acheron, a word associated with hell. She prepares the full force of her evil for Macbeth:

> *"Upon the corner of the moon*
> *There hangs a vaporous drop profound;*
> *I'll catch it ere it come to ground:"*

Her intentions towards Macbeth are malignant, her purpose is clear – to *"draw him on to his confusion."*

Hecate's speech contrasts with the rhythm of the other witches' speech in the earlier scenes and for this reason some critics contend that Shakespeare himself did not write this scene.

EXERCISES

1. (a) What do we learn of Hecate in this scene? Would you consider her to be more or
       less malignant than the other witches?
   (b) What are the intentions of the witches towards Macbeth?
2. What is the purpose of *Scene V*? Could it be omitted from the play?

Societal resentment towards Macbeth is growing - Scotland is boiling to kill Macbeth

Scene VI

Forres – A Room in the Palace.

Enter Lennox and another Lord.

Lennox	My former speeches have but hit your thoughts,[1]
	Which can interpret further: only, I say,
	Things have been strangely borne. The gracious Duncan
	Was pitied of Macbeth: marry, he was dead:
	And the right-valiant Banquo walk'd too late;
	Whom, you may say, if't please you, Fleance kill'd,
	For Fleance fled: men must not walk too late.
	Who cannot want the thought[2] how monstrous
	It was for Malcolm and for Donalbain
	To kill their gracious father? Damned fact! *10*
	How it did grieve Macbeth! Did he not straight,
	In pious rage, the two delinquents tear,
	That were slaves of drink and thralls[3] of sleep?
	Was not that nobly done? Ay, and wisely too;
	For 'twould have anger'd any heart alive
	To hear the men deny't. So that, I say,
	He has borne all things well; and I do think
	That, had he Duncan's sons under his key,–
	As, an't please heaven, he shall not, – they should find
	What 'twere to kill a father; so should Fleance. *20*
	But, peace! For from broad words,[4] and 'cause he fail'd
	His presence at the tyrant's feast, I hear,
	Macduff lives in disgrace. Sir, can you tell himself?
Lord	The son of Duncan,
	From whom this tyrant holds the due of birth,

Side notes:
[1] he has only said what is already in the lord's mind
[2] who cannot help thinking
[3] captives
[4] plain words

Handwritten annotations:
- *Things have worked-out strongly*
- *Hows it possible for sons to kill their fathers*

[5] Edward the Confessor
(reigned 1042–1066)

[6] honours due to free men

[7] gloomy
[8] mutters
[9] regret
[10] burdens

Hatred

✗ Macduff
is not is
Scotland ✗

Lives in the English court, and is receiv'd
Of the most pious Edward[5] with such grace
That the malevolence of fortune nothing
Takes from his high respect. Thither Macduff
Is gone to pray the holy King upon his aid   30
To wake Northumberland and war-like Siward:
That, by the help of these – with Him above
To ratify the work – we may again
Give to our tables meat, sleep to our nights,
Free from our feasts and banquets bloody knives,
Do faithful homage and receive free honours;[6]
All which we pine for now. And this report
Hath so exasperate the King that he
Prepares for some attempt at war.

Lennox   Sent he to Macduff?

Lord   He did: and with an absolute, 'Sir, not I!',   40
The cloudy[7] messenger turns me his back,
And hums,[8] as who should say, 'You'll rue[9] the time
That clogs[10] me with this answer?'

Lennox   And that well might
Advise him to a caution to hold what distance
His wisdom can provide. Some holy angel

illegitimate
King (L)

Fly to the court of England and unfold
His message ere he come, that a swift blessing
May soon return to this our suffering country
Under a hand accurs'd!

Lord *lennox prays*   I'll send my prayers with him!
for Macduffs sucess
                                          [Exeunt.

Scene Analysis

In *Scene VI* Lennox and another lord discuss happenings in Scotland. It is a short scene but it supplies important points of information. Lennox lists and comments on all the strange deeds that have taken place. The lord speaks of Malcolm's warm welcome at the court of King Edward in England. We learn of Macduff's journey there to seek English assistance against Macbeth and that Macbeth is preparing for war.

CHARACTERS
LENNOX

Lennox is a shrewd cautious character. He does not fully trust the lord to whom he is speaking in this scene and so his words are deliberately oblique. He allows the lord to draw his own conclusions:

> *"My former speeches have but hit your thoughts,*
> *Which can interpret further: only, I say,*
> *Things have been strangely borne."*

He speaks ironically of Macbeth's reaction to Duncan's murder:

> *"How it did grieve Macbeth!"*

It is obvious now that he was not fooled by Macbeth's killing the two grooms:

> *"...Ay, and wisely too;*
> *For 'twould have anger'd any heart alive*
> *To hear the men deny't."*

He can see through the theory that Duncan's sons were to blame and sarcastically observes that Banquo must have been killed by Fleance:

> *"For Fleance fled"*

Lennox is concerned about the state of Scotland, suffering *"Under a hand accurs'd"* and prays for the success of Macduff in his mission:

> *"Some holy angel*
> *Fly to the court of England and unfold*
> *His message ere he come, that a swift blessing*
> *May soon return to this our suffering country".*

EXERCISES

1. (a) What important facts do we learn from the conversation of Lennox and the lord?
   (b) What is the tone of Lennox's speech?
2. What dramatic impact have the references to Macduff in this scene?

REVISION

> *"Nought's had, all's spent,*
> *Where our desire is got without content"*   (Lady Macbeth, Act 3, Scene II)

Macbeth, suspicious of Banquo and mindful of the second part of the witches' prophesy, decides to kill Banquo and his son Fleance. He hires two murderers to kill them on the night he is holding a state banquet. Three murderers attack, killing Banquo, but Fleance escapes. That evening at the banquet the guilt-ridden Macbeth sees the ghost of Banquo. The guests disperse at the command of Lady Macbeth. Lennox discusses the situation with another lord and discloses that Macduff has refused all invitations to court.

POINTS TO NOTE

1. *Scene I* reminds the audience that it is Banquo's descendants who are to be future kings.
2. Banquo is now playing a similar role as insincere subject to King Macbeth as Macbeth played to King Duncan.
3. By killing Banquo and Fleance, Macbeth is in effect challenging fate, trying to belie the prophesies.
4. Macbeth's consciousness of good is not entirely destroyed, but goodness, tenderness and pity are deliberately suppressed.
5. Another example of dramatic irony – Banquo's promise to be present at the banquet.
6. The murder of Banquo and its consequences mark a transition from hidden criminality to open dictatorship.
7. The strain of events in the banquet scene has exhausted Lady Macbeth and this prepares us for her next appearance in the sleep-walking scene.

REVISION ASSIGNMENT

Give an account of Macbeth's rise to power from the murder of Duncan to the murder of Banquo. What indications of discontent are there? Would you agree that the murder of Banquo is the turning point of the play?

Act 4
Scene 1

A Cavern. In the middle, a boiling Cauldron.[1]

[1] large boiling pot

Thunder. Enter the three Witches.

1st Witch	Thrice the brinded[2] cat hath mew'd.
2nd Witch	Thrice and once the hedge-pig[3] whin'd.
3rd Witch	Harper[4] cries: 'Tis time, 'tis time.
1st Witch	Round about the cauldron go;
	In the poison'd entrails[5] throw.
	Toad that under cold stone
	Days and nights hast thirty-one
	Swelter'd venom sleeping got,[6]
	Boil thou first i' the charmed pot.
All	Double, double toil and trouble;
	Fire burn and cauldron bubble.
2nd Witch	Fillet of a fenny snake,[7]
	In the cauldron boil and bake;
	Eye of newt,[8] and toe of frog,
	Wool of bat, and tongue of dog,
	Adder's fork,[9] and blind-worm's sting,[10]
	Lizard's leg, and howlet's[11] wing,
	For a charm of powerful trouble,
	Like a hell-broth boil and bubble.
All	Double, double toil and trouble;
	Fire burn and cauldron bubble.
3rd Witch	Scale of dragon, tooth of wolf,
	Witch's mummy,[12] maw[13] and gulf[14]
	Of the ravin'd[15] salt-sea shark,
	Root of hemlock digg'd i' the dark,
	Liver of blaspheming Jew,
	Gall[16] of goat, and slips of yew[17]
	Sliver'd[18] in the moon's eclipse,[19]
	Nose of Turk, and Tartar's lips,
	Finger of birth-strangled babe
	Ditch-delivered[20] by a drab,[21]
	Make the gruel thick and slab:[22]
	Add thereto a tiger's chaudron,[23]
	For the ingredients of our cauldron.
All	Double, double toil and trouble;
	Fire burn and cauldron bubble.
2nd Witch	Cool it with a baboon's blood,
	Then the charm is firm and good.

10

20

30

[2] brindled, striped
[3] hedgehog
[4] one of the witches creatures

[5] bowels

[6] a toad which sleeping under cold stone for thirty-one days, has gathered poisonous sweat

[7] snake living in marshy-ground

[8] type of lizard

[9] fork-tongued
[10] worm believed poisonous
[11] owl

[12] dried corpse
[13] stomach
[14] gullet
[15] ravenous

[16] bitter fluid from the liver
[17] graveyard tree reputed to be poisonous
[18] sliced or shaved off
[19] an eclipse was a bad omen
[20] born in a ditch
[21] prostitute
[22] sticky
[23] entrails

✗IMAGES✗

Enter Hecate.

Hecate
O! well done! I commend your pains,
And every one shall share i' the gains.   40
And now about the cauldron sing,
Like elves and fairies in a ring,
Enchanting all that you put in.
                    [*Music and a song, 'Black Spirits,' etc.*
                                        [*Exit Hecate.*

2nd Witch
By the pricking of my thumbs,
Something wicked this way comes.
Open locks, whoever knocks.

Enter Macbeth.

Macbeth
How now, you secret, black, and mid-night hags!
What is't you do?

All   A deed without a name.

²⁴summon

Macbeth
I conjure²⁴ you, by that which you profess,–
Howe'er you come to know it, –answer me: 50
Though you untie the winds and let them fight
Against the churches; though the yesty waves
Confound and swallow navigation up;

²⁵young corn
²⁶beaten flat

Though bladed corn²⁵ be lodg'd²⁶ and trees
    blown down;
Though castles topple on their warders' heads;
Though palaces and pyramids do slope

²⁷the seeds of all living
    things
²⁸till destruction grows sick
    of destroying itself

Macbeth is demanding

Their heads to their foundations; though the
    treasure
Of nature's germens²⁷ tumble all together,
Even till destruction sicken;²⁸ answer me
To what I ask you.   60

1st Witch   Speak.
2nd Witch   Demand.
3rd Witch   We'll answer.
1st Witch
Say, if thou'dst rather hear it from our mouths,
Or from our masters?

Macbeth   Call 'em: let me see 'em.

²⁹litter of newly born piglets
³⁰gallows

1st Witch
Pour in sow's blood, that hath eaten
Her nine farrow;²⁹ grease, that's sweaten
From the murderer's gibbet³⁰ throw
Into the flame.

All   Come, high or low;

³¹skilfully

Thyself and office deftly³¹ show.

                                        macduff

Thunder. First Apparition – an Armed Head
                                ↓
                          ghost

Macbeth	Tell me, thou unknown power, –
1st Witch	He knows thy thought:
	Hear his speech, but say thou nought.
1st App.	Macbeth! Macbeth! Macbeth! beware
	Macduff; (L) 70
	Beware the Thane of Fife. Dismiss me. Enough.
	[Descends.
Macbeth	Whate'er thou art, for thy good caution, thanks;
	Thou hast harp'd[32] my fear aright. But one word
	more,–
1st Witch	He will not be commanded: here's another,
	More potent than the first.

strong

Thunder. Second Apparition – a Bloody Child.

2nd App.	Macbeth! Macbeth! Macbeth! –
Macbeth	Had I three ears, I'd hear thee.
2nd App.	Be bloody, bold, and resolute; laugh to scorn
	The power of man, for none of woman born
	Shall harm Macbeth. (L) 80
	[Descends.
Macbeth	Then live, Macduff: what need I fear of thee?
	But yet I'll make assurance double sure,
	And take a bond of fate:[33] thou shalt not live;
	That I may tell pale-hearted fear it lies,
	And sleep in spite of thunder.

No females will kill macbeth

as long as the trees don't uproot

Thunder. Third Apparition – a Child Crowned, with a tree in his hand

	What is this,
	That rises like the issue of a king,
	And wears upon his baby brow the round
	And top of sovereignty?[34]
All	Listen, but speak not to't.
3rd App.	Be lion-mettled,[35] proud, and take no care
	Who chafes,[36] who frets, or where conspirers
	are: 90
	Macbeth shall never vanquish'd be until
	Great Birnam wood to high Dunsinane Hill
	Shall come against him.
	[Descends.
Macbeth	That will never be:
	Who can impress[37] the forest, bid the tree
	Unfix his earth-bound root? Sweet bodements,[38]
	good!
	Rebellion's head rise never till the wood
	Of Birnam rise, and our high-plac'd Macbeth

[32] given expression to

[33] make an agreement with fate

[34] the crown

[35] have the qualities of a lion
[36] irritates

[37] impress into service
[38] prophesies

39 shall live the full term of life
40 natural death

Macbeth is never satisfied

Shall live the lease of nature,[39] pay his breath
To time and mortal custom.[40] Yet my heart
Throbs to know one thing: tell me, if your art   100
Can tell so much, – shall Banquo's issue ever
Reign in this kingdom?

All   Seek to know no more.

Macbeth   I will be satisfied: deny me this,
And an eternal curse fall on you! Let me know.
Why sinks that cauldron? and what noise is this?

                                                          [*Hautboys.*

1st Witch   Show!
2nd Witch   Show!
3rd Witch   Show!
All   Show his eyes, and grieve his heart;
Come like shadows, so depart.   *110*

41 the eight kings of the Stuart line

*A show of Eight Kings,[41] the last with a glass in his
hand: Banquo's Ghost following*

Macbeth   Thou art too like the spirit of Banquo; down!

42 scorch

Thy crown does sear[42] mine eyeballs: and thy hair,
Thou other gold-bound brow, is like the first:
A third is like the former. Filthy hags!

43 jump

Describing the kings

Why do you show me this! A fourth! Start, eyes![43]
What! will the line stretch out to the crack of
    doom?[44]

44 the thunder of the Last Judgement

Another yet? A seventh! I'll see no more:

45 mirror to reveal the future

And yet the eighth appears, who bears a glass[45]
Which shows me many more; and some I see

46 refers to the double coronation of King James at Stirling and Westminster, uniting the kingdoms of England and Scotland

That two-fold balls[46] and treble sceptres[47]
    carry.   *120*

47 England, Ireland and Scotland, the union of Great Britain under King James. The bell and sceptre were symbols of power carried at the coronation.

Horrible sight! Now, I see, 'tis true;
For the blood-bolter'd[48] Banquo smiles upon me,
And points at them for his.

48 with blood-clotted hair

                                                          [*Apparitions vanish.*

What! is this so?

1st Witch   Ay, sir, all this is so: but why
Stands Macbeth thus amazedly?
Come, sisters, cheer we up his sprites,
And show the best of our delights
I'll charm the air to give a sound,

49 strange dance

While you perform your antic round,[49]   *130*
That this great king may kindly say,

50 we fulfilled our duties to receive him hospitably

Our duties did his welcome pay.[50]

Music. The Witches dance, and then vanish.

Macbeth *looses* Where are they? Gone? Let this pernicious hour
all his humanity Stand aye[51] accursed in the calendar!   [51] forever
all his sense Come in, without there!
of self.

               Enter Lennox. *still loyalish to*
                                    macbeth

Lennox   What's your Grace's will?
Macbeth   Saw you the Weird Sisters?
Lennox   No, my lord.
Macbeth   Came they not by you?
Lennox   No, indeed, my lord.
Macbeth   Infected be the air whereon they ride,
               And damn'd all those that trust them! I did hear
               The galloping of horse: who was't came by! 140
Lennox   'Tis two or three, my lord, that bring you word
               Macduff is fled to England.
Macbeth   Fled to England!
Lennox   Ay, my good lord.
Macbeth   *[Aside]* Time, thou anticipat'st[52] my dread exploits;   [52] foretold
               The flighty purpose never is o'ertook
He is going Unless the deed go with it.[53] From this moment   [53] intentions are never
to kill macduf The very firstlings of my heart shall be   fulfilled unless they are
wife The firstlings of my hand.[54] And even now,   acted upon at once
+ kids To crown my thoughts with acts, be it thought   [54] his heart's wishes shall be
                and done: his hands' immediate
               The castle of Macduff I will surprise; 150   deeds
               Seize upon Fife; give to the edge of the sword
               His wife, his babes, and all unfortunate souls
               That trace him in his line.[55] No boasting like a   [55] are his closest relatives
                fool;
               This deed I'll do, before this purpose cool:
               But no more sights! Where are these gentlemen?
               Come, bring me where they are.
                           [Exeunt.

Scene Analysis

The dimension of Macbeth's evil is suggested by the hideous description of the witches' brew. Macbeth is desperate for knowledge of the future. He is prepared to have the whole universe reduced to chaos and disorder if it means the witches will tell him what he wants to know:

    "...though the treasure
    Of nature's germens tumble all together,
    Even till destruction sicken; answer me
    To what I ask you".

An apparition arises from the cauldron and warns him to beware Macduff, thus confirming Macbeth's fears of him. The second apparition is a bloody child and informs him that none of woman born will harm him. Macbeth takes this as a good omen, but to be fully sure he decides to kill Macduff anyway. The third apparition is a child carrying a tree, who predicts that Macbeth will not be vanquished until Birnam Wood moves to Dunsinane. At Macbeth's question about the reign of Banquo's successors, the witches conjure up apparitions of a line of Scottish kings with Banquo's ghost at the end. When the witches vanish, Lennox brings news of Macduff's flight. Macbeth is furious that he has not already killed him. His attempt to control the future has failed and he becomes savage in his desperation, deciding to kill Macduff's family without any apparent reason.

CHARACTERS
THE WITCHES

Macbeth calls the witches *"secret, black, and mid-night hags."* The witches are clearly ministers of evil. There is little doubt that they are conjuring up an evil spell. Their broth is *"Like a hell broth"*, a gruesome mixture of animal and human parts and entrails. (Hecate and the three extra witches who appear are generally considered to be a non-Shakespearian addition to the play).

This is the last scene in which the witches appear. They have had a significant influence on the action of the play. They do not control Macbeth, he is not powerless against them. He followed the course of the prophecies only because he was not an innocent man. The witches are the physical and symbolic representation of evil in the play. Once Macbeth commits himself totally to evil, they disappear. At the very moment they vanish, Lennox brings news of Macduff's escape to England – representing the coming to the fore of the forces for good and the ultimate defeat of the evil forces which the witches represent.

LENNOX

Lennox brings the news of Macduff's escape to Macbeth. Lennox, unlike Macduff, continues to serve Macbeth. He gives no hint of disloyalty:

"What's your Grace's will?"

But in the final showdown, men such as Lennox will side with Macduff.

MACBETH

By seeking out the witches, Macbeth acknowledges his total commitment to evil. He challenges the witches fearlessly, he demands to know the worst:

"I conjure you, by that which you profess, –
Howe'er you come to know it, – answer me:"

Sweet bodements, good!

(Macbeth, Act 4, Scene 1)

Macbeth's language conveys his urgency but also the turbulence of his mind. He evokes a picture of total destruction which shows a complete disregard for natural order in the universe:

> *"Though you untie the winds and let them fight*
> *Against the churches; though the yesty waves*
> *Confound and swallow navigation up;*
> *Though bladed corn be lodg'd and trees blown down;*
> *Though castles topple on their warders' heads;*
> *Though palaces and pyramids do slope*
> *Their heads to their foundations..."*

Such violence expresses his state of mind, which is fast degenerating into the mind of a heartless and destructive tyrant. The first apparition touches immediately on Macbeth's fear. *"Beware the Thane of Fife"*. The second apparition dismisses that fear as of no consequence. But even though the prophecy seems to favour him, Macbeth distrusts Macduff and he is now forcing fate to keep its promise:

> *"But yet I'll make assurance double sure,*
> *And take a bond of fate:"*

The third apparition convinces Macbeth that the prophecies are benign, that he is untouchable:

> *"Sweet bodements, good!*
> *Rebellion's head rise never till the wood*
> *Of Birnam rise, and our high-plac'd Macbeth*
> *Shall live the lease of nature, pay his breath*
> *To time and mortal custom."*

Macbeth is not afraid of the powers of the witches and defies their warning – *"Seek to know no more."* He commands them peremptorily:

> *"I will be satisfied: deny me this,*
> *And an eternal curse fall on you!"*

Yet he protests vehemently:

> *"...Filthy hags!*
> *Why do you show me this?"* –

when the vision shows *"the blood-bolter'd Banquo"* and his line. The witches wonder why Macbeth is so amazed since he already knew the prophecy concerning Banquo's issue. But Macbeth has been acting against fate ever since the murder of Duncan. He wishes to foresee his fate but curses it when it is contrary to his desire, – *"I'll see no more".* Macbeth has finished with the witches and the apparition and even as they disappear Lennox arrives with news of Macduff's escape. Just as the witches' first prediction was almost instantly fulfilled in *Act I, Scene III,* thus giving him confidence in their veracity, here the witches' first warning is given immediate fulfilment. He resolves from now on to make action precede thought. The powers of evil have had their full effect on him. His decision to have Lady Macduff and her children murdered is cruel and unnecessary. He murders now without conscience or concealment. The transition of Macbeth from a murderer beset by fears and guilt to a tyrant devoid of human feeling is now complete.

EXERCISES

1. What is the effect of the detailed description of the ingredients of the witches' cauldron?
2. Contrast Macbeth's treatment of the witches in this scene with his first encounter with them.
3. Describe and explain the apparitions which Macbeth sees.
4. Do the apparitions have the effect which the witches planned in *Act 3, Scene IV?*
5. (a) Why is Macbeth determined to kill Macduff?
   (b) Why does he decide to kill Macduff's wife and family?
6. Has Macbeth changed since the murder of Banquo?

Scene II

Fife — Macduff's Castle.

Enter Lady Macduff , her Son, and Ross.

Lady Macduff	What had he done to make him fly the land?
Ross	You must have patience, madam.
Lady Macduff	He had none:
	His flight was madness. When our actions do not,
	Our fears do make us traitors.
Ross	You know not
	Whether it was his wisdom or his fear.
Lady Macduff	Wisdom! To leave his wife, to leave his babes,
	His mansion, and his titles, in a place
	From whence himself does fly? He loves us not;
	He wants the natural touch;[1] for the poor wren,
	The most diminutive of birds, will fight, *10*
	Her young ones in her nest, against the owl.
	All is the fear, and nothing is the love;
	As little is the wisdom, where the flight
	So runs against all reason.
Ross	My dearest cos,[2]
	I pray you, school[3] yourself. But, for your husband,
	He is noble, wise, judicious, and best knows

[1] he lacks feeling of natural affection

[2] cousin; term of affection
[3] control

⁴ sudden disorders of the times

⁵ believe rumours because of fear

⁶ hither and thither, yet remaining on the spot

⁷ improve

⁸ Ross is near to tears

⁹ sticky substance used for catching small birds
¹⁰ fowler's trap
¹¹ snare

I will see you again things are so bad they'll have to get better

	The fits o' the season.⁴ I dare not speak much further:
	But cruel are the times, when we are traitors
	And do not know ourselves, when we hold rumour
	From what we fear,⁵ yet know not what we fear, *20*
	But float upon a wild and violent sea
	Each way and none.⁶ I take my leave of you:
	Shall not be long but I'll be here again.
	Things at the worst will cease, or else climb upward⁷
	To what they were before. My pretty cousin,
	Blessing upon you!
Lady Macduff	Father'd he is, and yet he's fatherless.
Ross	I am so much a fool, should I stay longer,
	It would be my disgrace⁸ and your discomfort:
	I take my leave at once. *30*
	[Exit.
Lady Macduff	Sirrah, your father's dead:
	And what will you do now? How will you live?
Son	As birds do, mother.
Lady Macduff	What! with worms and flies?
Son	With what I get, I mean; and so do they.
Lady Macduff	Poor bird! thou'dst never fear the net nor lime,⁹
	The pit-fall¹⁰ nor the gin.¹¹
Son	Why should I, mother? Poor birds they are not set for.
	My father is not dead, for all your saying.
Lady Macduff	Yes, he is dead: how wilt thou do for a father?*40*
Son	Nay, how will you do for a husband?
Lady Macduff	Why, I can buy me twenty at any market.
Son	Then you'll buy 'em to sell again.
Lady Macduff	Thou speak'st with all thy wit; and yet, i' faith,
	With wit enough for thee.
Son	Was my father a traitor, mother?
Lady Macduff	Ay, that he was.
Son	What is a traitor?
Lady Macduff	Why, one that swears and lies.
Son	And be all traitors that do so? *50*
Lady Macduff	Every one that does so is a traitor, and must be hang'd.
Son	And must they all be hang'd that swear and lie?
Lady Macduff	Every one.
Son	Who must hang them?
Lady Macduff	Why, the honest men.

Son	Then the liars and swearers are fools, for there are liars and swearers enow to beat the honest men, and hang up them.
Lady Macduff	Now God help thee, poor monkey! But how wilt thou do for a father? 60
Son.	If he were dead, you'd weep for him: if you would not, it were a good sign that I should quickly have a new father.
Lady Macduff	Poor prattler, how thou talk'st!

Enter a Messenger.

Messenger	Bless you, fair dame! I am not to you known, Though in your state of honour I am perfect.[12] I doubt some danger does approach you nearly: If you will take a homely man's advice, Be not found here; hence, with your little ones. To fright you thus, methinks, I am too savage; 70 To do worse[13] to you were fell[14] cruelty, Which is too nigh your person. Heaven preserve you! I dare abide no longer. [Exit.]
Lady Macduff	Whither should I fly? I have done no harm. But I remember now I am in this earthly world, where, to do harm Is often laudable, to do good sometime Accounted dangerous folly. Why then, alas, Do I put up that womanly defence, To say I have done no harm?

Enter Murderers.

What are these faces?

Murderer	Where is your husband? 80
Lady Macduff	I hope in no place so unsanctified Where such as thou mayst find him.
Murderer	He's a traitor.
Son	Thou liest, thou shag-hair'd villain
Murderer	What! you egg. Young fry[15] of treachery! [Stabs him.]
Son	He has killed me, mother: Run away, I pray you! [Dies.]

[Exit Lady Macduff, crying 'Murder!', and pursued by the Murderers.

[12] though he knows well what high rank she holds

[13] by not warning her
[14] terrible

[15] spawn

Sheer utter blood thirstyness

113

Scene Analysis

In this scene Ross and Lady Macduff discuss Macduff's departure which Lady Macduff sees as desertion. Ross describes the state of Scotland, a land of fear, suspicion, treachery and cruelty:

> *"But cruel are the times, when we are traitors*
> *And do not know ourselves, when we hold rumour*
> *From what we fear, yet know not what we fear,*
> *But float upon a wild and violent sea*
> *Each way and none."*

The dialogue between mother and son is a reminder of the values of tenderness and goodness which have been destroyed by treachery. There is humour in the teasing questions and answers which contrasts starkly with the grimness of the slaughter which follows.

CHARACTERS
ROSS

Macduff has sent Ross to explain his departure to Lady Macduff. Ross does his best to excuse Macduff, protesting:

> *"You know not*
> *Whether it was his wisdom or his fear."*

Ross clearly respects Macduff:

> *"...But, for your husband,*
> *He is noble, wise, judicious, and best knows*
> *The fits o' the season."*

Ross is embarrassed at Lady Macduff's bitter remarks:

> *"My dearest cos,*
> *I pray you, school yourself:"*

Ross has a clear idea of the extent of the breakdown of law and order in Scotland. He is careful not to give anything away and is circumspect in giving information regarding Macduff to Lady Macduff:

> *"I dare not speak much further..."*

Ross is so moved by the unhappiness of Lady Macduff that he abruptly takes his leave:

> *"I am so much a fool, should I stay longer,*
> *It would be my disgrace and your discomfort:"*

Whither should I fly?
I have done no harm.

(Lady Macduff, Act 4, Scene II)

LADY MACDUFF

Lady Macduff is a gentle and affectionate mother. She feels anger towards her husband, but it is an anger prompted by fear of being left at the mercy of a tyrant and hurt at not being taken into her husband's confidence. She enjoys her son's precociousness, entering into his spirit of fun:

> "...how will you do for a husband?"
> "Why, I can buy me twenty at any market."

She faces her murderers with courage and dignity:

> "Whither should I fly?
> I have done no harm."

Despite all she has said about Macduff she stands up for him when one of the murderers asks where her husband is:

> "I hope in no place so unsanctified
> Where such as thou mayst find him."

SON

The child is pert and clever. He seems unperturbed by his mother's statement:

> "Sirrah, your father's dead:
> And what will you do now? How will you live?"

His answer shows a child's innocence – "*As birds do, mother*" – yet he shows unusual wisdom for a child – "*Poor birds they are not set for.*" With knowing insight the child challenges the mother:

> "My father is not dead, for all your saying."
> "If he were dead, you'd weep for him:"

The boy does not understand the word traitor, yet he asks:

> "Was my father a traitor, mother?"

With a child's naivety, yet with relentless logic, he exclaims:

> "Then the liars and swearers are fools,
> for there are liars and swearers enow to
> beat the honest men, and hang up them."

This is bitterly ironic in the light of what happens to him and his mother. The little boy's chatter is not just idle prattle; it has a dramatic force and emphasizes the wanton cruelty of Macbeth. There is the added pathos of the little boy courageously defending his father's name before he is killed:

> "He's a traitor."

> *"Thou liest, thou shag-hair'd villain."*

He bravely calls out to his mother:

> *"Run away, I pray you!"*

The brief appearance of Macduff's little son in the play evokes a picture of innocence and defencelessness which only a heartless man would take advantage of.

EXERCISES

1. Do you agree with Lady Macduff that Macduff should not have fled to England?
2. What is your opinion of Lady Macduff?
3. What do you think of Lady Macduff's son? Do you consider his character credible?
4. Consider the conversation of Lady Macduff and her son. Is there any special significance in their words?
5. What is the dramatic relevance of Shakespeare allowing us to see the Macduffs before they are murdered?

Scene III

England – Before the King's Palace.

Enter Malcolm and Macduff.

Malcolm	Let us seek out some desolate shade! and there Weep our sad bosoms empty.
Macduff	Let us rather Hold fast the mortal[1] sword, and like good men Bestride[2] our down-fall'n birthdom.[3] Each new morn New widows howl, new orphans cry, new sorrows Strike heaven on the face, that it resounds As if it felt with Scotland and yell'd out Like syllable of dolour.[4]
Malcolm	What I believe, I'll wail, What know, believe, and what I can redress![5] As I shall find the time to friend, 1 will. 10 What you have spoke, it may be so perchance. This tyrant, whose sole[6] name blisters our tongues, Was once thought honest: you have lov'd him well, He hath not touch'd you yet. I am young; but something

[1] deadly
[2] defend
[3] land of our birth
[4] the same cry of pain
[5] set right
[6] mere

⁷ by betraying me

⁸ Even a good man may do evil if ordered by a king

⁹ change

¹⁰ even though evil men put on an appearance of virtue, good men must keep their virtuous appearance
¹¹ helplessness

¹² suspicions

¹³ legally assured

¹⁴ as well

¹⁵ moreover

¹⁶ various

Macduff	You may deserve of him through me,[7] and wisdom To offer up a weak, poor, innocent lamb To appease an angry god. I am not treacherous.
Malcolm	But Macbeth is. A good and virtuous nature may recoil In an imperial charge.[8] But I shall crave your pardon; 20 That which you are, my thoughts cannot transpose;[9] Angels are bright still, though the brightest fell; Though all things foul would wear the brows of grace, Yet grace must still look so.[10]
Macduff	I have lost my hopes.
Malcolm	Perchance even there where I did find my doubts. Why in that rawness[11] left you wife and child - Those precious motives, those strong knots of love – Without leave-taking? I pray you, Let not my jealousies[12] be your dishonours, But mine own safeties: you may be rightly just, 30 Whatever I shall think.
Macduff	Bleed, bleed, poor country! Great tyranny, lay thou thy basis sure, For goodness dares not check thee! Wear thou thy wrongs; The title is affeer'd![13] Fare thee well, lord: I would not be the villain that thou think'st For the whole space that's in the tyrant's grasp, And the rich East to boot.[14]
Malcolm	Be not offended: I speak not as in absolute fear of you. I think our country sinks beneath the yoke; It weeps, it bleeds, and each new day a gash 40 Is added to her wounds: I think withal,[15] There would be hands uplifted in my right; And here, from gracious England, have I offer Of goodly thousands. But, for all this, When I shall tread upon the tyrant's head, Or wear it on my sword, yet my poor country Shall have more vices than it had before, More suffer, and more sundry[16] ways than ever, By him that shall succeed.

Macduff	What should he be?
Malcolm	It is myself I mean; in whom I know 50
	All the particulars of vice so grafted,[17]
	That, when they shall be open'd,[18] black Macbeth
	Will seem as pure as snow, and the poor state
	Esteem him as a lamb, being compar'd
	With my confineless harms.
Macduff	Not in the legions
	Of horrid hell can come a devil more damn'd
	In evils to top[19] Macbeth.
Malcolm	I grant him bloody
	Luxurious, avaricious, false, deceitful,
	Sudden, malicious, smacking of every sin
	That has a name; but there's no bottom,
	none, 60
	In my voluptuousness: your wives, your
	daughters,
	Your matrons, and your maids, could not fill up
	The cistern of my lust; and my desire
	All continent[20] impediments would o'erbear
	That did oppose my will; better Macbeth
	Than such an one to reign.
Macduff	Boundless intemperance
	In nature is a tyranny; it hath been
	Th' untimely emptying of the happy throne,
	And fall of many kings. But fear not yet
	To take upon you what is yours. You may 70
	Convey your pleasures in a spacious plenty,[21]
	And yet seem cold, the time you may so hood-
	wink.
	We have willing dames enough; there cannot be
	That vulture in you, to devour so many
	As will to greatness dedicate themselves,
	Finding it so inclin'd.
Malcolm	With this there grows
	In my most ill-compos'd affection[22] such
	A stanchless[23] avarice that, were I King,
	I should cut off[24] the nobles for their lands,
	Desire his jewels, and this other's house; 80
	And my more-having would be as a sauce
	To make me hunger more, that I should forge
	Quarrels unjust against the good and loyal,
	Destroying them for wealth.
Macduff	This avarice
	Sticks deeper, grows with more pernicious root
	Than summer-seeming lust,[25] and it hath been

[17] made part of himself
[18] revealed

[19] surpass

[20] restaining

[21] in great number

[22] unbalanced disposition
[23] without end
[24] kill

[25] lust that only lasts as long as summer

26 plenty
27 bearable

28 goodness

29 separate

30 forbidding

31 by fasting and penance

32 devices

33 he takes back all the evil
things he said
34 renounce an oath

35 never perjured himself

The sword of our slain kings: yet do not fear;
Scotland hath foisons26 to fill up your will,
Of your mere own. All these are portable,27
With other graces weigh'd.   90

Malcolm (L) But I have none: the king-becoming graces,
As justice, verity, temperance, stableness,
Bounty,28 perseverance, mercy, lowliness,
Devotion, patience, courage, fortitude,
I have no relish of them, but abound
In the division of each several29 crime,
Acting it many ways. Nay, had I power, I should
Pour the sweet milk of concord into hell,
Uproar the universal peace, confound
All unity on earth.   100

Macduff   O Scotland, Scotland!
Malcolm If such a one be fit to govern, speak:
I am as I have spoken.

Macduff   Fit to govern!
No, not to live. O nation miserable,
With an untitled tyrant bloody-scepter'd,
When shalt thou see thy wholesome days again,
Since that the truest issue of thy throne
By his own interdiction30 stands accurs'd,
And does blaspheme his breed? Thy royal father
Was a most sainted king; the queen that bore
    thee,
Oft'ner upon her knees than on her feet,   110
Died31 every day she liv'd. Fare thee well!
These evils thou repeat'st upon thyself
Have banish'd me from Scotland. O my breast,
Thy hope ends here!

Malcolm   Macduff, this noble passion,
Child of integrity, hath from my soul
Wip'd the black scruples, reconcil'd my thoughts
To thy good truth and honour. Devilish Macbeth (L)
By many of these trains32 hath sought to win me
Into his power, and modest wisdom plucks me
From over-credulous haste. But God above   120
Deal between thee and me! for even now
I put myself to thy direction, and
Unspeak mine own detraction,33 here abjure34
The taints and blames I laid upon myself,
For strangers to my nature; I am yet
Unknown to woman, never was forsworn,35
Scarcely have coveted what was mine own;
At no time broke my faith, would not betray
The devil to his fellow, and delight

malcolm claims that Macduff Protestations have cleared him of any respected involvment with Macbeth

Malcom places his destiny in the hands of Macduff

take it all back

No less in truth than life; my first false
  speaking   *130*
Was this upon myself. What I am truly,
Is thine and my poor country's to command;
Whither indeed, before thy here-approach,
Old Siward,[36] with ten thousand warlike men,
Already at a point,[37] was setting forth.
Now we'll together, and the chance of goodness
Be like our warranted quarrel.[38] Why are you
  silent?

Macduff Such welcome and unwelcome things at once
'Tis hard to reconcile.

Enter a Doctor.

Malcolm Well; more anon. Comes the King forth, I pray
  you?   *140*

Doctor Ay, sir; there are a crew of wretched souls
That stay his cure;[39] their malady convinces[40]
The great assay[41] of art; but, at his touch,
Such sanctity hath heaven given his hand,
They presently amend.

Malcolm   I thank you, doctor.
                                      [Exit Doctor.

Macduff What's the disease he means? any Illness
Malcolm   'Tis call'd the evil:[42]
A most miraculous work in this good king,
Which often, since my here-remain in England,
I have seen him do. How he solicits heaven,
Himself best knows; but strangely-visited   *150*
  people,
All swoln and ulcerous, pitiful to the eye,
The mere despair of surgery, he cures;
Hanging a golden stamp[43] about their necks,
Put on with holy prayers; and 'tis spoken
To the succeeding royalty he leaves
The healing benediction. With this strange virtue,
He hath a heavenly gift of prophecy,
And sundry blessings hang about his throne
That speak him full of grace.

Enter Ross.

Macduff   See, who comes here?
Malcolm My countryman; but yet I know him not.   *160*
Macduff My ever-gentle cousin, welcome hither.
Malcolm I know him now. Good God betimes remove
The means that make us strangers!

General in the English army
[36] the son of Beorn, Earl of Northumberland
[37] ready

[38] he hopes that their chances of success be as great as the justice of their cause

[39] expect him to cure them
[40] defies
[41] attempt; their disease defeats the utmost attempt of science

King Edward the Confesser

[42] the King's evil was thought to be curable at the touch of any king descended from Edward the Confessor

[43] a gold coin

Ross	Sir, amen.
Macduff	Stands Scotland where it did?
Ross	Alas! poor country;

Almost afraid to know itself. It cannot
Be call'd our mother, but our grave; where
   nothing,
But who knows nothing, is once seen to smile;
Where sighs and groans and shrieks that rent
   the air

[44] noticed

Are made, not mark'd;[44] where violent sorrow
   seems

[45] an everyday emotion

A modern ecstasy;[45] the dead man's knell   170
Is there scarce ask'd for who; and good men's
   lives
Expire before the flowers in their caps,
Dying or ere they sicken.

Scotland is in a state of violend disorder

[46] report
[47] precise
[48] a man is derided for telling news an hour old
[49] gives birth to

Macduff	O! relation[46]

Too nice,[47] and yet too true!

Malcolm	What's the newest grief?
Ross	That of an hour's age doth hiss the speaker;[48]

Each minute teems[49] a new one.

Macduff	How does my wife?
Ross	Why, well.
Macduff	And all my children?
Ross	Well too.
Macduff	The tyrant has not batter'd at their peace?
Ross	No; they were well at peace when I did leave 'em.

[50] mean

Macduff	Be not a niggard[50] of your speech: how goes't? 180
Ross	When I came hither to transport the tidings,

"scotland needs your presence to rally the people to fight against Macbeth.

Which I have heavily borne, there ran a rumour
Of many worthy fellows that were out;[51]

[51] out in the battlefield

Which was to my belief witness'd the rather
For that I saw the tyrant's power a-foot.

[52] if you were in Scotland

Now is the time of help; your eye in Scotland[52]
Would create soldiers, make our women fight,

[53] get rid of

To doff[53] their dire distresses.

Malcolm	Be't their comfort,

We are coming thither. Gracious England hath
Lent us good Siward and ten thousand men;   190
An older and a better soldier none
That Christendom gives out.

Ross	Would I could answer

This comfort with the like! But I have words
That would be howl'd out in the desert air,

[54] catch

Where hearing should not latch[54] them.

Macduff	What concern they?
	The general cause? or is it a fee-grief[55]
	Due to some single breast?
Ross	No mind that's honest
	But in it shares some woe, though the main part
	Pertains to you alone.
Macduff	If it be mine
	Keep it not from me; quickly let me have it. *200*
Ross	Let not your ears despise my tongue for ever,
	Which shall possess them with the heaviest sound
	That ever yet they heard.
Macduff	Hum! I guess at it.
Ross	Your castle is surpris'd; your wife and babes
	Savagely slaughter'd: to relate the manner,
	Were, on the quarry[56] of these murder'd deer,
	To add the death of you.
Malcolm	Merciful heaven!
	What, man! Ne'er pull your hat upon your
	brows;
	Give sorrow words; the grief that does not
	speak
	Whispers the o'er-fraught[57] heart and bids it
	break. *210*
Macduff	My children too?
Ross	Wife, children, servants, all
	That could be found.
Macduff	And I must be from thence!
	My wife kill'd too?
Ross	I have said.
Malcolm	Be comforted:
	Let's make us medicine of our great revenge,
	To cure this deadly grief.
Macduff	He has no children. All my pretty ones?
	Did you say all? O hell-kite! All?
	What! all my pretty chickens and their dam[58]
	At one fell swoop?
Malcolm	Dispute it like a man. *220*
Macduff	I shall do so;
	But I must also feel it as a man:
	I cannot but remember such things were,
	That were most precious to me. Did heaven look
	on,
	And would not take their part? Sinful Macduff!
	They were all struck for thee. Naught that I am,
	Not for their own demerits, but for mine,
	Fell slaughter on their souls. Heaven rest them
	now!

[55] an individual grief

[56] game killed in hunting, victims

[57] over-burdened

[58] mother

Malcolm	Be this the whetstone of your sword. Let grief
	Convert to anger; blunt not the heart, enrage it.
Macduff	O! I could play the woman with mine eyes, *230*
	And braggart[59] with my tongue. But, gentle heavens,
	Cut short all intermission;[60] front to front
	Bring thou this fiend of Scotland and myself;
	Within my sword's length set him; if he 'scape,
	Heaven forgive him too!
Malcolm	This tune goes manly.
	Come, go we to the King. Our power is ready;
	Our lack is nothing but our leave.[61] Macbeth
	Is ripe for shaking, and the powers above
	Put on their instruments. Receive what cheer you may;
	The night is long that never finds the day. *240*

[Exeunt.

[59] boast

[60] interruption

[61] all they need is to take leave of the King

Handwritten margin note: Let this grief compel you to exact your revenge on Macbat

Handwritten note near "fiend of Scotland and myself": enemy

Handwritten note near "This tune": not our

Scene Analysis

Scene III marks the beginning of the counter action against Macbeth. Malcolm and Macduff meet up in England. Malcolm voices his suspicions of Macduff:

> *"Why in that rawness left you wife and child –*
> *Those precious motives, those strong knots of love –*
> *Without leave-taking?"*

Macduff's answers are sincere:

> *"I would not be the villain that thou think'st*
> *For the whole space that's in the tyrant's grasp*
> *And the rich East to boot."*

Yet Malcolm realizes:

> *"This tyrant, whose sole name blisters our tongues,*
> *Was once thought honest: you have lov'd him well;*
> *He hath not touch'd you yet."*

Macbeth's tyranny has made good men like Macduff suspect. To test Macduff's reaction Malcolm proceeds to blacken his own character and in order to appear a worse tyrant than Macbeth he describes himself as a man:

> *"...in whom I know*
> *All the particulars of vice so grafted,*
> *That, when they shall be open'd, black Macbeth*
> *Will seem as pure as snow, and the poor state*

> *Esteem him as a lamb, being compar'd*
> *With my confineless harms."*

Macduff is sure that no one could be worse than Macbeth:

> *"Not in the legions*
> *Of horrid hell can come a devil more damn'd*
> *In evils to top Macbeth."*

Malcolm exaggeratedly attributes vices to himself:

> *"...but there's no bottom, none*
> *In my voluptuousness."*

Yet Macduff is prepared to excuse Malcolm's vices, even to accommodate them:

> *"...But fear not yet*
> *To take upon you what is yours. You may*
> *Convey your pleasures in a spacious plenty,*
> *And yet seem cold, the time you may so hoodwink."*

When Malcolm accuses himself of *"A stanchless avarice"*, Macduff points out:

> *"Scotland hath foisons to fill up your will,*
> *Of your mere own. All these are portable,*
> *With other graces weigh 'd. "*

But he is deeply shocked at Malcolm's rejection of *"the king-becoming graces."* Malcolm's threat to:

> *"Pour the sweet milk of concord into hell,"*

to destroy the peaceful order of the whole universe, shatters Macduff's hopes. Macduff's cries of bitter disappointment *"O Scotland, Scotland!"* convince Malcolm of Macduff's loyalty and he retracts all that he has spoken. Once Malcolm has retracted his so-called vices, his virtues clearly contrast with the vices he previously admitted to. An important aspect of this scene is the debate on the ideal of kingship. The virtues denied by Malcolm are an indication of the ideal qualities of kingship. The vices which Malcolm has named and rejected clearly indict Macbeth. The concept of good is strengthened by the opposition of evil qualities. Malcolm's list of *"the king-becoming graces"*:

> *"As justice, verity, temperance, stableness,*
> *Bounty, perseverence, mercy, lowliness,*
> *Devotion, patience, courage, fortitude,"*

reinforce the theme of divine order. The entire conversation between Malcolm and Macduff accentuates the contrast between true royalty and tyranny.

A doctor enters and informs them that King Edward is about to work a miraculous cure. There is a pointed contrast between the good King Edward and the evil Macbeth. Edward

...there's no bottom, none,
In my voluptuousness   *(Malcolm, Act 4, Scene III)*

is a healer; Macbeth is a disease. Edward is a sanctified king, Macbeth is a usurper. Edward's court is sanctified, Macbeth's castle is hell. Edward solicits heaven; Macbeth relies on the forces of evil. When the doctor leaves, Ross arrives. Macduff inquires about the state of Scotland and Ross paints a picture of a country torn by suffering:

> "...where nothing
> But who knows nothing, is once seen to smile;
> Where sighs and groans and shrieks, that rent the air,
> Are made, not mark'd"

Ross breaks the news of the massacre of Macduff's family reluctantly. Macduff feels that the only way he can atone for their deaths is to kill Macbeth personally. By the end of the scene there is the confident promise of retribution. The movement against Macbeth is both political and personal.

CHARACTERS
MALCOLM

Scene III gives us the most detailed analysis of Malcolm's character in the play. Malcolm is a stronger character than Duncan. He does not judge by appearances:

> "Though all things foul would wear the brows of grace,
> Yet grace must still look so."

He has learned caution through experience and is very careful to check rumours:

> "What I believe I'll wail,
> What know, believe..."

His suspicion of Macduff, although unfounded, is justified:

> "...Devilish Macbeth
> By many of these trains hath sought to win me
> Into his power, and modest wisdom plucks me
> From over-credulous haste..."

Malcolm does not wish to offend Macduff:

> "...I pray you,
> Let not my jealousies be your dishonours,
> But mine own safeties: you may be rightly just,
> Whatever I shall think."

Malcolm's exaggerated description of himself as a voluptuous and avaricious person abounding:

> "In the division of each several crime"

is a striking contrast to his real character. The confession of innocence that Malcolm finally makes to Macduff points to exceptional qualities. He asserts that he has never broken his word or faith, that he delights no less in truth than in life and that his pretences to Macduff were the first lies that he ever told. He is deeply concerned about his country:

> *"I think our country sinks beneath the yoke;*
> *It weeps, it bleeds, and each new day a gash*
> *Is added to her wounds."*

He is determined to do what he can:

> *"...and what I can redress,*
> *As I shall find the time to friend, I will."*

Once he recognizes Macduff's integrity he willingly submits to his direction:

> *"...What I am truly,*
> *Is thine and my poor country's to command;"*

Malcolm is sympathetic to Macduff's personal grief and urges him to express it openly:

> *"Give sorrow words; the grief that does not speak*
> *Whispers the o'er-fraught heart and bids it break."*

Malcolm obviously inspires respect and confidence. He has successfully secured a force of ten thousand men and is confident of his future success:

> *"...Macbeth*
> *Is ripe for shaking, and the powers above*
> *Put on their instruments."*

MACDUFF

Macduff has a deep and patriotic love for his country and is prepared to fight for it rather than just weep for it:

> *"Let us rather*
> *Hold fast the mortal sword, and like good men*
> *Bestride our down-fall'n birthdom..."*

He is intensely loyal to his country and its rightful ruler. Honesty moves him to refuse to recognize Macbeth as his king and he shows courage in openly opposing him. He puts concern for his country before everything, and takes the drastic step of leaving his family in order to seek out Malcolm in England. This is his only mistake and he pays dearly for it. His replies to Malcolm's questions show him to be a man who cares about justice and who loves his country. Personal integrity is important to him and he is hurt and angry when Malcolm questions him about leaving his family:

> *"Fare thee well, lord:*
> *I would not be the villain that thou think'st"*

Scotland hath foisons to fill up your will,
Of your mere own. All these are portable,
With other graces weigh'd.   (Macduff, Act 4, Scene III)

His grief is deep when Malcolm declares himself to be an impossible ruler. His perfect honesty is seen in the fact that, although Malcolm is Duncan's son, Macduff cannot give his allegiance to one who had the vices Malcolm claims to have:

> *"Fit to govern!*
> *No, not to live. O nation miserable,*
> *With an untitled t'yrant bloody-scepter'd,*
> *When shalt thou see thy wholesome days again,*
> *Since that the finest issue of thy throne*
> *By his own interdiction stands accurs'd,*
> *And does blaspheme his breed?"*

He is very emotional. He is noticeably silent after Malcolm tells him the truth about his character:

> *"Such welcome and unwelcome things at once*
> *'Tis hard to reconcile."*

Macduff, who is a forthright person, is irritated at Ross's brief replies:

> *"Be not a niggard of your speech:"*

When Ross arrives he enquires about his country's welfare before he asks for his family but when he hears of the deaths of his wife and children his grief is boundless. In disbelief he asks over and over again if they have all been killed:

> *"...All my pretty ones?*
> *Did you say all? O hell-kite! All?*
> *What! all my pretty chickens and their dam*
> *At one fell swoop ?"*

Macduff's reaction to the news of his wife's death contrasts very much with that of Macbeth in the next act. Macduff answers Malcolm's words:

> *"Dispute it like a man."*

with the moving words:

> *"I shall do so;*
> *But I must also feel it as a man."*

Macbeth has lost all capacity for such feeling and can only say of Lady Macbeth's death:

> *"She should have died hereafter..."*

Macduff shows not only a willingness to face up to events but also to acknowledge his own part in causing them:

> *"Sinful Macduff!*
> *They were all struck for thee."*

Unlike Macbeth he has no wish to hide from his own guilt. The tragedy befallen him rouses him to personal revenge and the death of Macbeth at his hands is his attempt at retribution to his family.

ROSS

Ross again appears in his role as messenger. He has the difficult task of informing Macduff of the tragedy that has befallen his family. Ross quibbles with words to avoid telling Macduff and to control his own emotions. Twice he shies away from telling the bad news until he is finally ordered angrily by Macduff to tell it. He is obviously upset and so blurts out the news bluntly and without sensitivity:

> *"Your castle is surpris'd, your wife and babes*
> *Savagely slaughter'd: to relate the manner,*
> *Were, on the quarry of these murder'd deer,*
> *To add the death of you."*

EXERCISES

1. (a) Why does Macduff seek out Malcolm?
   (b) Do you think Malcolm was justifiably suspicious of Macduff?
2. (a) Describe the character of Malcolm as he portrays it to Macduff in order to deliberately mislead him.
   (b) What is the effect of the contrast between the true and false description of Malcolm?
3. (a) What important aspects of Macduff's character are in evidence in this scene?
   (b) How does Macduff convince Malcolm of his sincerity?
4. What is the purpose of (a) the conversation with the doctor; (b) the arrival of Ross?
5. What effect on Macduff has the news of the murder of his family?
6. Would you agree with the view that Macbeth is *"ripe for shaking"* at this stage of the play?

REVISION

> *"...an untitled tyrant bloody-scepter'd"*   *(Macduff, Act 4, Scene III)*

Macbeth returns to the witches who warn him to beware Macduff and assure him that he cannot be killed by any man of woman born, nor until Birnam Wood comes to Dunsinane. When Macbeth learns from Lennox that Macduff has fled to England, he orders the death of Macduff's family. In England Malcolm questions Macduff's loyalty at first but is then reassured. Plans are made to lead an army against Macbeth.

POINTS TO NOTE

1. The three apparitions in the cauldron scene are the counterpart of the three prophecies in the first act, but whereas the prophecies foretold Macbeth's rise to the throne, the apparitions foretell his downfall, even though he fails to interpret them correctly.

2. The murder of Lady Macduff provides an actual example of Macbeth's new-found and unbounded cruelty.

3. The qualities of evil that Malcolm attributes to himself in fact fit the description of the tyrant Macbeth.

4. Malcolm's speech on "*the king-becoming graces*" is an exposition of the qualities a king should have.

5. *Scene III* clearly establishes Malcolm's fitness for kingship.

6. The forces of good have begun to fight back, and the moral darkness is about to lift:

   "The night is long that never finds the day".

REVISION ASSIGNMENT

Assess the importance of Macbeth's second meeting with the witches. Trace the growing tyranny of Macbeth in this act and the increasing importance of the role played by the virtuous characters in the play.

Act 5
Scene I

re-introduction of Lady Macbeth

Dunsinane – A Room in the Castle.

Lady M · Servent

Enter a Doctor of Physic and a Waiting-Gentlewoman

Doctor	I have two nights watched with you, but can perceive no truth in your report. When was it she last walked?
Gen.Wm	Since his Majesty went into the field, I have seen her rise from her bed, throw her night-gown upon her, unlock her closet, take forth paper, fold it, write upon't, read it, afterwards seal it, and again return to bed; yet all this while in a most fast sleep.

Lady Macbeth Sleepwalking

Doctor	A great perturbation in nature,[1] to receive at *10* once the benefit of sleep and do the effects of watching![2] In this slumbery agitation, besides her walking and other actual performances, what, at any time, have you heard her say?
Gen.Wm	That, sir, which I will not report after her.
Doctor	You may to me, and 'tis most meet[3] you should.
Gen.Wm	Neither to you nor any one, having no witness to confirm my speech.

[1] disturbance of her constitution

[2] act as if aware

[3] proper

Enter Lady Macbeth, with a taper.

[4] appearance

	Lo you! here she comes. This is her very guise,[4] and, upon my life, fast asleep. Observe her; *20* stand close.
Doctor	How came she by that light?
Gen.Wm	Why, it stood by her. She has light by her continually; 'tis her command.
Doctor	You see, her eyes are open.
Gen.Wm	Ay, but their sense is shut.
Doctor	What is it she does now? Look, how she rubs her hands.
Gen.Wm	It is an accustomed action with her, to seem thus washing her hands. I have known her to *30* continue in this a quarter of an hour.
Lady Macbeth	Yet here's a spot.
Doctor	Hark! she speaks. I will set down what comes from her, to satisfy my remembrance the more strongly.

⁵ dark	

Lady Macbeth Out, damned spot! out, I say! One; two: why, then, 'tis time to do't. Hell is murky!⁵ Fie, my lord, fie! a soldier, and afeard? What need we fear who knows it, when none can call our power to account? Yet who would have *40* thought the old man to have had so much blood in him?

Doctor Do you mark that?

⁶ Macduff

Blood is a symbol of her guilt

Lady Macbeth The Thane of Fife⁶ had a wife: where is she now? What! will these hands ne'er be clean? No more o' that, my lord, no more o' that: you mar all with this starting.

Doctor Go to, go to; you have known what you should not.

Gen.Wm She has spoke what she should not, I am sure of that. Heaven knows what she has known. *50*

Lady Macbeth Here's the smell of the blood still. All the perfumes of Arabia will not sweeten this little hand. Oh! oh! oh!

⁷ heavily burdened

Doctor What a sigh is there! The heart is sorely charged.⁷

Gen.Wm I would not have such a heart in my bosom for the dignity of the whole body.

Doctor Well, well, well.

Gen.Wm Pray God it be, sir.

Doctor This disease is beyond my practice. Yet I *60* have known those which have walked in their sleep who have died holily in their beds.

Lady Macbeth Wash your hands, put on your night-gown; look not so pale. I tell you yet again, Banquo's buried; he cannot come out on's grave.

⁸ Really?

Doctor Even so?⁸

Lady Macbeth To bed, to bed: there's knocking at the gate. Come, come, come, come, give me your hand. What's done cannot be undone. To bed, to bed, to bed.

[*Exit.*

Doctor Will she go now to bed? *70*

Gen.Wm Directly.

⁹ foul rumours are circulating

Doctor Foul whisperings are abroad.⁹ Unnatural deeds Do breed unnatural troubles; infected minds To their deaf pillows will discharge their secrets:

¹⁰ priest

More needs she the divine¹⁰ than the physician. God, God forgive us all! Look after her;

¹¹ injury

Remove from her the means of all annoyance,¹¹ And still keep eyes upon her. So, good night:

¹² confused

My mind she has mated,¹² and amaz'd my sight. I think, but dare not speak. *80*

Gen.Wm Good night, good doctor. [*Exeunt.*

Scene Analysis

In this scene Lady Macbeth appears for the last time. In her sleep-walking trance she relives the crimes of the past and articulates the thoughts that have tormented her since the murder. She is mostly concerned about the impossibility of getting the blood off her hands, and she repeatedly goes through the motions of washing them. We witness the complete reversal of all her utterances. She once called for the *"blanket of the dark"*, now *"She has light by her continually"*. She once asked for *"the dunnest smoke of hell"* to surround her, now it is an image of her fear – *"Hell is murky"*. Her former words – *"A little water clears us of this deed"* are now belied by her pathetic attempts to wash the blood from her hands. Bearing in mind Lady Macbeth's earlier comments and behaviour, this scene is charged with irony.

CHARACTERS
DOCTOR AND GENTLEWOMAN

The gentlewoman has obviously reported Lady Macbeth's sleep-walking to the doctor. The doctor, in order to verify the report, watches with the gentlewoman for two nights. The gentle-woman is loyal to her mistress and when the doctor asks what she has overheard she replies:

> *"That, sir, which I will not report after her."*

The doctor is amazed by what he sees and recognizes his limitations as a physician:

> *"This disease is beyond my practice..."*

He is overawed by her guilty secret:

> *"God, God forgive us all!"*

but like the gentlewoman has the quality of discretion:

> *"I think, but dare not speak."*

LADY MACBETH

In the sleep-walking scene Lady Macbeth at last betrays herself. The sleep-walking is a visual representation of the horror, guilt and remorse which weighs her down. Her mind has given way under the strain, she is now at the mercy of *"a mind diseased"*. Her first words:

> *"Yet here's a spot."*

and the continuous rubbing of her hands for up to a quarter of an hour at a time, show the extent of her obsession with blood. Unlike her husband, she suppressed any revulsion of blood, taunting Macbeth:

> *"A foolish thought to say a sorry sight."*

What! will these hands ne'er be clean?   (Lady Macbeth, Act 5, Scene I)

Yet the "*sorry sight*" is now an obsession:

> "*...all the perfumes of Arabia will not sweeten this little hand. Oh! Oh! Oh!*"

The disorder of her mind is shown in the way she moves from one idea to another with little logical progression, yet she re-enacts one by one the events of the night of murder. She imagines that she hears the bell which was the summons for the murder. She recalls the horror of having to smear the grooms with the blood of Duncan who so resembled her father that it made a deep and lasting impression on her mind:

> "Yet who would have thought the old man to have had so much blood in him?"

Likewise she is haunted by the murder of Lady Macduff, even though she herself had no active part in it:

> "*The Thane of Fife had a wife: where is she now?*"

It is especially significant that not only does she re-enact the horror of the murder but she relives the strain of having to exhort her husband to action:

> "*Fie, my lord, fie! a soldier, and afeard?*"
> "*No more o' that, my lord, no more o' that: you mar all with this starting.*"
> "*Wash your hands, put on your night-gown; look not so pale. I tell you yet again, Banquo's buried; he cannot come out on's grave.*"

These exclamations are disjointed and show the terrible burden she carries – not just her own guilt but also the constant fear of her husband's self-betrayal. Her words – "*What's done cannot be undone*" – is almost an exact repetition of her words to Macbeth in *Act 3, Scene II* – "*What's done is done...*" but whereas then it seemed matter of fact and indifferent, here it is a tragic acknowledgement of failure. Her will power has given way to helplessness. Lady Macbeth has kept her self-control outwardly but she has cracked inwardly. Her self-control has given way to a pathetic vulnerability:

> "*Come, come, come, come, give me your hand.*"

Lady Macbeth commands the same fascination in her sleep-walking as she did in her awe-inspiring role in the early part of the play.

EXERCISES
1. Describe the sleep-walking of Lady Macbeth. Examine what she says and relate her words to earlier incidents in the play.
2. Does this scene change your view of Lady Macbeth?

Scene II

The Country near Dunsinane — *Macbeths Castle* (handwritten)

Enter, with drum and colours,[1] *Menteith,*
Caithness, Angus, Lennox and Soldiers.

Plotting their (handwritten)
Path towards (handwritten)
Macbeths castle (handwritten)

Menteith	The English power is near, led on by Malcolm,
	His uncle Siward, and the good Macduff.
	Revenges burn in them; for their dear causes
	Would to the bleeding and the grim alarm[2]
	Excite the mortified man.[3]
Angus	Near Birnam wood
	Shall we well meet them; that way are they
	coming.
Caithness	Who knows if Donalbain be with his brother?
Lennox	For certain, sir, he is not: I have a file
	Of all the gentry. There is Siward's son,
	And many unrough[4] youths that even now *10*
	Protest[5] their first of manhood.
Menteith	What does the tyrant?
Caithness	Great Dunsinane he strongly fortifies. *(strengthening the castle — handwritten)*
	Some say he's mad; others that lesser hate him,
	Do call it valiant fury; but, for certain,
	He cannot buckle his distemper'd[6] cause
	Within the belt of rule.
Angus	Now does he feel
	His secret murders sticking on his hands;
	Now minutely revolts[7] upbraid[8] his faith-breach;
	Those he commands move only in command,
	Nothing in love. Now does he feel his title *20*
	Hang loose about him, like a giant's robe
	Upon a dwarfish thief.
Menteith	Who then shall blame
	His pester'd senses to recoil and start,
	When all that is within him does condemn
	Itself for being there?
Caithness	Well, march we on,
	To give obedience where 'tis truly ow'd;
	Meet we the medicine of the sickly weal,
	And with him pour we in our country's purge
	Each drop of us.
Lennox	Or so much as it needs
	To dew the sovereign flower and drown the *30*
	weeds.
	Make we our march towards Birnam.
	[Exeunt, marching.

Side notes:
[1] flags
[2] fight
[3] man accustomed to repress his natural feelings
[4] beardless
[5] assert
[6] sick
[7] revolts breaking out every minute
[8] denounce

Scene Analysis

Scene II is short but significant as we learn of the desertion of the Scottish lords to Malcolm. Menteith reports the nearness of the English force under Malcolm, Siward and Macduff. Their motivation is revenge and there is no lack of support for their cause:

> *"...for their dear causes*
> *Would to the bleeding and the grim alarm*
> *Excite the mortified man."*

The image of bleeding the country in order to purge it of evil is used, and reference is made once again to the image of clothing which gives some indication of Macbeth's state of mind:

> *"...now does he feel his title*
> *Hang loose about him, like a giant's robe*
> *Upon a dwarfish thief."*

The Scottish army under Menteith, Caithness, Angus and Lennox will meet the English army at Birnam Wood – this immediately brings to mind the prophecy of the witches. Macbeth is prepared for attack and is fortifying Dunsinane. However, he is having difficulty commanding his followers:

> *"He cannot buckle his distemper'd cause*
> *Within the belt of rule."*

CHARACTERS

THE SCOTTISH LORDS

The lords are organized and united in their cause against Macbeth. Their role in this scene is to advance the action quickly and by means of their conversation to let us know the latest state of affairs. Angus and Lennox play very minor roles in the play but their presence is essential to the unfolding of the drama. Angus and Lennox represent the loyal thanes of Scotland. They served Duncan and they admired and respected Macbeth. They seemed prepared to acknow-ledge Macbeth as king, unlike Macduff, until Macbeth became an open tyrant and they realized that Scotland was suffering *"under a hand accurs'd"*. In *Act 3*, Lennox prayed for the success of Macduff's mission. Here he actively supports it:

> *"Or so much as it needs*
> *To dew the sovereign flower and drown the weeds.*
> *Make we our march towards Birnam."*

EXERCISES

1. Why has Malcolm now taken the lead in the fight against Macbeth?
2. Would you agree that Macbeth's conduct is due to either *"madness"* or *"valiant fury"*?
3. How does this scene advance the action?
4. Comment on the two clothing images which occur in this scene.

Scene III

Dunsinane – A room in the Castle.

Enter Macbeth, Doctor, and Attendants.

Macbeth   Bring me no more reports; let them fly all:
Till Birnam wood remove to Dunsinane
I cannot taint with fear. What's the boy Malcolm?
Was he not born of woman? The spirits that know
All mortal consequences have pronounc'd me
   thus:
'Fear not, Macbeth; no man that's born of woman
Shall e'er have power upon thee.' Then fly, false
   thanes,
And mingle with the English epicures:
The mind I sway by and the heart I bear
Shall never sag with doubt nor shake with
   fear.   *10*

          Enter a Servant.

The devil damn thee black, thou cream-fac'd
   loon!
Where gott'st thou that goose look?

Servant   There is ten thousand. –

Macbeth   Geese, villain?

Servant   Soldiers, sir.

Macbeth   Go, prick thy face, and over-red thy fear,
Thou lily-liver'd boy. What soldiers, patch?
Death of thy soul! Those linen cheeks of thine
Are counsellors to fear. What soldiers, whey-face?

Servant   The English force, so please you.

Macbeth   Take thy face hence.
                         [Exit Servant.

Seyton! – I am sick at heart   *20*
When I behold – Seyton, I say! – This push[1]
Will cheer me ever, or disseat[2] me now.
I have liv'd long enough. My way of life
Is fall'n into the sear, [3] the yellow leaf;
And that which should accompany old age,
As honour, love, obedience, troops of friends,
I must not look to have; but, in their stead,
Curses, not loud but deep, mouth-honour, breath,
Which the poor heart would fain[4] deny, and
   dare not.
Seyton!   *30*

[1] assault
[2] dethrone
[3] old
[4] gladly

Enter Seyton.

Seyton	What is your gracious pleasure?
Macbeth	What news more?
Seyton	All is confirm'd, my lord, which was reported.
Macbeth	I'll fight till from my bones my flesh be hack'd.
	Give me my armour. *Courageous*
Seyton	'Tis not needed yet.
Macbeth	I'll put it on.

Send out more horses, skirr[5] the country round;   [5] scour
Hang those that talk of fear. Give me mine
  armour.
How does your patient, doctor?

Doctor   Not so sick, my lord,
As she is troubled with thick-coming fancies,
That keep her from her rest.   40

Macbeth   Cure her of that:
Canst thou not minister[6] to a mind diseas'd,   [6] treat
Pluck from the memory a rooted sorrow,
Raze out the written troubles of the brain,
And with some sweet oblivious antidote[7]   [7] medicine to cause
Cleanse the stuff'd bosom of that perilous stuff   forgetfulness
Which weighs upon the heart?

Doctor   Therein the patient
Must minister to himself.

Macbeth Throw physic to the dogs; I'll none of it.
Come, put mine armour on; give me my staff.
Seyton, send out. – Doctor, the thanes fly from
  me.   50
Come, sir, dispatch. If thou couldst, doctor, cast
The water of my land,[8] find her disease   [8] a medical term for
And purge it to a sound and pristine[9] health,   diagnosis; illness was
I would applaud thee to the very echo,   diagnosed by an
That should applaud again. – Pull't off, I say. –   examination of the urine
What rhubarb, senna,[10] or what purgative drug   [9] original good
Would scour these English hence? Hear'st thou   [10] dried leaves used as a
  of them?   laxative

Doctor Ay, my good lord. Your royal preparation
Makes us hear something.

Macbeth   Bring it after me.
I will not be afraid of death and bane[11]   60   [11] ruin
Till Birnam Forest come to Dunsinane.
                [Exeunt all but the Doctor.

Doctor *[Aside]* Were I from Dunsinane away and clear,
Profit again should hardly draw me here.
                    [Exit.

Scene Analysis

At the beginning of *Scene III* Macbeth is defiant and fearless but he is shaken by the messenger's news that the English force is in sight:

> *"This push*
> *Will cheer me ever, or disseat me now."*

Admitting to himself that he is "*sick at heart*", he thinks of what is missing from his life – love, friendship and honour. When Seyton confirms the messenger's report he becomes defiant again. He enquires of the doctor about Lady Macbeth but is contemptuous of the doctor and his "*physic*" which cannot:

> *"Raze out the written troubles of the brain".*

He wishes the doctor could diagnose the disease of his country:

> *"And purge it to a sound and pristine health."*

CHARACTERS

DOCTOR

The doctor quietly reports to Macbeth, explaining that Lady Macbeth is:

> *"Not so sick, my lord,*
> *As she is troubled with thick-coming fancies,*
> *That keep her from her rest."*

Again we see the doctor as discreet and showing considerable understanding of a delicate situation. There is no criticism of Lady Macbeth, only a recognition that:

> *"Therein the patient*
> *Must minister to himself."*

The doctor distinguishes between physical and mental ills and does not offer any facile cure for "*the written troubles of the brain.*"

MACBETH

In *Scene II* it was reported that Macbeth had lost control of the situation. It was rumoured that he had become mad but:

> *"...others that lesser hate him*
> *Do call it valiant fury..."*

This valiant fury is clearly seen in *Scene III* when Macbeth defies all reports, defies the fleeing thanes, berates his servants, and insults the doctor. He is reckless in his confidence in the witches' prophecy:

> *"Till Birnam wood remove to Dunsinane*
> *I cannot taint with fear."*

But his reiteration of the witches' prophecy shows his utter dependence on it:

> *"The spirits that know*
> *All mortal consequences have pronounc'd me thus:*
> *'Fear not, Macbeth; no man that's born of woman*
> *Shall e'er have power upon thee'."*

The courage that earned him the admiration of the king and all the thanes is still very much in evidence:

> *"The mind I sway by and the heart I bear*
> *Shall never sag with doubt nor shake with fear."*

One sees how utterly tyrannical Macbeth has become in his unnecessarily hard treatment of the servant. The servant is fearful of having to report to the furious Macbeth the news of the approach of ten thousand soldiers. Macbeth is merciless in his contempt for his fear:

> *"Go, prick thy face, and over-red thy fear,*
> *Thou lily-liver'd boy. What soldiers, patch?*
> *Death of thy soul! Those linen cheeks of thine*
> *Are counsellors to fear. What soldiers, whey-face?"*

His defiance expends itself in his insults, however, and his mood changes to one of despair – "*I am sick at heart.*" There is an element of self-pity in the realization:

> *"And that which should accompany old age,*
> *As honour, love, obedience, troops of friends,*
> *I must not look to have..."*

yet one feels that Macbeth regrets very deeply the qualities of honour, love and obedience which he has sacrificed and he bitterly suffers:

> *"Curses, not loud but deep, mouth-honour, breath,*
> *Which the poor heart would fain deny, and dare not."*

When Seyton confirms the reports, Macbeth asserts himself again:

> *"I'll fight till from my bones my flesh be hack'd."*

Yet the fact that he insists on putting on his armour when it is not yet needed is an indication of his insecurity. He is abrupt with the doctor, yet shows a sensitive awareness of the nature of Lady Macbeth's suffering:

> *"Canst thou not minister to a mind diseas'd,*
> *Pluck from the memory a rooted sorrow,*
> *Raze out the written troubles of the brain,*
> *And with some sweet oblivious antidote*
> *Cleanse the stuff'd bosom of that perilous stuff*
> *Which weighs upon the heart?"*

The doctor's helplessness angers him and he dismisses him rudely:

> *"Throw physic to the dogs; I'll none of it."*

He shows considerable agitation, orders Seyton to help him with his armour, then shouts at him

> – *"Pull 't off, I say."*

To reassure himself, Macbeth repeats the witches' rhyme:

> *"I will not be afraid of death and bane*
> *Till Birnam Forest come to Dunsinane."*

EXERCISES

1. (a) What has happened since we last saw Macbeth?
    (b) Has Macbeth changed much?
2. Is Macbeth as confident as he claims in this scene? How would you describe his state of mind?

Scene IV

Country near Birnam Wood.

Enter, with drum and colours, Malcolm, Siward and his Son,
Macduff, Menteith, Caithness, Angus, Lennox, Ross and
Soldiers marching.

Malcolm	Cousins, I hope the days are near at hand
	That chambers will be safe.
Menteith	We doubt it nothing.
Siward	What wood is this before us?
Menteith	The wood of Birnam.
Malcolm	Let every soldier hew him down a bough
	And bear't before him: thereby shall we shadow
Soldier	The numbers of our host, and make discovery
	Err in report of us.
Soldier	It shall be done.
Siward	We learn no other but the confident tyrant
	Keeps still in Dunsinane, and will endure
	Our setting down[1] before't. 10
Malcolm	'Tis his main hope;
	For where there is advantage to be given,

Cutt a branch off

[1] laying siege

	Both more and less[2] have given him the revolt,	[2] high and low in rank
	And none serve with him but constrained[3] things	[3] acting under compulsion
	Whose hearts are absent too.	
Macduff	Let our just censures[4]	[4] judgement
	Attend the true event,[5] and put we on	[5] the end of the battle
	Industrious soldiership.	
Siward	The time approaches	
	That will with due decision make us know	
	What we shall say we have and what we owe.[6]	[6] what we have gained and lost
	Thoughts speculative their unsure hopes relate,	
	But certain issue strokes must arbitrate;[7] 20	[7] speculation puts forward unreliable hopes, but the battle will decide the outcome
	Towards which advance the war.	
	[Exeunt, marching.	

Scene Analysis

Scene IV is important in that it effectively disposes of one part of the witches' prophesy. The English and Scottish forces meet at Birnam Wood and Malcolm instructs every soldier to carry the branch of a tree before him. We learn that Macbeth has been deserted:

> *"Both more and less have given him the revolt,*
> *And none serve with him but constrained things*
> *Whose hearts are absent too."*

CHARACTERS
MALCOLM

Malcolm is identified with the representatives of order and goodness and he expresses the hope that men will be able to sleep in safety, bringing again to mind the murder of innocent people like Duncan and the Macduff family:

> *"Cousins, I hope the days are near at hand*
> *That chambers will be safe."*

Malcolm shows himself to be a skilful soldier, taking care to camouflage his army to conceal their number and so surprise the enemy:

> *"Let every soldier hew him down a bough*
> *And bear't before him; thereby shall we shadow*
> *The numbers of our host, and make discovery*
> *Err in report of us."*

Malcolm is confident and optimistic.

Let every soldier hew him down a bough
And bear't before him   (Malcolm, Act 5, Scene IV)

MACDUFF

Macduff is cautious and realizes that they will have to put on "*industrious soldiership*" in the fight with Macbeth. He warns Malcolm:

> *"Let our just censures*
> *Attend the true event..."*

Macduff is silent and tense throughout the short scene.

EXERCISES

1. Discuss the importance of the incident of cutting down the boughs.
2. Show how this scene knits together the various strands of the plot.

Scene V

Dunsinane – Within the Castle.

Enter, with drum and colours, Macbeth, Seyton, and Soldiers.

Macbeth *is*   Hang out our banners on the outward walls;
utterley   The cry is still, 'They come'. Our castle's strength
defiant and   Will laugh a siege to scorn. Here let them lie
determent   Till famine and the ague[1] eat them up;   [1] fever
             Were they not forc'd[2] with those that should be   [2] reinforced
               ours,
             We might have met them dareful, beard to beard,
             And beat them backward home.
                     [A cry of women within.
                        What is that noise?

Seyton   It is the cry of women, my good lord.
                                [Exit.

Macbeth   I have almost forgot the taste of fears.
             The time has been my senses would have cool'd 10
             To hear a night-shriek, and my fell of hair[3]   [3] scalp
Soliloquy   Would at a dismal treatise[4] rouse and stir   [4] story
             As life were in't. I have supp'd full[5] with horrors;   [5] eaten my fill
             Direness,[6] familiar to my slaughterous thoughts,   [6] horror
             Cannot once start me.

             Re-enter Seyton.

                    Wherefore was that cry?
Seyton   The Queen, my lord, is dead.
Macbeth   She should have died hereafter;[7]   [7] later
             There would have been a time for such a word.
             To-morrow, and to-morrow, and to-morrow,
             Creeps in this petty[8] pace from day to day,   20   [8] trivial
             To the last syllable of recorded time;[9]   [9] till the end of time forced
             And all our yesterdays have lighted fools   by fate
             The way to dusty death. Out, out, brief candle![10]   [10] short life
             Life's but a walking shadow, a poor player
             That struts and frets his hour upon the stage,
             And then is heard no more; it is a tale
             Told by an idiot, full of sound and fury,
             Signifying nothing.

             Enter a Messenger.

             Thou com'st to use thy tongue; thy story quickly.

[Handwritten annotations: "Macbeth is utterley defiant and determent"; "Soliloquy"; "There is a complete lack of empathy in macbeths reaction to his wife's death"; "actor"; "pointing towards the Futility of life"]

This scene represents Macbeths lack of humanity

Messenger	Gracious my lord,	30
	I should report that which I say I saw,	
	But know not how to do it.	
Macbeth	Well, say, sir.	
Messenger	As I did stand my watch upon the hill,	
	I look'd towards Birnam, and anon, methought,	
	The wood began to move.	
Macbeth	Liar and slave!	
Messenger	Let me endure your wrath if't be not so:	
	Within this three mile may you see it coming;	
	I say, a moving grove.	
Macbeth	If thou speak'st false,	

Upon the next tree shalt thou hang alive,
Till famine cling[11] thee. If thy speech be sooth,[12] 40
I care not if thou dost for me as much.
I pull[13] in resolution and begin
To doubt the equivocation of the fiend *the witche*
That lies like truth; 'Fear not, till Birnam wood
Do come to Dunsinane,' and now a wood
Comes toward Dunsinane. Arm, arm, and out!
If this which he avouches[14] does appear,
There is nor flying hence, nor tarrying[15] here.
I 'gin to be aweary of the sun,
And wish the estate o' the world were now
 undone.   50
Ring the alarum bell! Blow, wind! come, wrack![16]
At least we'll die with harness[17] on our back.

[Exeunt.

[11]shrivel
[12]truth
[13]draw back

[14]affirms
[15]delaying

[16]wreck
[17]armour

Scene Analysis

In *Scene V* Macbeth prepares for the coming siege and orders the flag to be raised. A cry is heard and Seyton brings news of the death of Lady Macbeth. This moves Macbeth to thoughts about the futility of life. A messenger reports that Birnam Wood has moved, and, as always when desperate, Macbeth resorts to impulsive action. He decides to take on Malcolm's forces in open battle and he rushes out defiantly.

CHARACTERS
MACBETH

Siward referred to Macbeth in the previous scene as "*the confident tyrant*". His confidence is evident in this scene as he defiantly prepares for battle:

> "...our castle's strength
> Will laugh a siege to scorn;"

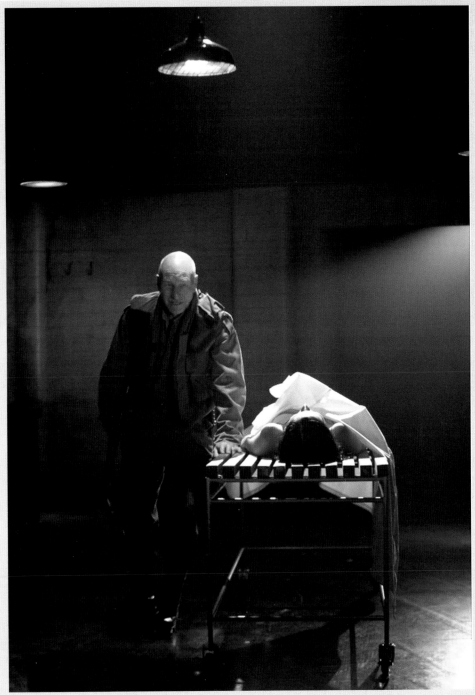

Life's but a walking shadow, a poor player
That struts and frets his hour upon the stage,
And then is heard no more   (Macbeth, Act 5, Scene V)

He realizes that he has almost forgotten the emotion of fear. He is unmoved by the cry of the women, he whose:

> *"...senses would have cool'd.*
> *To hear a night-shriek..."*

It is a measure of how much he has changed that he can now say:

> *"Direness, familiar to my slaughterous thoughts,*
> *Cannot once start me."*

His comment on learning of his wife's death is ambiguous:

> *"She should have died hereafter;*
> *There would have been a time for such a word."*

If he means simply that she would have died anyway, he would appear to be showing little feeling. If he means that she has chosen an inconvenient time to die, it seems equally callous but at least expresses a wish to mourn her as was her due. "*...supp'd full with horrors*", he seems beyond feeling. Perhaps unconsciously, the death of Lady Macbeth evokes in Macbeth a spiritual emptiness which he expresses in his last soliloquy in which life is portrayed as totally meaningless. He sees one day creeping after another in a "*petty*" way. Life is a shadow, it is a candle flame blowing out all too quickly, it is a meaningless story "*signifying nothing*". This is a despairing speech and having just uttered it he learns that Birnam Wood is moving. Macbeth rages against the messenger who brings the news, yet he begins now to doubt:

> *"I pull in resolution and begin*
> *To doubt the equivocation of the fiend*
> *That lies like truth..."*

He senses that his hour has come but is resigned to death:

> *"I 'gin to be aweary of the sun,*
> *And wish the estate o' the world were now undone."*

Yet although he is trapped:

> *"There is nor flying hence, nor tarrying here."*

He is determined to put up a good fight:

> *"At least we'll die with harness on our back."*

EXERCISES

1. Are you surprised to learn of Lady Macbeth's death?
2. Discuss the effect of Lady Macbeth's death on Macbeth.
3. Outline briefly Macbeth's thoughts on the vanity of human life.
4. How does Macbeth react when he hears the news that Birnam Wood is moving?

Scene VI

The Same – A Plain before the Castle.

Enter, with drum and colours, Malcolm,
Siward, Macduff, and their Army, with boughs.

Malcolm	Now near enough; your leavy screens throw down,
	And show like those you are. You, worthy uncle,[1]
	Shall, with my cousin, your right-noble son,
	Lead our first battle; worthy Macduff and we
	Shall take upon's what else remains to do,
	According to our order.
Siward	Fare you well.
	Do we but find the tyrant's power to-night,
	Let us be beaten, if we cannot fight.
Macduff	Make all our trumpets speak; give them all breath,
	Those clamorous harbingers[2] of blood and death.

10

[Exeunt.

[1] Siward

[2] heralds

Scene Analysis

In *Scene VI* the army has reached Dunsinane. The soldiers cast away their branches and the signal for battle is sounded.

CHARACTERS
MALCOLM

Malcolm instructs his soldiers clearly

> *"...your leavy screens throw down,*
> *And show like those you are."*

He directs Siward and his son to lead the first battle while he and Macduff:

> *"Shall take upon's what else remains to do,*
> *According to our order."*

EXERCISES
1. What is the dramatic effectiveness of such a short scene?

Scene VII

The Same – Another Part of the Plain.

Enter Macbeth.

Macbeth *continues* They have tied me to a stake; I cannot fly,
to desperately But bear-like I must fight the course.[1] What's he
cling to the That was not born of woman? Such a one
1st of the Am I to fear, or none.
witches prophecies

Enter Young Siward.

Yng Siward   What is thy name?
Macbeth   Thou'lt be afraid to hear it.
Yng Siward   No; though thou call'st thyself a hotter name
                   Than any is in hell.
Macbeth   My name's Macbeth.
Yng Siward   The devil himself could not pronounce a title
                   More hateful to mine ear.
Macbeth   *threatning* — No, nor more fearful.
Yng Siward   Thou liest, abhorred tyrant; with my sword   10
                   I'll prove the lie thou speak'st.   *murdered*

                   [They fight and Young Siward is slain.

Macbeth   Thou wast born of woman:
                   But swords I smile at, weapons laugh to scorn,
                   Brandish'd by man that's of a woman born.
                                                          [Exit.

Alarums. Enter Macduff

Macduff   That way the noise is. Tyrant, show thy face:
desperate   If thou be'st slain and with no stroke of mine,
for revenge   My wife and children's ghosts will haunt me still.
                   I cannot strike at wretched kerns, whose arms
                   Are hir'd to bear their staves:[2] either thou,
                     Macbeth,
                   Or else my sword with an unbatter'd edge
                   I sheathe again undeeded.[3] There thou shouldst
                     be;   20
                   By this great clatter, one of greatest note[4]
                   Seems bruited.[5] Let me find him, Fortune!
                   And more I beg not.
                                              [Exit. Alarums.

[1] in Elizabethan bearbaiting, the bear was tied to a stake and the dogs were set loose on him. An assault of ten dogs was called a course

[2] spear shafts

[3] unused

[4] importance
[5] announced

Enter Malcolm and Old Siward.

Siward   This way, my lord; the castle's gently render'd:[6] [6]surrendered
         The tyrant's people on both sides do fight;

The battle is almost won The noble thanes do bravely in the war,
         The day almost itself professes yours,[7] [7]you have almost won the day
         And little is to do.

Malcolm   We have met with foes
         That strike beside us.

Siward   Enter, sir, the castle.
            [*Exeunt. Alarums.*

Scene Analysis

Macbeth appears alone, feeling trapped like a bear but still believing in the witches' last prophecy that none of woman born can harm him. Siward's son challenges Macbeth to fight but is killed. Young Siward associates Macbeth with hell:

> *"The devil himself could not pronounce a title*
> *More hateful to mine ear."*

As Macduff is seeking out Macbeth, the surrender of Macbeth's castle is reported by Siward. It was an easy victory as Macbeth's people are still deserting him:

> *"We have met with foes*
> *That strike beside us."*

CHARACTERS
MACBETH

In *Scene VII* Macbeth is like a cornered animal, desperate and savage:

> *"They have tied me to a stake; I cannot fly,*
> *But bear-like I must fight the course."*

Despite his disillusionment at the witches' prophecies regarding the moving of Birnam Wood – which seemed an impossibility yet has come true – Macbeth still clings to the final prophecy:

> *"What's he*
> *That was not born of woman? Such a one*
> *Am I to fear, or none."*

Siward's son bravely fights Macbeth but is slain. This easy victory by one that was "*born of woman*" increases Macbeth's confidence:

> *"But swords I smile at, weapons laugh to scorn,*
> *Brandish'd by man that's of a woman born."*

*If thou be'st slain and with no
stroke of mine,
My wife and children's ghosts
will haunt me still.*
(Macduff, Act 5, Scene VII)

YOUNG SIWARD AND MACDUFF

Siward and Macduff are both unafraid of the tyrant Macbeth. Young Siward does not flinch when confronted with Macbeth himself and attempts to *"prove the lie"* that he is afraid of the *"abhorred tyrant"*.

Macduff is motivated by a desire for revenge which is as personal as it is intense. It is not sufficient that Macbeth be slain:

> *"If thou be'st slain and with no stroke of mine,*
> *My wife and children's ghosts will haunt me still."*

EXERCISES

1. What purpose is served by the death of Siward in this scene?
2. Has Macbeth still confidence in the witches at this point?
3. Comment on the effect of Macbeth's last words before the arrival of Macduff –
   "...Swords I smile at, weapons laugh to scorn,/Brandish'd by man that's of a woman born."

Scene VIII

The Battlefield.

Enter Macbeth.

Macbeth   Why should I play the Roman fool,[1] and die
On mine own sword? Whiles I see lives, the
  gashes
Do better upon them.

Re-enter Macduff.

Macduff *I don't want*   Turn, hell-hound, turn!
Macbeth *to win you* Of all men else I have avoided thee:
But get thee back, my soul is too much charg'd
With blood of thine already.
Macduff   I have no words;
My voice is in my sword, thou bloodier villain
Than terms[2] can give thee out![3]
                               [They fight.

Macbeth   Thou losest labour:
As easy mayst thou the intrenchant[4] air
With thy keen sword impress[5] as make me
  bleed: 10
Let fall thy blade on vulnerable crests;[6]
Protected I bear a charmed life, which must not yield
To one of woman born.
Macduff *mother had a C-Section* Despair thy charm;
And let the angel whom thou still hast serv'd
Tell thee, Macduff was from his mother's womb
Untimely[7] ripp'd.
Macbeth   Accursed be that tongue that tells me so,
For it hath cow'd my better part of man;[8]
And be these juggling[9] fiends no more believ'd,
That palter with us in a double sense;[10]   20
That keep the word of promise to our ear,
And break it to our hope. I'll not fight with thee.
Macduff   Then yield thee, coward, *—changes Macbeths mind*
And live to be the show and gaze o' the time:
We'll have thee, as our rarer monsters are,
Painted upon a pole,[11] and underwrit,
'Here may you see the tyrant.'
Macbeth   I will not yield,
To kiss the ground before young Malcolm's feet
And to be baited with the rabble's curse.

[1] Roman heroes committed suicide when the battle was lost

[2] words
[3] call you

[4] cannot be cut
[5] cut

[6] helmets

[7] prematurely

[8] frightened my manhood
[9] deceitful
[10] cheat

[11] painted on a board and hung up on a pole

although I have no chance I will not give up

¹²fight

Though Birnam wood be come to Dunsinane, 30
And thou oppos'd, being of no woman born,
Yet I will try the last. Before my body
I throw my war-like shield. Lay on,¹² Macduff,
And damn'd be him that first cries, 'Hold
        enough!'
                                    [*Exeunt, fighting.*

*Retreat. Flourish. Re-enter, with drum and colours,
Malcolm, Siward, Ross, Lennox, Angus, Caithness,
Menteith, and Soldiers*

Malcolm	I would the friends we miss were safe arriv'd.
Siward	Some must go off;¹³ and yet, by these I see,
	So great a day as this is cheaply bought.
Malcolm	Macduff is missing, and your noble son.
Ross	Your son, my lord, has paid a soldier's debt:
	He only liv'd but till he was a man; 40
	The which no sooner had his prowess confirm'd
	In the unshrinking station¹⁴ where he fought,
	But like a man he died.
Siward	Then he is dead?
Ross	Ay, and brought off the field. Your cause of
	sorrow
	Must not be measur'd by his worth, for then
	It hath no end.
Siward	Had he his hurts before?¹⁵
Ross	Ay, on the front.
Siward	Why then. God's soldier be he!
	Had I as many sons as I have hairs,
	I would not wish them to a fairer death:
	And so, his knell is knoll'd. 50
Malcolm	He's worth more sorrow,
	And that I'll spend for him.
Siward	He's worth no more;
	They say, he parted well, and paid his score:¹⁶
	And so, God be with him! Here comes newer
	comfort.

¹³die

¹⁴in the spot from which he did not shrink

¹⁵in front

¹⁶did his duty

Re-enter Macduff, with Macbeth's head.

¹⁷surrounded
¹⁸best men

Macduff	Hail, King! for so thou art. Behold, where stands
	The usurper's cursed head. The time is free:
	I see thee compass'd¹⁷ with thy kingdom's pearl,¹⁸
	That speak my salutation in their minds;
	Whose voices I desire aloud with mine,
	Hail, King of Scotland!

All   Hail, King of Scotland!

Newly crowned king   [Flourish.

Malcolm   We shall not spend a large expense of time   60
                 Before we reckon with your several loves,[19]   [19] the loves of each of you

NB   And make us even with you. My Thanes and
                    kinsmen,
                 Henceforth be Earls, the first that ever
                    Scotland
                 In such an honour nam'd. What's more to do,
                 Which would be planted newly with the time,
                 As calling home our exil'd friends abroad — *Donalblain*
                 That fled the snares of watchful tyranny;
                 Producing forth the cruel ministers
        (L)   Of this dead butcher and his fiend-like queen,
                 Who, as 'tis thought, by self and violent hands   70
        suicide Took off her life; this, and what needful else
                 That calls upon us, by the grace of Grace,[20]   [20] grace of God
                 We will perform in measure,[21] time, and place: [21] appropriately
                 So, thanks to all at once and to each one,
                 Whom we invite to see us crown'd at Scone.

                                    [Flourish. Exeunt.

Scene Analysis

In the last scene Macbeth and Macduff finally confront each other face to face. Macbeth is reluctant to fight Macduff saying:

> "...my soul is too much charg'd
> With blood of thine already."

But Macduff is determined that they will fight. When Macduff reveals the manner of his birth, thus breaking Macbeth's final hope of being saved by the charm, Macbeth is shaken and refuses to fight. However he is roused again by Macduff's taunt of "*coward*" and the promise of future humiliation and he fights to the end.

Macduff appears before the victorious army with the head of Macbeth. Malcolm is proclaimed king of Scotland. Order and normality are restored and this is the theme of Malcolm's last speech. The nobles will be rewarded for their services and friends recalled from exile:

> "...this, and what needful else
> That calls upon us, by the grace of Grace,
> We will perform in measure, time and place:"

CHARACTERS
MACBETH

Macbeth does not intend to surrender or to give in by committing suicide even though capture seems imminent. It is in this mood of defiance that Macduff finds him:

> *"Why should I play the Roman fool, and die*
> *On mine own sword? Whiles I see lives, the gashes*
> *Do better upon them."*

Macbeth's reluctance to fight Macduff shows an unusual stab of conscience. He does not doubt that he will kill Macduff and he confidently fights asserting:

> *"As easy mayst thou the intrenchant air*
> *With thy keen sword impress as make me bleed."*

At Macduff's answer:

> *"Despair thy charm;*
> *And let the angel whom thou still hast serv'd*
> *Tell thee, Macduff was from his mother's womb*
> *Untimely ripp'd."*

Macbeth is truly shaken:

> *"Accursed be that tongue that tells me so,*
> *For it hath cow'd my better part of man;"*

At last he recognizes the evil power of the witches:

> *"And be these juggling fiends no more believ'd,*
> *That palter with us in a double sense;*
> *That keep the word of promise to our ear,*
> *And break it to our hope".*

With the shock of insight comes a refusal to fight. Nevertheless when Macduff accuses him of cowardice he refuses to yield:

> *"To kiss the ground before young Malcolm's feet,*
> *And to be baited with the rabble's curse."*

With courage and determination he faces Macduff:

> *"Though Birnam wood be come to Dunsinane,*
> *And thou oppos'd, being of no woman born,*
> *Yet I will try the last. Before my body*
> *I throw my war-like shield."*

Our last picture of Macbeth recalls the first description of him as *"Bellona's bridegroom"* – proud and fearless in battle.

*I bear a charmed life, which must not yield
To one of woman born.*

(Macbeth, Act 5, Scene VIII)

MACDUFF

Macduff confronts Macbeth, determined only to kill him:

> *"I have no words,*
> *My voice is in my sword..."*

When Macbeth refuses to fight, he offers him his life but it is a cruel alternative to death:

> *"We'll have thee, as our rarer monsters are,*
> *Painted upon a pole, and underwrit,*
> *'Here may you see the tyrant," '*

They fight to the bitter end and Macduff presents Macbeth's head to Malcolm. It is fitting that it is Macduff who proclaims Malcolm King of Scotland and triumphantly announces:

> *"...The time is free:"*

MALCOLM

Malcolm is concerned about those not accounted for – Macduff and the young Siward whose death Ross announces. He grieves for young Siward:

> *"He's worth more sorrow,*
> *And that I'll spend for him."*

Malcolm, *"compass'd with thy kingdom's pearl"*, makes it clear that he will repay the loyalty of the thanes:

> *"We shall not spend a large expense of time*
> *Before we reckon with your several loves,*
> *And make us even with you."*

Order will be established, exiled friends called back to be

> *"...planted newly with the time."*

He refers to Macbeth and Lady Macbeth harshly as:

> *"this dead butcher and his fiend-like queen."*

Macbeth and Lady Macbeth must be seen as the epitome of evil whereas Malcolm is the epitome of goodness:

> *"...by the grace of Grace"*

EXERCISES

1. Describe the encounter of Macbeth and Macduff. At what point does Macbeth lose confidence?
2. What is your opinion of Macbeth during the last phase of his life?

3. Would you agree with Malcolm's view of Macbeth as a "*butcher*" and Lady Macbeth as a "*fiend-like queen*"?
4. Do the audience and Malcolm share the same perspective?

REVISION

"...this even-handed justice
Commends th' ingredients of our poison'd chalice
To our own lips"   (Macbeth, Act 1, Scene VII)

Lady Macbeth, distraught with guilt and remorse, is watched by a doctor and gentlewoman who tells him that every night Lady Macbeth walks in her sleep. Macbeth, learning of the approach of the English army, prepares for battle. At Birnam Wood, Malcolm orders the army to camouflage its approach by bearing branches in front. Macbeth learns of Lady Macbeth's death and the approach to Birnam Wood but still trusts the witches' promise that he has a charmed life. Meeting Macduff in battle, he learns that Macduff was not "*born*" but "*untimely ripped*" from his mother's womb. With the last witches' prophesy fulfilled, Macduff kills Macbeth and presents his head to the victorious Malcolm, now acclaimed King of Scotland.

POINTS TO NOTE

1. In her sleep Lady Macbeth expresses her horror at the sight and smell of blood which she had to suppress on the night of the murder.
2. The glory of Macbeth's action in fixing the head of Macdonwald upon the battlements is completely reversed when his own head is displayed by Macduff.
3. *Scene II* ends with images of life, growth, cure and healing.
4. The kingship of Malcolm will restore order and harmony to Scotland.

REVISION ASSIGNMENT

In what different ways are Macbeth and Lady Macbeth punished for their crimes?

Part 3

Further Study

The Plot

In the Chronicle of Scottish History, Holinshed tells the story of the historical Macbeth. He was King of Northern Scotland, he killed Duncan who was King of all Scotland and for the next seventeen years ruled the whole of Scotland until he too was killed in battle fighting Duncan's son.

Holinshed tells the story of the three witches and of their prophecies regarding the future of Macbeth and Banquo. When acts of Duncan seem to make the fulfilment of the prophecy impossible, Macbeth, supported by Banquo, is provoked into rebellion and he kills the king in battle at Inverness.

Holinshed's chronicle also relates the story of King Duffe who lived before the time of Macbeth and was murdered by his castellan Donwald and his wife. While the king was on a visit to them, they made his guards drunk, sent henchmen to kill him and then Donwald murdered the guards.

Shakespeare took these separate stories as his plot for *Macbeth*. The real historical Macbeth was totally unlike the Macbeth of the play. He killed Duncan in open war, not by stealthily murdering the sleeping king. In Shakespeare's conception, Macbeth is a most sensitive and imaginative man, a man of reflection and imagination, a soldier and a poet.

Macbeth is the shortest of the tragedies. It is not much more than half as long as *Hamlet*. Structurally, the play divides into two parts – the rise and fall of Macbeth – but the initial simplicity of the plot of *Macbeth* is enriched by an intricate development of themes, the dramatic complexity of character and the vividness of the language and symbolism.

Structure

Structurally, *Macbeth* follows the pattern of most tragedies – exposition, conflict and catastrophe.

In *Act 1*, the situation is expounded out of which the conflict arises. The witches prophesy two honours for Macbeth, one of which is fulfiled immediately; the other Macbeth decides to fulfil himself by murder. In spite of much inward resistance in Macbeth's mind, the action moves swiftly through seven brief scenes in *Act I* to the moment of crisis in *Act 2, Scene I*, when Macbeth sees the visionary dagger and moves after it to murder Duncan.

Throughout the next three acts we see the development and consequences of Macbeth's inner conflict. The turning point of the play comes in *Act 3, Scene IV*. Fleance has escaped and Macbeth has lost control. Macbeth's action in the first part of the tragedy follows on the prediction of the witches who promise him the kingship. When the action moves forward again after the banquet scene, Macbeth seeks out the witches who make false promises which again drive him forward. The impression of rapidity of action is maintained as Macbeth hastens to his ruin. The catastrophe begins in *Act 5*. In *Scene I*, we see the consequences of the crime in the sleep-walking torment of Lady Macbeth. In *Scene V,* Birnam Wood does indeed move to Dunsinane and in *Scene VIII* Macbeth is slain by *"one not of woman born"*.

Themes

Good vs Evil

The play centres around the concepts of good and evil and there is a clear contrast between two opposed orders. Duncan and Malcolm represent order, loyalty and goodness; Macbeth and Lady Macbeth stand for disorder, treachery and evil.

Shakespeare ultimately believed in a harmonious universe, but he also believed in the power of evil which can destroy goodness. The witches are the embodiment of this evil and evil is presented as ugly and deformed.

Macbeth enters a world of evil when he consorts with the witches. Lady Macbeth identifies with this evil when she evokes the aid of evil spirits – *"murdering ministers"*, *"sightless substances"*, *"nature's mischief"*. Evil is represented by the deformed creatures which are thrown into the witches' cauldron in *Act 4, Scene I:*

> *"Fillet of a fenny snake,*
> *In the cauldron boil and bake;*
> *Eye of newt, and toe of frog,*
> *Wool of bat, and tongue of dog,*
> *Adder's fork, and blind worm's sting,*
> *Lizard's leg, and howlet's wing..."*

This supernatural evil is opposed by the supernatural grace represented by Duncan, Malcolm and the King of England. At the death of Duncan *"reknown and grace are dead"* and Malcolm describes England's holy king as having power over evil:

> *"...but, at his touch,*
> *Such sanctity hath heaven given his hand,*
> *They presently amend."*   (Act 4, Scene III)

Against such grace evil cannot triumph. Good rejects evil and fights evil with the virtues of courage and loyalty. The balance of good and evil is disrupted by the overwhelming evil of Macbeth's deed but the defeat of Macbeth and the coming of Malcolm to the throne restores the predominance of good, and the natural order functions properly again. At the end of the play Macbeth is denounced as a *"dead butcher"* which is a clear moral rejection of the force of evil.

Macbeth is not just about the external struggle of the forces of good and evil, but of the conflict of good and evil in the mind of the character Macbeth. Macbeth chooses evil when he allies himself with the witches, but his moral sense struggles with his ambition. The evil thought is so abhorrent to his essential goodness that the very suggestion unnerves him.

Macbeth suffers even before he commits the murder of Duncan, but as evil increasingly dominates his nature he suffers less. With each new murder Macbeth's moral sense becomes less sensitive and his conscience, his essential goodness, is smothered; but he suffers the torment of his own spiritual destruction. The defeat of his better nature leaves him utterly wretched and empty. He becomes a man who is *"weary of the sun"*, whose life has withered away. Macbeth's tragedy is that the evil he reluctantly embraces destroys him. In the inner conflict between good and evil, evil wins; but the defeat of Macbeth in fact marks the defeat of evil in the wider context of the play's theme.

Appearance vs Reality

A sense of mystery is in the play from the beginning. Banquo questions the reality of the witches:

> *"Were such things here as we do speak about?"*   *(Act I, Scene III)*

There is amazement at the murder of Duncan, and at the strange happenings on the night of the murder. Fear predominates and fear gives rise to an atmosphere of doubt and uncertainty which is reflected in the continual questions throughout *Macbeth*, tense and powerful:

> *"But wherefore could not I pronounce Amen'?"*

> *"Will all great Neptune's ocean wash this blood*
> *Clean from my hand?"*

> *"The Thane of Fife had a wife: where is she now?"*
> *"What's the newest grief ?"*

> *"Can such things be,*
> *And overcome us like a summer's cloud.*
> *Without our special wonder?"*

It is a world of rumours and fears, vague knowledge and uncertainties, riddles and half truths. The witches are *"imperfect speakers"* and equivocation and ambiguity runs right through the play. The porter admits an equivocator into hell and equivocation predominates in the play – the battle is *"lost and won"*, *"Fair is foul, and foul is fair"*. Appearance is deceptive:

> *"...look like the innocent flower,*
> *But be the serpent under't."*   *(Act 1, Scene V)*

Things are made to appear what they are not. Lady Macbeth decides:

> *"I'll gild the faces of the grooms withal;*
> *For it must seem their guilt."*   *(Act 2, Scene II)*

Malcolm seems to be an even greater tyrant than Macbeth by *"false speaking"*. Macbeth realizes:

> *"False face must hide what the false heart doth know."*   *(Act 1, Scene VII)*

Eventually appearance cannot be distinguished from reality. Macbeth follows an imaginary dagger to commit Duncan's murder asking:

> *"Is this a dagger which I see before me,*
> *The handle toward my hand?"*   *(Act 2, Scene I)*

He sees and talks to Banquo's ghost and wonders how the others:

> *"...can behold such sights,*
> *And keep the natural ruby of your cheeks."*   *(Act 3, Scene IV)*

Lady Macbeth sees an invisible spot on her hand – *"Out, damned spot!"*. It is hard to judge between appearance and reality in a world where *"nothing is but what is not."* The prophecies are ambiguous, true but misleading because of their hidden meanings:

> *"Macbeth shall never vanquish'd be until*
> *Great Birnam Wood to high Dunsinane hill*
> *Shall come against him."*   *(Act 4, Scene I)*

Macbeth is confident *"That will never be"*, but Birnam Wood does come against him – *"The wood began to move"*. The witches also promise that:

> *"...none of woman born*
> *Shall harm Macbeth."*

Macbeth therefore assumes that he can:

> *"...weapons laugh to scorn,*
> *Brandish'd by man that's of a woman born."*   *(Act 5, Scene VII)*

But this *"charm"* does not apply to Macduff who:

> *"...was from his mother's womb*
> *Untimely ripp'd."*   *(Act 4, Scene VII)*

Only at the very end of the play does Macbeth begin to doubt:

> *"...the equivocation of the fiend*
> *That lies like truth..."*   *(Act 4, Scene IV)*

He recognises that the witches are forces of evil:

> *"That palter with us in a double sense..."*   *(Act 5, Scene VII)*

In *Macbeth*, false appearances and equivocation are inseparable from evil.

Disorder

In Elizabethan times, the universe was considered to be divinely ordered into degrees linked in a great chain of being. The stability of the universe depended on the balance of opposites. Disturbances in the microcosm, i.e. man, affected the macrocosm and vice versa. Any unnatural action was believed to break the chain and disturb the divine order.

The murder of Duncan is explicitly presented as a violation of the natural order. Macbeth violates his ties of loyalty to Duncan as king, kinsman and guest. It is Macbeth himself who articulates the very sentiments of duty and loyalty by which his crime must be judged:

> *"Your highness' part*
> *Is to receive our duties; and our duties*
> *Are to your throne and state, children and servants;*
> *Which do but what they should, by doing everything*
> *Safe toward your love and honour."*   (Act 1, Scene IV)

The sanctity of Duncan, the natural fertility which he manifests, clearly represent the natural order. Duncan's wounds are *"a breach in nature"* and this is reflected in the upheaval in the elements and among the animals:

> *"The obscure bird*
> *Clamour'd the live long night: some say the earth*
> *Was feverous and did shake."*   (Act 2, Scene III)

The murder of Duncan is accompanied by extraordinary manifestations:

> *"Lamentings heard i'the air; strange screams of death..."*

The conversation between Ross and the old man in *Act 2, Scene IV,* depicts the disturbance in the universe which seems to parallel Duncan's death. We are clearly told in this short scene that these strange events reflect the essential unnaturalness of murder:

> *"'Tis unnatural,*
> *Even like the deed that's done."*

The enormity of Macbeth's evil is emphasised by the universal element. Acts of violence and murder result in disturbances in nature itself.

This outward manifestation of disorder effectively mirrors the inner conflict of the characters. When Lady Macbeth sleep-walks, it is *"A great perturbation in nature"*. Sleeplessness is another aspect of disorder. Sleep is natural and Macbeth is aware that he has interfered with the:

> *"Balm of hurt minds, great nature's second course."*   (Act 2, Scene II)

Macbeth has *"murder'd sleep"* and so soothing sleep is replaced by hideous dreams, *"the torture of the mind"*. Macbeth calls on night to break *"the bond of nature"* and in *Act 5,*

Scene V, he actually wishes:

> "...the estate o' the world were now undone".

In the banquet scene we see how disorder is permeating the very structure of society. Lady Macbeth explicitly states:

> "Stand not upon the order of your going".

and the banquet breaks up in disorder. Disorder disrupts family life. Lady Macduff looks at her little boy and thinks:

> "Father'd he is, and yet he's fatherless."   (Act 4, Scene II)

Her husband has behaved contrary to the natural order of things:

> "...for the poor wren,
> The most diminutive of birds, will fight –
> Her young ones in her nest – against the owl."   (Act 4, Scene II)

Macbeth has disrupted the great chain of being in the universe. By unbalancing the divine order – man, society, living creatures, the heavens – all are thrown into disharmony. The moral order in the universe can only be restored by the death of Macbeth and Lady Macbeth.

The Imperial Theme

Macbeth is not just the tragedy of one man but of a whole state. In the sixteenth century, kings were considered to be God's regents and to rebel against a king was to rebel against God. When Macbeth:

> "...broke ope
> The Lord's annointed temple, and stole thence
> The life o' the building."   (Act 2, Scene III)

he cut off *"The spring, the head,"* *"the very source"* of life not just from Duncan's sons but from the whole state. Macbeth says that Duncan's murder shakes his state of man. In fact it shakes the whole state. The murder of the king is *"the great doom's image!"* and the whole moral order is disrupted, *"reknown and grace is dead"* and *"nature seems dead"*.

Spiritual evil is put into a political context:

> "Alas! Poor country;
> Almost afraid to know itself. It cannot
> Be call'd our mother, but our grave:"   (Act 4, Scene III)

By murdering his rightful king, Macbeth lets loose in his own nature and hence into Scotland a disrupting evil force. The personal and national turmoil develop together and culminate in the murder of Macduff's family in *Act 4, Scene II*. This action marks the lowest depth in Macbeth's crimes against conscience and humanity and is the lowest point in Scotland's misery. The degree of evil is such that:

> *"Things at the worst will cease, or else climb upward*
> *To what they were before."*   *(Act 4, Scene II)*

Macbeth has been unable to:

> *"...buckle his distemper'd cause*
> *Within the belt of rule."*   *(Act 5, Scene II)*

But Malcolm will perform his actions *"in measure, time, and place"*. Macbeth's rule has been associated with witches and friends but the rightful ruler will rule by *"the grace of Grace"*. Duncan was the source of growth. Macbeth cut off the source and interfered with *"the imperial theme"*. Malcolm is the new source of growth and at the end his thoughts are of planting afresh:

> *"What's more to do,*
> *Which would be planted newly with the time,"*   *(Act 5, Scene VIII)*

Order and peace in Scotland will be restored by Duncan's rightful successor.

Language: Imagery and Symbolism

The imagery in *Macbeth* reinforces and highlights the themes in the play. Opposing images of good and evil suggest political and moral conflicts. The direct opposition of good and evil, appearance and reality, lawful and corrupt rule, order and disorder, are reflected in opposing images – light and darkness, grace and sin, fertility and disease. The association between evil and darkness is constantly stressed. Macbeth's crime is given a cosmic significance by images of the unnatural. The same kind of correlation between evil deeds and disorder within the individual is conveyed through images of disturbed sleep. The imagery of blood reinforces the nightmare quality of the play.

"The medicine of the sickly weal..."

Duncan is not really developed as a character, rather he has a symbolic value. He is the symbol of order, authority and goodness. The kingship of Duncan is lawful and beneficent and his vitality and goodness find expression in the imagery of fertility. He uses an image of harvest fullness when addressing Macbeth:

> *"I have begun to plant thee, and will labour*
> *For make thee full of growing."*   *(Act 1, Scene IV)*

The quality of his speech is life-giving, fertile:

> *"My plenteous joys*
> *Wanton in fullness, seek to hide themselves*
> *In drops of sorrow."*

This imagery of fertility is twisted by Lady Macbeth when she cries to the spirits:

> *"...unsex me here...make thick my blood,*
> *Stop up th' access and passage to remorse...*
> *Come to my woman's breasts*
> *And take my milk for gall."*   (Act 1, Scene V)

Contrasting with the images of bounty and fertility which surround Duncan is the disease imagery which suggests the tyranny of Macbeth. Images of sterility replace those of growth. Macbeth is referred to by Lennox in terms of a weed which has taken the place of *"the sovereign flower"* – Malcolm. During Macbeth's reign:

> *"...good men's lives*
> *Expire before the flowers in their caps,*
> *Dying or ere they sicken."*   (Act 4, Scene III)

Macbeth too speaks of the disease of Scotland:

> *"If thou couldst, doctor, cast*
> *The water of my land, find her disease,*
> *And purge it to a sound and pristine health..."*   (Act 5, Scene III)

But it is Macbeth's rule that is *"distempered"*. The disease of tyranny has spread throughout the whole country and so, like a disease, Scotland must be purged. Lennox and Caithness are prepared to help Malcolm:

> *"And with him pour we in our country's purge,*
> *Each drop of us..."*
>
> *"...Or so much as it needs,*
> *To dew the sovereign flower, and drown the weeds."*   (Act 5, Scene II)

Life itself is seen as one long illness by Macbeth who envies Duncan's escape from *"life's fitful fever"*. Macbeth tells the murderers that as long as Banquo lives he wears his *"health but sickly"*. In *Act 5, Scene III*, Macbeth asks the doctor:

> *"Canst thou not minister to a mind diseased,"*

The doctor can do nothing for *"infected minds"* which he thinks need divine help. But Scotland's disease can be cured by Malcolm *"the medicine of the sickly weal"*. Health and disease, fertility and sterility, are symbolically related to moral good and evil.

"The instruments of darkness..."

The Witches appear in the very first scene of the play and immediately we are in the realm of the supernatural. They prepare the way for the atmosphere of evil and disruption which is the spirit of the play. They are ambivalent creatures. Banquo questions them:

> *"Are ye fantastical, or that indeed*
> *which outwardly ye show?"*   *(Act I, Scene III)*

The Witches are intimations of a world beyond the real world, a manifestation of the evil in the universe, the agents of Fate.

But the Witches are more than a symbolic force in the play. The prophecy is the very pivot on which the play revolves. From the moment that Macbeth hears the prophecy of the Witches he is in their power:

> *"Stay, you imperfect speakers, tell me more"*   *(Act 1, Scene III)*

The first partial fulfilment of the prophecy makes him feel that Fate means him to be King:

> *"Two truths are told,*
> *As happy prorogues to the swelling act*
> *Of the imperial theme".*

Realising that *"The greatest is behind"*, he rushes to fulfil a destiny which he wants to believe and control. Besides the promise of the crown there is the revelation that Banquo will beget kings. Macbeth acts in order to fulfil the first part of the prophecy. He then acts to prevent the fulfilment of the second part. He believes in Fate on the one hand and yet, ironically, would try to change what, by definition, is pre-ordained.

In *Act 3, Scene V*, Hecate promises that Macbeth:

> *"...shall spurn fate, scorn death, and bear*
> *His hopes 'bove wisdom, grace and fear"*

This indeed he does when in *Act 5, Scene VIII*, he faces Macduff and says:

> *"Though Birnam Wood be come to Dunsinane,*
> *And thou oppos'd, being of no woman born,*
> *Yet I will try the last..."*

In *Act 1, Scene I*, Banquo surmises about the Witches' prophecies. He recognises the possibility of the oracle coming true for him too, but in his case he leaves it to chance. Lady Macbeth attributes what happens to *"fate and metaphysical aid"*, and sees Duncan's arrival at the castle as being part of the unfolding of that fate:

> *"I feel now*
> *The future in the instant."*   *(Act 1, Scene V)*

Greek tragedy was dominated by the idea of *Destiny* and man's struggle against an inexorable fate was shown to be useless, pitiful, tragic. The identification of the three Weird Sisters with the *Parcae* is unmistakable, but Shakespeare recognises and gives prominence to the concept of free will. If man's choices are determined, they can only be partially tragic. The Shakespearean hero is sublimely tragic because he is free, he is responsible for his own tragedy.

In spite of the prophecy of the Witches and the encouragement from Lady Macbeth, Macbeth is totally free. The supernatural solicitations of the witches could only bring temptation to an ambitious man who would willingly seize any opportunity for power. The witches simply announce events. When the proclamation of Duncan regarding Malcolm removes all apparent chance of succession, Macbeth's thoughts turn to treason and murder. That Macbeth should fulfil the prophecy by murdering the king is of his own free will. If Banquo is ambitious, there is no guilt in his ambition and he is not in the power of the witches:

> "He chid the sisters
> When first they put the name of king upon me,
> And have them speak to him..."   (Act 3, Scene I)

He silently submits to Macbeth's succession to the throne even though he suspects the truth, but though his honesty may be questioned he has no thought of acting to bring about the fulfilment of the prophecy.

The Witches give tangible form to Macbeth's subconscious thoughts. Macbeth echoes the very words of the witches when he says:

> "So foul and fair a day I have not seen"   (Act 1, Scene III)

He himself knows that he is entertaining a suggestion that cannot be right:

> "If good, why do I yield to that suggestion
> Whose horrid image doth unfix my hair..."

The vision which warns of Macduff, in *Act 4, Scene I*, is only confirming Macbeth's already acknowledged fear:

> "Thou hast harp'd my fear aright."

Macbeth says of the witches:

> "...they have more in them than mortal knowledge"   (Act 1, Scene V)

and Banquo asks them:

> "Live you? or are you aught that man may question?"   (Act 1, Scene III)

It is indeed Banquo himself who comes nearest to the truth when he says:

> "But 'tis strange:
> And oftentimes, to win us to our harm,
> The instruments of darkness tell us truths,
> Win us with honest trifles, to betray's
> In deepest consequence."   (Act 1, Scene III)

"The blanket of the dark..."

The opposition between good and evil in the play is highlighted by contrasts between day and night, light and darkness.

Night and darkness are associated with evil. The *"midnight hags"* are the *"instruments of darkness"*. The most significant scenes take place at night – the vision of the dagger, the murder of Duncan, the murder of Banquo, the sleep-walking of Lady Macbeth.

> Macbeth: *"Stars, hide your fires!*
> *Let not light see my black and deep desires"* (Act 1, Scene IV)
>
> Lady Macbeth: *"Come, thick night,*
> *And pall thee in the dunnest smoke of hell,*
> *That my keen knife see not the wound it makes,*
> *Nor heaven peep through the blanket of the dark..."* (Act I, Scene V)

invoke the blackness of night to conceal their crime. The night of Duncan's murder is a night of darkness *"The moon is down"* and there are no stars:

> *"There's husbandry in heaven,*
> *Their candles are all out."* (Act 2, Scene I)

Duncan's murder is followed by darkness at noon:

> *"...by the clock 'tis day,*
> *And yet dark night strangles the travelling lamp"* (Act 2, Scene IV)

As the play continues *"light thickens"*. The sun seems to shine only twice in the whole play – in *Act I, Scene VI* where Duncan and Banquo admire the pleasant surroundings of the castle at Inverness, and in the last act as the victory of the advancing army seems imminent.

The imagery of light does not so much relieve the darkness as heighten its effect. Lady Macbeth, who sought *"thick night"*, later is reported to have light by her continually. Fleance carries a torch which is dashed out at the moment of his father's murder.

Similarly, the moral darkness is contrasted with imagery of purity and virtue. The pastoral imagery of *Act 1, Scene IV,* is an ironic opposition to the imagery of blood and darkness that follows. Lady Macduff's gentle maternal love is set against Lady Macbeth's rejection of it. Just as Malcolm's father, Duncan, is the personification of goodness, his mother is the essence of virtue:

> *"Thy royal father*
> *Was a most sainted king, the queen that bore thee,*
> *Oft'ner upon her knees than on her feet,*
> *Died every day she lived."* (Act 4, Scene III)

Macduff's description of the tyrant Macbeth:

> *"Not in the legions*
> *Of horrid hell can come a devil more damn'd*
> *In evils to top Macbeth"*   *(Act 4, Scene III)*

is a striking contrast to Malcolm's description of England's holy king:

> *"And sundry blessings hang about his throne*
> *That speak him full of grace."*   *(Act 4, Scene III)*

At the close of the play the darkness seems to thin. As the army approaches, the imaginative darkness that has enveloped Scotland is dispelled.

"Blood will have blood..."

The world of *Macbeth* is a sinister world and the imagery of blood which permeates the play adds to the horror. In the second scene of the play, the savage imagery of war is given full rein in the description of battle given by the bloody sergeant. Macbeth's sword is *"smok'd with bloody execution"*. Macbeth and Banquo *"bathe in reeking wounds"*. The fainting sergeant says *"my gashes cry for help"*. This foreshadows the later image of a bleeding Scotland,

> *"...each new day a gash*
> *Is added to her wounds."*   *(Act 4, Scene III)*

The physical reality of the theme of murder is bloody and violent. Lady Macbeth says of Duncan:

> *"...who would have thought the old man to have had so much*
> *blood in him"*   *(Act 5, Scene I)*

There is blood on the murderer's face when he comes to report to Macbeth that Banquo's body is in a ditch *"With twenty trenched gashes on his head"*. Banquo's ghost shakes his *"gory locks"* at Macbeth. Macbeth's consciousness of the horror of murder is evident from his almost obsessive use of the image of blood in his language. The dagger of his vision has *"gouts of blood"*. Before Banquo's murder he thinks of the *"bloody and invisible hand"* of night. He realizes that *"blood will have blood"*. Macbeth is *"Stepped in so far"* in blood that even if he should *"wade no more, Returning were as tedious as go o'er"*. The imagery of blood is visual, sensory and tactile. Macbeth envisages his crime as an ocean of blood:

> *"...this my hand will rather he multitudinous seas incarnadine,*
> *Making the green one red."*   *(Act 2, Scene II)*

Lady Macbeth, in her nightmare of blood, tries to remove the imaginary *"damned spot"* from her hands and says:

> *"Here's the smell of the blood still: all the perfumes of Arabia will*
> *not sweeten this little hand."* *(Act 5, Scene I)*

The final image is the physical bloody illustration of evil uprooted, as Macbeth's severed head is displayed on a pole.

"The affliction of these terrible dreams..."

The atmosphere of darkness, pervaded by continual references to blood and creatures of ill omen, gives the play a nightmare quality. A nightmare signifies the abnormal disturbance of sleep and there are constant allusions to sleep, sleeplessness and the terrible dreams of remorse. In *Act I, Scene III,* the first Witch, as a punishment for the sailor's wife, threatens:

> *"Sleep shall neither night nor day*
> *Hang upon his pent-house lid,*
> *He shall live a man forbid*
> *Weary se'n nights nine times nine*
> *Shall he dwindle, peak and pine:"*

A terrible element in the punishment of Macbeth and Lady Macbeth is a loss of sleep. Macbeth murders a sleeping man and it is as if he has murdered sleep itself. After Duncan's murder he tells Lady Macbeth:

> *"Me thought I heard a voice cry 'sleep no more!'"* *(Act 2, Scene II)*

Indeed after this they:

> *"...sleep*
> *In the affliction of these terrible dreams"* *(Act 3, Scene II)*

Lady Macbeth tells her husband:

> *"You lack the season of all natures, sleep."* *(Act 3, Scene IV)*

By violating the *"innocent sleep,"* which is nature's repose, Macbeth deprives himself of that balm, *"chief nourisher in life's feast"*. The extreme agony of sleep that is not the *"Balm of hurt minds"* is depicted in the sleep-walking of Lady Macbeth.

The illusion of the dagger in the air suddenly splashed with blood, the sound of a voice from nowhere crying *"Sleep no more"*, the ghost of Banquo – all are part of this nightmare world.

"The sweet milk of concord..."

The imagery of sleep suggests the innocence and peace destroyed by the crime of Macbeth and Lady Macbeth. Other images point to the qualities of tenderness and pity which have no place in a world where *"reknown and grace is dead"*.

The imagery of the baby and milk are suggestive of natural human and tender feelings. Lady Macbeth denies her very nature when she prays:

> *"...unsex me here"*

and rejects her natural instincts as she adds:

> *"Come to my woman's breasts,*
> *And take my milk for gall,"*   *(Act 1, Scene V)*

When prompting Macbeth to the murder of Duncan she says:

> *"I have given suck, and know*
> *How tender 'tis to love the babe that milks me:*
> *I would, while it was smiling in my face,*
> *Have pluck'd my nipple from his boneless gums,*
> *And dash'd the brains out.."*   *(Act 1, Scene VII)*

The most tender human feeling of all, that of the mother for her child, is scorned here. Lady Macbeth uses the same image to describe her husband's nature:

> *"It is too full o' the milk of human kindness"*   *(Act 1, Scene V)*

Macbeth too evokes the image of the baby when he compares pity to a:

> *"...naked new-born babe"*   *(Act 1, Scene VII)*

Just as Lady Macbeth can only steel herself to murder by not succumbing to natural feelings of tenderness and sympathy, so too Macbeth must ignore his feelings of human kindness and pity. By denying their natural feelings, Macbeth and Lady Macbeth transgress not only nature but their very humanity.

"Nothing is but what is not..."

In *Macbeth* reality is not what it seems to be and various images point to the deception, lies and hypocrisy. Duncan, having discovered Cawdor's treachery says:

> *"There's no art*
> *To find the mind's construction in the face:"*   *(Act 1, Scene IV)*

This is the first of several images which highlight the idea of the face as a mask. At first Macbeth is not good at concealing his feelings. Banquo notices his reaction to the witches and to the news of his new title:

> *"Look, how our partner's rapt."*   *(Act 1, Scene III)*

Lady Macbeth tells him:

> *"Your face, my thane, is as a book where men*
> *May read strange matters."*   *(Act 1, Scene V)*

She advises him in the art of deception:

> "...look like the innocent flower,
> But be the serpent under't..."   (Act 1, Scene V)

As he progresses in crime, Macbeth becomes aware of the need to maintain a false appearance:

> "False face must hide what the false heart doth know."   (Act 1, Scene VII)

He repeats that image in *Scene II* of *Act 3*:

> "...And make our faces vizards to our hearts,
> Disguising what they are."

References to Macbeth's clothes draw attention to the fact that he is not what he seems. The images of borrowed clothes point to the fact that Macbeth has taken what does not rightfully belong to him. He himself uses the image of borrowed clothes to express his disbelief when Ross informs him that he is Thane of Cawdor:

> "The Thane of Cawdor lives: why do you dress me
> In borrow'd robes?"   (Act 1, Scene III)

Banquo uses the image of new clothes in which one is ill at ease to describe the effect of Macbeth's new titles on him:

> "New honours come upon him,
> Like our strange garments, cleave not to their mould
> But with the aid of use."   (Act 1, Scene III)

Macbeth tries to persuade Lady Macbeth that he should not murder Duncan just when his victory has won him the highest respect:

> "...and I have bought
> Golden opinions from all sorts of people,
> Which would be worn now in their newest gloss,
> Not cast aside so soon."   (Act 1, Scene VII)

The most striking clothes image is used by Angus in *Scene II* of the last act when he speaks of Macbeth's ill fitting garments:

> "...now does he feel his title
> Hang loose about him, like a giant's robe
> Upon a dwarfish thief."

Macbeth stole the title so the clothes do not belong to him. He is a petty tyrant with none of Duncan's regal grandeur. The badly fitting robe is the visual symbol that Macbeth is not the true king.

Macbeth commits himself to hypocrisy from the moment he murders Duncan. An example of the doubleness of words occurs in *Act 2, Scene III* when Macbeth utters his sentiments about Duncan's murder to convince the others of his innocence:

> *"Had I but died an hour before this chance*
> *I had liv'd a blessed time; for, from this instant,*
> *There's nothing serious in mortality,*
> *All is but toys; reknown and grace is dead..."*

The words are meant to deceive, but there is an underlying sense of truth in what he says. Malcolm realizes how easy it is to appear to feel what you do not feel.

It is a measure of the change in Macbeth that with each murder he finds it easier to lie and deceive. He beguiles Banquo with a flattering invitation to a banquet which is to take place after Banquo has been murdered. But the turning point is reached after Banquo's murder. When Macbeth makes no further attempts to hide his crimes there is no longer the same need for concealment and so there are fewer images of deception.

"A breach in nature..."

Macbeth's revolt against lawful authority releases forces of universal disorder. One of the key words in *Macbeth* is *"unnatural"*. In Ross's words, the whole crime is *"Gainst nature still"*. The moral upheaval is symbolized by the disharmony in nature. Weird phenomena in the animal and stellar worlds strike fear and awe. On the night of Duncan's murder there is a violent tempest:

> *"Lamentings heard i' th' air; strange screams of death..."*   (Act 2, Scene III)

When Macbeth revisits the Witches in *Act 4, Scene I*, he tells them that he must have satisfaction, no matter what disorder or confusion may follow:

> *"Though you untie the winds, and let them fight*
> *Against the churches...*
> *Though palaces and pyramids do slope*
> *Their heads to their foundations..."*

The comparison of these outward manifestations in the natural world to the central act of disorder is clearly pointed:

> *"Unnatural deeds*
> *Do breed unnatural troubles"*   (Act 5, Scene I)

Vivid animal disorder symbolism is recurrent in the play. A falcon is killed by an owl. Duncan's horses eat each other, *"unnatural,/Even like the deed that's done"*.

The sense of mystery and evil associated with the Weird Sisters is heightened by their reference to animals of unnatural form or unpleasant association. In the cauldron scene, *Act 4, Scene I*, the list of creatures is gruesome – toad, snake, newt, bat, blind-worm, lizard.

Throughout the play, the animals mentioned are for the most part fierce, ugly or of ill-omened significance. We hear of the *"hycran tiger"*, the *"arm'd rhinocerous"* and the *"rugged russian bear"*. There are *"maggot-pies"* and *"choughs"* and *"rooks"* and *"bats"*. The raven ominously croaks the entrance of Duncan, and the owl is *"the fatal bellman, Which gives the stern'st goodnight"*. Macbeth says *"night's black agents to their preys do rouse"*, thus linking the animal imagery to the powers of darkness – the Witches.

Language: Dramatic Expression

The language of *Macbeth* is illustrative of the themes of the play and the qualities of the characters.

The themes – good v evil, appearance v reality, equivocation and disorder – are reflected in the equivocation, enigmas and ambiguities of the play's language. Throughout the play, there is the juxtaposition of opposites, inversion of meaning, paradox and antithesis. Shakespeare's use of language intensifies the total impression of the reversal of values in the play.

There is a very clear juxtaposition of opposing and contrasting sets of symbols – grace/evil, fertility/disease, light/darkness, sleep/nightmare. This juxtaposition of various concepts gives rise to an intricate web of imagery which enriches the themes of the play. This is reinforced by the use of inversion, antithesis and paradox, the contradictory phrases pointing clearly to the reversal of values in the world of *Macbeth*. In the very first scene there is a striking example of inversion. We are introduced to a world where *"Fair is foul, and foul is fair."* It is a paradoxical world where *"...nothing is/But what is not"*, *"...the battle's lost and won"*, the future replaces the present, where:

> *"...by the clock 'tis day,*
> *And yet dark night strangles the travelling lamp."*   (Act 2, Scene IV)

The confusion is emphasised by the predominance of antithesis in the play. Macbeth puzzles over his temptation:

> *"This supernatural soliciting*
> *Cannot be ill, cannot he good:"*   (Act 1, Scene III)

The theme of equivocation in the porter's scene is expressed by his use of antithesis:

> *"Lechery, sir, it provokes, and unprovokes; it provokes the*
> *desire, but it takes away the performance. Therefore much*
> *drink may be said to be an equivocator with lechery; it makes him,*
> *and it mars him; it sets him on, and it takes him off; it*
> *persuades him, and disheartens him; makes him*
> *stand to, and not stand to; in conclusion, equivocates him in a sleep, and,*
> *giving him the lie, leaves him."*   (Act 2, Scene III)

The porter defines an equivocator as one:

> *"...that could swear in both the scales against either scale"*

After the murder of Duncan, Macbeth becomes an equivocator:

> *"Had I but died an hour before this chance*
> *I had liv'd a blessed time; for, from this instant,*
> *There's nothing serious in mortality..."*   (Act 2, Scene III)

The ostensible truth reflects a deeper truth. Macbeth realizes too late that equivocation *"lies like truth"*. The enigmatic riddles of the witches are full of ambiguities. Banquo is:

> *"Lesser than Macbeth, and greater."*
> *"Not so happy, yet much happier."*   (Act 1, Scene III)

"None of woman born" can harm Macbeth. Banquo refers to the witches as *"imperfect speakers"*, just as Macduff accuses Ross of being *"niggard"* in his speech. Indeed Ross quibbles with words, answering Macduff's query about his murdered wife with the words:

> *"Why, well."*

Words have no true meaning in a world where the face is a vizard to the heart, the innocent flower disguises the serpent and the tongue equivocates. The confusion and mistrust which is engendered by the murder of Duncan is caught up and expressed through the language of the play.

Language is illustrative not only of the mood and themes of the play but of the characters. The rich ordered poetry of Duncan is very different from the abrupt and disjointed language of Macbeth, whose speeches reflect the nervous tension of his mind. The quality of Duncan's speech and indeed that of his son, Malcolm, is that of order and strength of purpose:

> *"Sons, kinsmen, thanes,*
> *And you whose places are the nearest, know*
> *We will establish our estate upon*
> *Our eldest, Malcolm, whom we name hereafter*
> *The Prince of Cumberland; which honour must*
> *Not unaccompanied invest him only,*
> *But signs of nobleness, like stars, shall shine*
> *On all deservers."*   (Act 1, Scene IV)

The quality of Macbeth's speech is that of anarchy and disturbance. He struggles to get his own motives clear in the soliloquy in *Act I, Scene VII*:

> *"If it were done when 'tis done; then 'twere well*
> *It were done quickly;"*   (Act 1, Scene III)

and the speech is rhythmically uneven and jerky. This disjointed intensity of Macbeth's speeches reflects the tangled chaos of ideas in his mind. In the soliloquy in which he confronts his temptation:

> *"This supernatural soliciting*
> *Cannot be ill, cannot be good, if ill,*
> *Why hath it given me earnest of success,*
> *Commencing in a truth?"*   (Act 1, Scene III)

Macbeth's nervous disturbance at the very idea of such an act is reflected in the disjointed phrases, the questions, the juxtaposition of thoughts. A terrifying apprehension of evil is ex-pressed in the soliloquy where he sees the vision of the dagger. The sentences are short and abrupt to begin with as he tries to come to terms with the meaning of the vision:

> *"Is this a dagger which I see before me,*
> *The handle toward my hand? Come, let me clutch thee:*
> *I have thee not, and yet I see thee still...*
> *And on thy blade and dudgeon gouts of blood,*
> *Which was not so before. There's no such thing:*
> *It is the bloody business which informs*
> *Thus to mine eyes now o'er the one half world*
> *Nature seems dead.....*
> *Thou sure and firm-set earth.*
> *Hear not my steps..."*   (Act 2, Scene I)

Macbeth's sensibility is jolted by the confrontation with evil and the soliloquies reflect unrest, indecision, and fear in a style of broken, meditative flashes of thought. Macbeth's poetry is an expression of his spiritual conflict. The magnificence of his poetry is a measure of his sensitive soul. His emotional states are reflected in the rhythms of his speech. As Macbeth feels the moment of crime draw near, the language rises and the imagery begins to flow:

> *"...and wither'd murder,*
> *Alarum'd by his sentinel, the wolf,*
> *Whose howl's his watch, thus with his stealthy pace,*
> *With Tarquin's ravishing strides, toward his design*
> *Moves like a ghost."*   (Act 2, Scene I)

The same meditative eloquence can be seen just before Banquo's murder:

> *"Light thickens, and the crow*
> *Makes wing to th' rooky wood;*
> *Good things of day begin to droop and drowse;*
> *Whiles night's black agents to their preys do rouse."*   (Act 3, Scene II)

Macbeth's language always shows a strain of hyperbole when he is under pressure. After Duncan's murder he launches into a poetic description of sleep:

> *"... the innocent sleep,*
> *Sleep that knits up the ravell'd sleave of care...*
> *The death of each day's life, sore labour's bath,*
> *Balm of hurt minds, great nature's second course,*
> *Chief nourisher in life's feast, –"*   (Act 2, Scene II)

When forced to explain why he murdered the two grooms he comes out with a highly descriptive picture of Duncan's dead body:

> *"Here lay Duncan,*
> *His silver skin lac'd with his golden blood;*
> *And his gash'd stabs look'd like a breach in nature*
> *For ruin's wasteful entrance:"*   (Act 2, Scene III)

Macbeth's torture of mind gives rise to a profusion of images. But as his imagination is replaced by a mere weary lack of feeling, the rhythm of his speech becomes monotonous. There is a slow hopeless beat in:

> *"To-morrow, and to-morrow, and to-morrow,*
> *Creeps in this petty pace from day to day,"*   (Act 5, Scene V)

Nevertheless Macbeth is still a poet:

> *"Out, out, brief candle!*
> *Life's but a walking shadow; a poor player*
> *That struts and frets his hour upon the stage,*
> *And then is heard no more;"*   (Act 5, Scene V)

and there is a dignity in his calm acceptance of the dreadful finality of nothingness.

Lady Macbeth's language is in stark contrast to that of Macbeth. Whereas Macbeth utters the most profound responses of the play, Lady Macbeth's language contains a literalness which is indicative of her character. Lady Macbeth sees nothing but the promise of the crown. She has no imaginative flights of fancy, experiences no torture of the mind. She is a forthright person and for the most part utters simple forthright statements. Her images are simple, almost commonplace:

> *"Your face, my thane, is as a book where men*
> *May read strange matters."*   (Act 1, Scene V)

Her speech is sarcastic, argumentative and to the point:

> *"O proper stuff!*
> *This is the very painting of your fear;*
> *This is the air-drawn dagger which, you said,*
> *Led you to Duncan. O! these flaws and starts –*
> *Imposters to true fear – would well become*
> *A woman's story at a winter's fire,*
> *Authoriz'd by her grandam. Shame itself!*
> *Why do you make such faces? when all's done*
> *You look but on a stool."*   (Act 3, Scene IV)

Her speech is dramatic, taut and tense but it is not poetic. Her language is an indication of her limitations – her inability to feel beyond the immediate, to imagine the consequences, to appreciate her husband's agony of mind. Her inability to really communicate with Macbeth is her tragedy. Her total lack of comprehension is a barrier between them. Her literal interpretation of the world cannot come to terms with Macbeth's consciousness:

> "Me thought I heard a voice cry 'Sleep no more!
> Macbeth does murder sleep,' the innocent sleep,
> Sleep that knits up the ravell'd sleave of care,
> The death of each day's life..."
>
> "What do you mean?"
>
> "Still it cried, 'Sleep no more!' to all the house..."
>
> "Glamis hath murder'd sleep..."
>
> "Who was it that thus cried?"   (Act 2, Scene II)

In the sleep-walking scene Lady Macbeth speaks in prose. This is an indication of the disordered mentality of her mind as verse is the medium of the play.

Characterization

Macbeth

Macbeth is described as a tyrant, a madman, a dwarfish thief, a hell-hound and a dead butcher by various characters. He is a murderer and usurper. But Macbeth is the dominant consciousness of the play; the audience identifies with the consciousness of Macbeth and it is not the consciousness of a monster. Up until the banquet scene, we view events through the consciousness of Macbeth, but after the scene with the witches in *Act 4, Scene I*, there is a shift of perspective. Knowing that his spiritual destruction is complete, we see Macbeth through the eyes of his enemies, as the representative of evil which must be overcome.

Ambition vs "...the milk of human kindness..."

It is Lady Macbeth who gives us the greatest insight into Macbeth's character:

> "Glamis thou art, and Cawdor; and shalt be
> What thou art promis'd. Yet do I fear thy nature;
> It is too full o' the milk of human kindness
> To catch the nearest way; thou wouldst be great,
> Art not without ambition, but without
> The illness should attend it; what thou wouldst highly
> That thou wouldst holily; wouldst not play false,
> And yet wouldst wrongly win; thou'dst have, great Glamis,
> That which cries, 'Thus thou must do, if thou have it';

> *And that which rather thou dost fear to do*
> *Than wishest should be undone."*   *(Act 1, Scene V)*

Lady Macbeth never doubts for one moment that Macbeth will be king. She does not fear Macbeth's lack of ambition – it is his nature that she fears. She sees clearly that Macbeth's feelings stand in the way of expediency, that he is ambitious without being ruthless, that he craves greatness without wishing to lose his integrity, seeks power without wishing to pay the price. She pinpoints exactly Macbeth's predicament, his conflicting passions, his complex motives. She seems to think that Macbeth's kindlier qualities would outweigh his ambition.

The effect of the Witches' prophecy on him causes Banquo to ask:

> *"Good sir, why do you start, and seem to fear*
> *Things that do sound so fair?"*   *(Act 1, Scene III)*

That Macbeth should be startled is feasible, yet Banquo remains quite unmoved throughout the scene, even though the prophecy also concerns him. Banquo is not without ambition (we see later in the play that he too is giving careful consideration to the prophecy of the weird sisters – *Act 3, Scene I)* but he is perfectly honest and can address the witches with composure. There is no reason why Macbeth should fear the prophesy of the witches unless he instantaneously conceives of the idea of foul play. When it is announced that he is now *"Thane of Cawdor"*, he is beset by an immediate feeling of guilt. Already Macbeth's thoughts are subconsciously treacherous and are disturbing him. Already he is wondering if chance will crown him *"without my stir."* When the chance is diminished by the announcement that Malcolm is to be *"Prince of Cumberland"* he immediately realizes:

> *"....that is a step*
> *On which I must fall down, or else o'erleap,*
> *For in my way it lies."*   *(Act 1, Scene IV)*

He confirms Lady Macbeth's opinion of him when he says:

> *"The eye wink at the hand; yet let that be*
> *Which the eye fears, when it is done, to see."*   *(ibid)*

The sensitive Macbeth longs for a worthy motive but is forced to admit that it is the despicable motive of mere *"vaulting ambition"* that is impelling him to such an act. The course of action suggested by his ambition is abhorrent to his better feelings. It is the conflict between his *"black and deep desires"* and *"the milk of human kindness"* that gives Macbeth his tragic grandeur. Even after Duncan's murder, he is aware of a bond of sympathy with mankind and he asks that the hand of night would *"cancel and tear to pieces that great bond /Which keeps me pale"* – the bond of human fellowship and love, the bond which Lady Macbeth recognises as *"the milk of human kindness"*. Macbeth is no longer in conflict with himself when he becomes a total tyrant. He confronts his evilness head-on and achieves tragic recognition when he says:

> *"I have liv'd long enough".*   (Act 5, Scene III)

The murder of Duncan is motivated by ambition. The other murders are born out of fear.

Courage vs Cowardice

In the first act of the play, Macbeth is presented to us as a man of courage. The many epithets all testify to his fearlessness:— *"brave Macbeth – well he deserves that name"; "valour's minion"; "valiant cousin"*. He excels himself in the battle against *"The merciless Macdonwald"* and:

> *"Disdaining fortune, with his brandish'd steel,*
> *Which smok'd with bloody execution,*
> *Like valour's minion; carv'd out his passage*
> *Till he faced the slave"*   (Act 1, Scene II)

He is undismayed on hearing of a fresh assault by the Norweyan lord but *"doubly redoubled strokes upon the foe"*. Yet the man who, savagely fighting Macdonwald *"unseamed him from the nave to the chaps"*, is appalled as the terrible image of Duncan's murder confronts him, so much so that his hair stands on end and his heart hammers against his ribs. He can contend with palpable dangers and, even at the end when all seems lost, he fights bravely. His physical courage contrasts with his moral irresolution.

Macbeth is no coward, yet Lady Macbeth's main argument in winning over Macbeth is that only cowardice could prevent him from acting. There is some truth in Lady Macbeth's taunt:

> *"Art thou afeard*
> *To be the same in thine own act and valour*
> *As thou art in desire?"*   (Act 1, Scene VII)

But Lady Macbeth's notion of manliness is not the same as Macbeth's – *"Who dares do more is none"* – but a blind courage that demands insensibility and must exclude conscience. She says:

> *"...to be more than what you were, you would*
> *Be so much more the man."*

but it is because Macbeth denies the very feelings which make him a man and not a tyrant or a beast that he becomes very much less a man. That is his tragedy. He dies like a hunted beast, not like *"Bellona's bridegroom"*. His courage becomes desperation. His bravery turns to cruelty. In the last act his conscience is quite deadened and he can say:

> *"Direness, familiar to my slaughterous thoughts,*

Cannot once start me".   *(Act 4, Scene V)*

The man who starts and seems to fear the prophecy of the Witches, who is terrified by the temptation of murder, who is tortured by the agony of guilt, was a man. His very fears were the reflection of his conscience. Afraid of being thought afraid, he acts; he adds crime to crime until he can say:

"I have almost forgot the taste of fears".

He loses the timidity his wife complained of and becomes hard and ruthless. What appears to be cowardice is conscience, what appears to be fearlessness is heartlessness.

Conscience and Imagination

Lady Macbeth confuses Macbeth's imagination with nervous fear. The terrifying images which deter him from murder and follow it are really the protest of his deepest self, his conscience. In *Act I, Scene VII,* Macbeth struggles with his conscience. At first he considers all the obvious prudential reasons for not killing Duncan and it would seem as if he only fears immediate and personal punishment. But Macbeth is not a coward: neither is he calculating, cold-blooded or pitiless. His conscience revolts against the crime and in the second half of the soliloquy he speaks with passionate sincerity of Duncan's virtues, seeing them as angels pleading against the crime. His conscious mind considers the crime in terms of success or failure, but he reveals by the imagery he employs that his unconscious mind is horrified at the thought of murder. Convulsed by conscience, Macbeth's better nature comes to the surface in images which alarm and terrify. It is through his imagination that his conscience suggests what is noble and honourable in his character. His imagination is his link with goodness. It is a form of embodying the truth, but Macbeth ignores the principles of truth which take shape in his imagination. The pressure of imagination heightens into illusion. The vision of the dagger enacts Macbeth's fear in an intense form. The deed is done in horror and all nature seems to reflect it for him:

"Now o'er the one half-world
Nature seems dead."   *(Act 2, Scene I)*

Macbeth breaks down under the strain of the struggle with his conscience. He is tormented at the idea of not being able to say *"Amen"*. He forgets the plan of action and takes away the daggers instead of leaving them with the grooms. He is afraid to return to complete what he should have done. In the scene of discovery, the crisis proves too much for him and he kills the grooms. His guilt-ridden conscience could not endure their protests of innocence. Whenever his imagination stirs, he acts badly.

Macbeth tries to escape his conscience. He thinks that if he does not murder Banquo himself, then the murder will not trouble him. But his conscience awakens and his deed confronts him in the form of Banquo's ghost. Again it is left to Lady Macbeth to rise to the occasion and show the presence of mind that is required. Macbeth rejects the truth of his conscience. He tells himself that his:

> *"...strange and self-abuse*
> *Is the initiate fear that wants hard use:"*   *(Act 3, Scene IV)*

By ignoring the moral truths of his imagination, by denying his conscience, Macbeth discards his better self. With each murder, Macbeth's chaotic imaginings, his hallucinations and revulsion give way to insensitivity. He does not baulk at killing Macduff. Learning of Macduff's flight he says:

> *"..from this moment*
> *The very firstlings of my heart shall be*
> *The firstlings of my hand."*   *(Act 4, Scene I)*

Neither before nor after the murder of Lady Macduff and her children does he imagine the event.

When Macbeth's imagination ceases to stir his conscience, he is spiritually dead:

> *"...a poor player*
> *That struts and frets his hour upon the stage,*
> *And then is heard no more;"*   *(Act 5, Scene V)*

Lady Macbeth

"...undaunted mettle..."

Macbeth's admiration for his wife is prompted by her confidence, her decisiveness and the sheer force of her argumentative powers. From the moment she receives Macbeth's letter, Lady Macbeth knows what she must do. Her decision is instant, unlike that of Macbeth who wonders if *"chance"* will crown him. She knows her husband's "weakness" so she resolves to imbue him with her strength of purpose:

> *"Hie thee hither,*
> *That I may pour my spirits in thine ear,*
> *And chastise with the valour of my tongue*
> *All that impedes thee from the golden round,"*   *(Act 2, Scene I)*

She is quite undaunted at the prospect of the murder of Duncan. Unlike Macbeth, she does not examine the deterrents to the murder. When Macbeth appears to have changed his mind, she attacks his manhood, seeing his reluctance as fear. Lady Macbeth's strongest argument is that of cowardice. Macbeth is a general and would not want to *"live a coward"* in his *"own esteem"*. Nor would he want to live as a coward in the esteem of his wife. She measures her intrepidity against his. Having challenged his manhood she shows how she is prepared to sacrifice her womanhood:

> *"I have given suck, and know*
> *How tender 'tis to love the babe that milks me:*
> *I would, while it was smiling in my face,*
> *Have pluck'd my nipple from his boneless gums,*
> *And dash'd the brains out, had I so sworn as you*
> *Have done to this."*   (Act 1, Scene VII)

Macbeth offers no more arguments about honour or *"Golden opinions"*. Her merciless attack on his pride does not allow for such considerations. When he asks:

> *"If we should fail,"*

she has already won her case. She dismisses the idea of failure, having shown a coolness and a confidence that Macbeth never possesses. She associates failure with cowardice; success is a simple matter of courage.

> *"But screw your courage to the sticking-place,*
> *And we'll not fail."*   (Act 1, Scene VII)

Murder is straightforward:

> *"When Duncan is asleep,*
> *Whereto the rather shall his day's hard journey*
> *Soundly invite him, his two chamberlains*
> *Will I with wine and wassail so convince*
> *That memory, the warder of the brain,*
> *Shall be a fume, and the receipt of reason*
> *A limbeck only; when in swinish sleep*
> *Their drenched natures lie, as in a death,*
> *What cannot you and I perform upon*
> *The unguarded Duncan?"*   (ibid)

Macbeth's vacillating nature is vulnerable to such relentless will power and he declares himself *"settled"*.

Having won Macbeth over, Lady Macbeth plans and supervises the murder of Duncan without a qualm, while her husband is in the grip of doubts, guilt and uncertainty. Although ultimately she could not bring herself to commit the murder because of Duncan's resemblance to her father, we see that she was initially prepared to commit the murder herself with remarkable ease. After the murder of Duncan she exerts all her powers to give Macbeth courage. However when she cannot infuse her strength of will into her husband she again displays her *"undaunted mettle"* by returning to the room, despite her personal dread of the memory of her father. Unlike Macbeth, who acts badly under pressure, she never loses her common sense:

> "Get on your night-gown, lest occasion call us,
> And show us to be watchers." (Act 2, Scene II)

As queen she is dignified and composed, flattering Banquo and extending the utmost courtesy to the lords of the land. She realizes in *Act 3, Scene II*, that their *"desire is got without content"*, but again she takes the practical approach:

> "Things without all remedy
> Should be without regard: what's done is done." (Act 3, Scene II)

She strives to comfort Macbeth and again points out an obvious and apparently easy solution to the problem of Banquo and Fleance:

> "...in them nature's copy's not eterne."

This time she cannot advise her husband as he does not confide in her. During the banquet scene she makes a tremendous effort to calm Macbeth. With remarkable composure she expertly reassures the company and exhorts Macbeth aside, *"Are you a man?"*. However this time her accusations of cowardice have no effect and with a perfect sense of timing she dismisses the lords before Macbeth says what he should not. Her *"undaunted mettle"* rises to the occasion but she can do no more to help Macbeth who is now:

> "...bent to know,
> By the worst means, the worst." (Act 3, Scene IV)

From now on it is the prophecies of the witches which imbue Macbeth with a false sense of courage. For Lady Macbeth, *"the compunctious visitings of nature"*, which she had so dreaded, begin to undermine her *"undaunted mettle"* until she is driven to take her own life.

The "...fiend-like..." Queen

G. Wilson Knight refers to Lady Macbeth as *"a woman possessed of evil passion... the embodiment of evil, absolute and extreme"*. Many critics adopt this view of Lady Macbeth as being inhuman and even fiendish in her wickedness. What shocks most is her invocation to the evil spirits to possess her, but what appears as strength is in fact indicative of her weakness:

> "And fill me, from the crown to the toe, top full
> Of direst cruelty; make thick my blood,
> Stop up the access and passage to remorse,
> That no compunctious visitings of nature
> Shake my fell purpose..." (Act 1, Scene V)

If she pleads to be filled with cruelty it is because she is not cruel by nature. She says she knows *"How tender 'tis to love the babe that milks"* her. She wishes that her blood might be thickened in order not to feel the remorse that would be natural to her. She invokes the darkness so that *"my keen knife see not the wound it makes"*. She could not bring herself to murder Duncan because she was struck by a ressemblance to her father. In order to steel herself to do her part in the deed she has to resort to fortification:

> *"That which hath made them drunk hath made me bold"*   *(Act 2, Scene II)*

Lady Macbeth dominates her feelings before the arrival of Macbeth in order to give him the strength of purpose which he lacks. She is extreme in her persistence, scathing in rebuking him, but she is simply endorsing an already deep-rooted guilty ambition. It is an over simplification to see her in terms of the evil temptress who pushes him against his will to satisfy her own passionate ambition. She outlines the plan of murder, but he agrees when he is reassured that they will not fail. Lady Macbeth is enduring no conflict or chaos of soul and so appears to be coldly realistic at the time of the murder. She is fully in command. She carefully prepares the way for Macbeth. A moment of great dramatic tension in the play is when the two confront each other after the murder. Lady Macbeth knows instinctively that she must not allow Macbeth to give way to his sensibility:

> *"Consider it not so deeply."*   *(Act 2, Scene II)*

She does not understand the profundity of her husband's thoughts – *"What do you mean?"* – but she clearly understands the depth of horror in which they cannot afford to indulge:

> *"These deeds must not be thought*
> *After these ways; so, it will make us mad"*

Her language is as prosaic as his is poetic. She is both practical and realistic. While he is reflecting on the significance of not being able to pronounce *"Amen"*, it is she who thinks of the necessity of washing the blood from their hands and putting on their nightgowns. He hears a voice crying *"Sleep no more:"* what she hears is the scream of the owl and the cry of crickets. Her lack of imagination is an asset and accordingly she has no doubts or scruples. She says *"...the attempt and not the deed/Confounds us."*, whereas for Macbeth the deed itself is the crux of the matter. While Macbeth is tortured by ideas of retribution, Lady Macbeth does not think beyond the obvious.

> *"What need we fear who knows it, when none can call our power to account?"*
> *(Act 5, Scene I)*

It is Macbeth's utter powerlessness that puts his wife under the strain that results in near madness. She has to endure the strain of perfect self-control and the ordeal of infusing some of her own tenacity into her husband.

She may not understand his thoughts about murdering sleep but it is she who has later to act out the very embodiment of Macbeth's image. She says it is *"A foolish thought to say a sorry sight"* when Macbeth looks at the blood on his hands, but she herself is to be tormented by the image of bloody hands. The Gentlewoman tells the doctor:

> *"It is an accustom'd action with her, to seem thus washing her hands.*
> *I have known her continue in this a quarter of an hour."*   (Act 5, Scene I)

At the time of the murder she is superb in her strength of purpose, returning to the chamber where murder has been done, when Macbeth the valiant warrior does not dare. Then for her it is all over:

> *"A little water clears us of this deed;*
> *How easy it is, then!"*   (Act 2, Scene II)

Unlike Macbeth, she refuses to dwell on the horror and this is her undoing. Later her nature rises up against the foulness of the violent deed and her mind gives way under the terrible strain. In her sleep-walking, not only does she reproduce the horrible scene of the murder but she re-enacts the struggle of keeping her husband from betraying himself:

> *"No more o' that, my lord, no more o' that: you mar all with this starting."*
>   (Act 5, Scene I)

Lady Macbeth's greatness lies not in any superiority of strength or pitilessness, but in her ability to rise above her very nature and in her courage in nerving herself in the face of the necessity of the situation, so as to ensure the success of Macbeth.

"...My dearest partner of greatness..."

Macbeth and Lady Macbeth are moved by one and the same ambition and are alike in tragic grandeur. They compliment each other in many ways but the action is built on a strong contrast of character. In the earlier part of the play, they are of equal importance but as Macbeth proceeds from crime to crime Lady Macbeth fades into the background. It is as if his very weakness gives her strength; when he becomes strong in purpose he does not need her. Lady Macbeth is a good foil for Macbeth's feelings. Her apparent insensitivity highlights his depth of feeling, her lack of imagination emphasizes the extraordinary quality of his. Their attitudes towards the projected murder of Duncan are quite different and it produces in them equally different reactions, yet ultimately the effect of the murder on them is not so very different. Lady Macbeth deliberately suppresses her feelings before, during and immediately after the murder of Duncan, whereas Macbeth gives his imaginative fancies free rein. Later Macbeth's imagination is replaced by indifference while Lady Macbeth imaginatively re-enacts the murder – the result of a nervous intensity which has to play itself out. Just as one could say that Macbeth is spiritually dead when he undertakes the murder of Lady Macduff without a qualm, in the sleep-walking scene Lady Macbeth is also spiritually dead. Her suicide is the counterpart of his defeat and death.

Conclusion

Macbeth – a total, poetic experience

The action of the play turns on a deed of disorder. Duncan's murder and its results are felt as a violation of nature and are therefore related to the disorder symbols of the unnatural behaviour in man, animals and the elements.

By his crime Macbeth has cut himself off from everything natural. Sleep takes on the quality of nightmare and the blackness of night is a thing of fear. The essence of evil has communicated itself from Macbeth to the whole realm.

The poetic symbolism and imaginative atmosphere mirrors the spiritual conflict. The outer conflict is a symbol of the inner conflict. The language tends away from realism to pure poetic symbolism. Not only is the function of the poetry to highlight character and action, but it is also essential to the indefinable atmosphere that envelops *Macbeth,* investing it with great intensity and significance. We are confronted by mystery, darkness, abnormality, hideousness.

Shakespeare had the task of making a tragic hero out of a murderer. By giving Macbeth a sensitive conscience Shakespeare endowed him with nobility: by giving him the speech of a poet, he endowed him with grandeur. *Macbeth* is the portrait of the destruction of a fine, impressive spirit.

Glossary of Dramatic Terms

Action:
: the sequence of important events on which the interest depends. The action in *Macbeth* moves swiftly.

Acts:
: the Elizabethan dramatists followed Horace's dictate of five acts in a play.

Allusion:
: a casual reference to a well-known individual or event as for example the porter's reference to the equivocator, Farmer, who was hanged on the 3rd of May 1606 for his part in the gunpowder plot.

Anachronism:
: the relating of an event, custom, idiom or allusion to a period of time when it was not yet in existence, as for example the reference to the dollar in *Act 1, Scene II.* The dollar was a silver coin used in the reign of Elizabeth the First and could not possibly have been in use in the time of Macbeth.

Aside:
: a speech or a remark made in a lower tone and not intended to be heard generally. It is a useful dramatic device. In *Act 1, Scene III,* Macbeth's aside permits the audience to know what he is thinking and it is of course extremely important that Banquo and the others should have no idea what is going on in Macbeth's mind.

Atmosphere:
: the spirit which pervades a play; an atmosphere of darkness and the unnatural pervades *Macbeth.*

Catastrophe:
: an event which overturns the order of things – the final outcome of a dramatic play. Macbeth's catastrophe is his fatal battle with Macduff who is *"not of woman born".*

Catharsis:
: Aristotle's belief that the spectator was purified by the emotions of terror and pity and the overwhelming spectacle of sadness in tragedy.

Characterization:
: it is important that the audience believes in the characters, otherwise they cannot experience pity or terror. What a character does and says must be rigidly true to his own character. Macbeth is a totally credible ambitious general. It is the characterisation of Macbeth and Lady Macbeth which engrosses us most in *Macbeth.* A character undergoes profound modification in a play. Macbeth is a very different man at the end of the play from what he was in *Act 1.*

Chorus:	in Greek tragedy the chorus provided a commentary on the action of the play. In ancient English drama an actor would take the part of the chorus, giving a prologue or making comments either between the acts or at the end of the play. Shakespeare uses his characters occasionally to provide a commentary as for example in the conversation in *Act 2, Scene IV* between Ross and the Old Man, which does not advance the action but provides a commentary on it.
Comic Relief:	a diversion which provokes laughter and releases the audience momentarily from the tension of the tragedy. The porter scene in *Macbeth* is an example of comic relief.
Conflict:	struggle; the essence of all drama. In classical tragedy the hero was in conflict with Fate. In modern tragedy the hero is in conflict with his own nature. Macbeth's ambition is in conflict with all that is noble in his nature.
Contrast:	to compare in order to state the difference between; to show the opposition of certain qualities. In *Macbeth* there are numerous examples of contrasting images, symbols and characters.
Crisis:	a critical or decisive moment as of danger or suspense; a turning point. In *Macbeth* the banquet is the crisis point of the plot – Macbeth having very nearly betrayed himself resolves from now on *"to know/By the worst means the worst"*. He has reached the point of no return, *"I am in blood/Stepp'd in so far that, should I wade no more,/Returning were as tedious as go o'er"*. From this point he rushes towards his catastrophe.
Dénouement:	the unravelling of the plot, the outcome of the action; the dénouement is synonymous with the catastrophe in tragedy.
Dialogue:	John Galsworthy defined good dramatic dialogue as *"Good dialogue, again, is character, marshalled so as continually to stimulate interest or excitement"*. Dramatic dialogue reveals the character of the speaker and unfolds the plot simultaneously. We discover the character through the dialogue.
Dramatic Irony:	occurs when the audience recognises that the facts are not what the characters believe them to be. An audience can recognise that the opinions expressed by a character are the opposite to truth. An

example of dramatic irony in *Macbeth* is Macbeth's entrance at the very moment of Duncan's comment on the treachery of the Thane of Cawdor. The audience knows that this Thane of Cawdor is guilty of treachery – treacherous thoughts – but Duncan can have no idea of this.

The conversation between Lady Macbeth and Duncan is another example of dramatic irony. She says to him *"All our service/In every point twice done, and then done double, / Were poor and single business..."* but the audience knows that she has arranged to have him murdered.

The porter's scene is a striking example of dramatic irony. He is drunk and has no idea of what has happened within the castle yet the audience realizes the irony of the fact that he imagines himself to be the porter of hell.

Dramatis Personae:	*personae* is a Latin word for the mask worn by the actor in classical Greek drama and represented the characteristics of the person whose part he was taking. *Dramatis Personae* in Shakespeare's time meant the characters in the drama.
Effective:	for a scene to be dramatically effective, it must produce a definite impression. The porter scene is dramatically effective because it heightens the suspense of the discovery of the murder.
Exposition:	the explication and development of the plot.
Hero:	hero in the sense of the tragic hero means more than simply a man of courage, or the main protagonist. The tragic hero is always a man of high degree, a man of exceptional nature who has a divided soul.
Plot:	the arrangement of the incidents in the play, the design of the story. The nature of the characters determines the progress of the plot. The plot of *Macbeth* is spun out of Macbeth's ambition. Shakespeare cared little about his plots as such, taking them from stories already well-known and altering them to suit his purpose. He focuses on character and the plot unfolds through characterisation.
Retribution:	reward or punishment for good or bad actions. In tragedy, the hero's death is his retribution for his tragic flaw and is consequently acceptable as inevitable.

Soliloquy: a monologue addressed to the self. In *Macbeth* the hero's soliloquies reveal his inner self and ensure the sympathy of the audience.

Stage: the Shakespearean stage was like an apron and partly projected into the auditorium. In the prologue to *King Henry V,* the stage is referred to as a *"...wooden O...".* The chorus asks the audience *"...can this cockpit hold/The vasty fields of France? or may we cram/Within this wooden O the very casques/That did affright the air at Agincourt?"*

Symbolism: a symbol is a concrete thing which is at the same time itself and representative of something else. In *Macbeth* the witches may be regarded as symbols of the evil ambition in Macbeth's heart and of the evil temptation that is ever present in the world. There is an accumulation of symbolic references to night and darkness in *Macbeth.* In fact most of the important scenes take place at night, but the darkness corresponds to the blackness of the souls of Macbeth and Lady Macbeth.

Symmetry: a due proportion between the parts of a whole; balance. The structure of *Macbeth* is a perfectly symmetrical arc – the rise and fall of Macbeth; the turning point in *Act 3, Scene III,* marks the exact mid point of the play. Characters are also carefully balanced against one another. Lady Macbeth and Macbeth are balanced against Banquo and Macduff, Duncan is balanced by Malcolm after his death.

Sympathy: sharing another's emotions; being affected by the suffering of another. The sympathy of the audience with the tragic hero is essential for catharsis. In *Macbeth* the audience identifies with Macbeth rather than with Duncan or Banquo because Macbeth is the dominant consciousness through which we see the action.

Theme: the central idea.

Time: according to Holinshed, after Macbeth killed Duncan in battle he ruled Scotland for seventeen years but the dramatic time of Shakespeare's *Macbeth* extends over about two or three months. The events take place on nine separate days according to Shakespearian scholars. The events in the play appear to succeed one another rapidly.

Tragedy: the essence of tragedy is the death of a great soul which fills the audience with such pity and terror that it purifies the mind.

Questions and Sample Answers

Sample Exam Question for Ordinary Level

1. (a) Describe the scene in which Macbeth first meets the Witches. (10)

    (b) With which character in *Macbeth* do you feel the most sympathy? (10)

2. From the following statements, choose the one which best describes Lady Macbeth's character: (10)
    *   Lady Macbeth is a loving wife who supports her husband.
    *   Lady Macbeth is a wicked and evil woman.
    *   Lady Macbeth is a naive and tragic character.

3. Answer one of the following: [Each part carries 30 marks]

    (i) "Banquo is a good friend to Macbeth."

    Write a response to this statement supporting your points by reference to the play.

    OR

    (ii) Imagine you are a servant living in the castle of Dunsinane. Describe what happened the morning after Duncan's body was found in the castle.

    OR

    (iii) "Malcolm will make a good King of Scotland."

    To what extent would you agree with this statement? Support your view by reference to the play.

Sample Exam Question for Ordinary Level

1. (a) Write a short account of an important moment or scene from Shakespeare's *Macbeth*. (10)

    (b) Why, in your view, was that moment or scene an important one? (10)

2. Macduff paid dearly for going to England to join Malcolm. Briefly describe what happens to Macduff's family, and say what these events say about Macbeth as king. (10)

3. Answer one of the following: [Each part carries 30 marks]

    (i) "Lady Macbeth is the most interesting character in *Macbeth*."

    Do you agree with this statement? Support your answer with reference to the play.

    OR

    (ii) Your school magazine has asked you to write an article entitled "My Favourite Play." Write the article and explain what you particularly liked about *Macbeth*.

    OR

    (iii) "The play Macbeth shows us the danger of too much ambition."

    Do you agree with this statement? Support your answer with reference to the play.

Sample Answer to 2007 Ordinary Level Exam Question

1. (a) *In Act 2, Scene III,* **Macduff discovers Duncan's body. Describe Macbeth's reaction to this event.** (10)

This scene takes place the morning after the murder. Macduff is greeted by Lennox and Macbeth. Macbeth does not show any signs of guilt when Lennox comments on disturbances in the natural world the previous night. Macduff has been instructed to wake the king, and comes rushing back to Lennox and Macbeth bearing the terrible news of the murder. He says, *"Most sacrilegious murder hath broke ope / The Lord's anointed temple, and stole thence / The life of the building!"* Macbeth pretends to be surprised and rushes off with Lennox to see for himself. Lady Macbeth then enters and also pretends to be shocked at the news. Donalbain and Malcolm enter and Macduff informs them of their father's murder.

When he comes back Macbeth says that in a fit of rage brought on by the sight of the king's bloody body he killed the guards. He says, *"O, yet I do repent me of my fury / That I did kill them."* Of course he had to do this to cover up the murder. Macduff questions his reasons for this, and Macbeth becomes uncomfortable. Lady Macbeth then faints, probably to distract attention from her husband.

(b) **Why, in your opinion, does Macbeth decide to murder Banquo?** (10)

After Macbeth has been crowned King of Scotland, Banquo is concerned that Macbeth may have killed Duncan in order to make the Witches' prophecy came true. He says, *"Thou hast it now: King, Cawdor, Glamis, / All as the weird women promis'd; and, I fear / Thou play'dst most foully for't".* Macbeth comes on stage and appears to be in good humour. He welcomes Banquo and asks him to come to a feast to be held in the castle later that night.

Banquo tells Macbeth he intends to go riding before the feast. He will be accompanied by his son, Fleance. When Banquo leaves, Macbeth begins his soliloquy. We hear how he fears the prophecy that Banquo's descendents will be kings. He feels that he will have killed Duncan for nothing if his heirs cannot inherit the throne. Macbeth says, *"To be thus is nothing; / But to be safely thus."* He also reveals his fear of his friend. He sees that Banquo's strength is a threat to his position as king. He says, *"There is none but he whose being I do fear : and, under him, my genius is rebuked".* He is determined to kill Banquo to eliminate the threat.

2. **Do you feel pity for Lady Macbeth in the sleepwalking scene in Act 5?**
   Explain your answer. (10)

   In Acts 1 and 2, Lady Macbeth was happy to plan and take part in Duncan's murder. When Macbeth said he was afraid of the results of killing the king, he asked *"Will all great Neptune's ocean wash this blood clean from my hand?"* Lady Macbeth responded saying, *"A little water clears us of this deed ; I How easy is it then!"* Her attitude was simple – kill Duncan, seize the throne, and forget about it. However the first scene of Act 5 proves that she underestimated the effects of the murder on her own conscience.

   This is a scene where I felt sympathy for Lady Macbeth. The scene opens with a discussion between a doctor and one of Lady Macbeth's ladies-in-waiting. Lady Macbeth has been sleepwalking, a sure sign of a guilty conscience. Lady Macbeth then enters. She carries a candle, because she cannot bear the darkness. Her servant says, *"she has light by her continually; 'tis her command."* This fear of darkness is a sign of her guilty conscience. Lady Macbeth is seen trying to clean a spot of blood from her hands. She says, *"Out, damned spot! out, I say!... I yet who would have thought the old man to have so much blood in him?"* She is tortured by guilt and is being driven towards madness. Even though Lady Macbeth was wicked earlier in the play, it is hard not to feel pity for her in Act 5.

3. (i) **"Although Macbeth is guilty of many evil deeds, he is a brave man."**
   Would you agree with this opinion of Macbeth? Give reasons for your answer based on your knowledge of the play. (30)

   Yes, I do agree with this opinion of Macbeth. He is guilty of many evil deeds in the play. He murders the king, Duncan, and steals the crown of Scotland. Then, in order to try to hold on to his position as king, he organizes the murder of Banquo his best friend, and of Macduff's family. The play clearly shows he is a corrupt man. However, he is also brave. His bravery is most clearly shown at the beginning and at the end of the play.

   At the beginning of the play, the sergeant describes Macbeth as a brave warrior. He led Duncan's army in the battles against the Norwegian invaders and against the traitor Macdonwald. The sergeant describes how *"brave Macbeth, – well he deserves that name"* fought until his sword *"smoked with bloody execution"*. Macbeth fought his way through Macdonwald's army until he found the traitor and *"unseam'd him from the nave to the chaps, I And fix'd his head upon our battlements."* Clearly Macbeth is a brave warrior and a hero.

   Duncan is impressed by Macbeth's bravery. He says Macbeth is *"O valiant cousin! worthy gentleman!"* However, Duncan doesn't know that Macbeth is also corrupt. The Witches can see that Macbeth is evil. As he approaches the second Witch says, *"By the pricking of my thumbs, I Something wicked this way comes."* At the start of the play, Lady Macbeth thinks her husband is too cowardly to kill the king. She says his character is too full of *"the milk of human kindness"*. She is wrong and Macbeth does commit the terrible crime of killing the king, and takes the throne.

When Macbeth becomes king, the evil side of his character is clear. He arranges the murder of his friend, Banquo, because the Witches told him *"Thou shalt get kings, though thou be none"*. He even orders the murder of Banquo's son, the boy Fleance, saying he also "*must embrace the fate of that dark hour"*. This clearly shows Macbeth is evil. Later in the play, he also orders the murder of Macduff's children. Ross reports the terrible news to Macduff, saying *"Your castle is surprised; your wife and babes I Savagely slaughter'd"*. These actions show that Macbeth is a coward and is totally corrupt.

Despite these cowardly actions, Macbeth dies bravely. In Act 5 he realizes that the Witches have tricked him when Birnam Wood begins to move to Dunsinane. He is a warrior and says, *"I'll fight till from my bones my flesh be hack'd. I Give me my armour."* At the end, he learns that *"Macduff was from his mother's womb I Untimely ripp'd."* He dies bravely, saying, *"Yet I will try the last. Before my body I I throw my war-like shield. Lay on, Macduff, I And damn'd be him that first cries, 'Hold, enough!'"* This clearly shows that, although Macbeth is definitely an evil character, he is also brave.

Sample Questions for Higher Level

1. Discuss the theme of deception in Shakespeare's *Macbeth*.
    Support your answer with reference to the play.

2. "Macbeth is an intriguing character because he is both a deeply corrupt and deeply sympathetic man."
    Discuss this statement with reference to the play.

3. "Lady Macbeth is a complex character who inspires both loathing and pity in the audience."
    Do you agree with this statement? Support your answer with reference to the play.

4. "The play *Macbeth* is a brilliant description of what happens when one man puts personal ambition above the greater good by disrupting the natural order."
    Do you agree with this statement? Support your answer with reference to the play.

5. "The appeal of the play *Macbeth* lies in its depiction of the world of the Supernatural."
    Discuss this statement with reference to the play.

Past Higher Level Exam Questions

2007 Exam

(i) "The relationship between Macbeth and Lady Macbeth undergoes significant change during the course of the play."
Discuss this statement supporting your answer with the aid of suitable reference to the text.

OR

(ii) "Essentially the play *Macbeth* is about power, its use and abuse."
Discuss this view of the play, supporting your answer with the aid of suitable reference to the text.

2004 Exam

(i) "Shakespeare's *Macbeth* invites us to look into the world of a man driven on by ruthless ambition and tortured by regret."
Write a response to this view of the play, *Macbeth*, supporting the points you make by reference to the text.

OR

(ii) "The play *Macbeth* has many scenes of compelling drama."
Choose one scene that you found compelling and say why you found it to be so. Support your answer by reference to the play.

2003 Exam

(i) "We feel very little pity for the central characters of Macbeth and Lady Macbeth in Shakespeare's play."
To what extent would you agree with the above view? Support your answer by reference to the play.

OR

(ii) "In *Macbeth*, Shakespeare presents us with a powerful vision of evil."
Write your response to the above statement. Textual support may include reference to a particular performance of the play you have seen.

Sample Higher Level Answers

"The power of evil and the supernatural is a major theme in Shakespeare's *Macbeth*."
Discuss this statement with reference to the play.

> *Live you? or are you aught*
> *That man may question? ...*
> *you should be women,*
> *And yet your beards forbid me to interpret*
> *That you are so.*

Macbeth is a play about one man's descent into moral corruption and **evil**. Throughout the play, Shakespeare leaves us in no doubt about the intrinsic connection that exists between **supernatural** forces and **malevolence**. Philosophically, *Macbeth* is a Christian play, concerned with the natural order and God's omnipresence and omnipotence. The 'natural' world is the world that obeys the laws laid down for man by God. It is a world of duty and of honour, where kings are divinely appointed and an eternity of suffering awaits anyone who breaches the natural order. The '**supernatural**' world represents forces beyond these laws. The existence of the **supernatural** in the play is reinforced by the sight of Lady Macbeth calling on **evil** forces to give her strength, and by the appearance of Banquo's ghost, which reminds Macbeth of the suffering that awaits him in the afterlife. However, it is clear that in *Macbeth* the **supernatural** is primarily embodied by the Witches, **wicked** creatures whose *raison d'être* is to bring chaos and anarchy to the world of man. They are connected to the devil, and their temptation of Macbeth is very much in the tradition of the biblical story of Jesus' forty days and nights of temptation. Jesus is able to resist the lure of sin, but Macbeth is not. He is a fundamentally corrupt man, undone by vaulting ambition, and this is his fatal flaw. The ease with which he descends into **amorality** is shocking and is evidence of the clear connection between **evil** and the **supernatural** in the play.

Lady Macbeth appears to be **evil**. Her first appearance, in *Act 1, Scene V,* is shocking and memorable. She is excited by her husband's letter and appears to have no moral objection to the prospect of regicide, a crime for which there can be no forgiveness. She is linked to the Witches when she says of her husband, *"Hie thee hither, / That I may pour my spirits in thine ear"*. She is aware of the enormity of her proposed crime, and memorably calls on the forces of evil that exist in the natural world to help her overcome her natural abhorrence at such a terrible sin. She calls out to the *"spirits / That tend on mortal thoughts"*, and asks that they fill her *"from the crown to toe top-full / Of direst cruelty! Stop up the access and passage to remorse, / That no compunctious visitings of nature / Shake my fell purpose"*. She recognizes that her plan – to help her husband kill Duncan and usurp the throne – is "*fell*", or **evil**, and calls on **supernatural** forces to give her the power to overcome conscience. In this way,

Shakespeare leaves the audience in no doubt about two things, firstly, that wicked **supernatural** forces exist in the world of the play, and secondly, that **there is an intrinsic link between those supernatural forces and the power of evil**.

Lady Macbeth's call to **supernatural** forces is instigated by receipt of her husband's letter. The letter describes his encounter with the Witches, who Shakespeare intends as the physical embodiment of both the **supernatural** and **evil**. The Witches have powers beyond those given to man under God's law. They can fly, as we see in *Act 1, Scene I*, when the second Witch states her intention to *"Hover through the fog and filthy air."* Later, in *Act 3, Scene V*, Hecate states her intention to fly when she tells the weird sisters, *"I am for the air"*. The Witches have a variety of other **supernatural** abilities. They can appear and disappear at will. Banquo is amazed by their sudden disappearance in *Act 1, Scene III*, when he asks, *"The earth hath bubbles, as the water has, / And these are of them. Whither are they vanish'd?"* The Witches also have the ability to read men's minds and hearts, and appear to have a gift for understanding and recognising corruption in others. Hecate brilliantly sums up Macbeth's character in *Act 3, Scene V*, when she says, *"He shall spurn fate, scorn death, and bear / His hopes 'bove wisdom, grace and fear"*. However, nowhere is the **supernatural** power of the Witches more evident than in *Act 4, Scene I*, when they concoct the potion from which they summon the Apparitions.

Shakespeare uses *Act 4, Scene I*, to reinforce the twin points that the Witches are **supernatural** and that they are fundamentally **evil**. The Witches' brew contains horrific ingredients – *"Eye of newt and toe of frog... Scale of dragon, tooth of wolf... Liver of blaspheming Jew... Finger of birth-strangled babe..."* The fact that they concoct the potion is indicative of their **malevolence**. They use an incantation – *"And now around a cauldron sing, / Like elves and fairies in a ring, / Enchanting all that you put in"* – to conjure the Apparitions. The fact that the Apparitions can accurately predict the future (*"Macbeth shall never vanquish'd be until / Great Birnam wood to high Dunsinane Hill / Shall come against him."*) is further evidence of their **supernatural** abilities. Macbeth is led towards his doom and Banquo's warning from *Act 1, Scene III*, rings out to the audience; *"The instruments of darkness tell us truths, / Win us with honest trifles, to betray's / In deepest consequence."*

The Witches tempt Macbeth because their purpose is to cause *"hurlyburly"* in the world of man. Their cruelty and **supernatural** abilities are established when the first Witch reacts to a slight by a sailor's wife by saying, *"Her husband's to Aleppo gone, master o' th' Tiger: / But in a sieve I'll thither sail, / And, like a rat without a tail, / I'll do, I'll do, and I'll do."* They can manipulate the weather and cause havoc, but an important point is also made about the limitations of their **supernatural** powers in this scene. The first Witch says, *"Though his bark cannot be lost, / Yet it shall be tempest-tost."* This is important because it indicates that the Witches' **supernatural** powers are limited by free will. If the sailor is strong enough to stay awake the ship will not sink. This is crucial because it means Macbeth is not forced to corruption by the Witches. He is manipulated and led by them but were his character not undermined by vaulting ambition, he could, like Banquo, have resisted the Witches' temptations.

However, Macbeth's ambition is overwhelming and his descent into **tyranny** following the regicide is astonishing. His moral ambivalence is clear in *Act 3, Scene IV*, when he tells the murderer, *"better thee without than he within"*, referring to Banquo's blood, and later says, *"I am in blood / Stepp'd in so far that, should I wade no more, / Returning were as tedious as go o'er"*. This is shocking evidence of **corruption** and **evil**, and, significantly, the words are not spoken by a **supernatural**, **malevolent** creature, but by Macbeth, a previously heroic character undone by a fatal flaw. Perhaps the best example of how evil can enter the human heart comes in *Act 4, Scene I*, when, having met with the Witches, he says of Macduff, *"The castle of Macduff I will surprise; / Seize upon Fife; give to the edge o' the sword / His wife, his babes, and all unfortunate souls / That trace him in his line."* The Witches succeed in using their **supernatural** powers to tempt Macbeth to corruption, but their success would not have been possible had he not wanted the crown so desperately. Macbeth was willing to breach the natural order, God's law.

Macbeth is fully aware of God's omniscience and is fully aware of the consequences of his crime. In *Act 1, Scene VII*, he talks of the *"deep damnation"* that awaits him should he kill Duncan. A reminder of his fate emerges in another manifestation of the **supernatural** when Banquo's ghost appears in *Act 3, Scene IV*. Macbeth is the only character to see the ghost and he is shocked by its *"blood-bolted"* appearance. He desperately tells the ghost, *"never shake / Thy gory locks at me"*, but his denial is futile. The ghost is proof of an afterlife. The afterlife that awaits Macbeth is an eternity of suffering for his terrible crimes. The ghost, therefore, is a **supernatural** signal to Macbeth that he can expect God's retribution for his **evil** offences against the natural order. God is, after all, a very real presence in this play. In *Act 2, Scene III*, Macduff refers to the *"Most sacreligious murder"* which *"hath broke ope / The Lord's anointed temple, and stole thence / The life o' the building."* It is clear that Macbeth's error was underestimating, or of deliberately choosing to ignore, the power of the **supernatural**, both in the form of the malevolent Witches and in the form of a vengeful God.

It is therefore clear that *Macbeth* is a play dominated by the **supernatural**. The world Shakespeare depicts is recognisably Christian. It is a place where a weak humanity is given a strict set of rules by a benevolent God, whose natural laws bring order. It is also a world in which the presence of the **supernatural** and **evil** are everywhere. A world where even the most heroic of men can be undone by a combination of their internal weakness and the **supernatural** temptations of **evil**.

"In *Macbeth*, Shakespeare does not present Macbeth as a mere villain, but succeeds in arousing some measure of *sympathy* for him."

Discuss the character of Macbeth in the light of this statement, supporting your answer by relevant quotation or reference.

> *To-morrow, and to-morrow, and to-morrow,*
> *Creeps in this petty pace from day to day,*
> *To the last syllable of recorded time;*
> *And all our yesterdays have lighted fools*
> *The way to dusty death. Out, out, brief candle!*
> *Life's but a walking shadow, a poor player*
> *That struts and frets his hour upon the stage,*
> *And then is heard no more; it is a tale*
> *Told by an idiot, full of sound and fury,*
> *Signifying nothing.*

Macbeth is a tragic hero. He is a man capable of enunciating the most wonderful and mesmerising speeches that are filled with eloquence, insight and beauty. He is a brave warrior, hailed as the hero whose strength, endurance and determination saves Scotland from the machinations of traitors and invaders. He is a loving husband, who treats his wife as an equal. He is a nobleman, aware of God's law, of the natural order, and of his role within that natural order. And yet, Macbeth is also a reprehensible villain, a devil driven by ambition and egoism to regicide and tyranny. The play *Macbeth* is fascinating precisely because of the protagonist's complex character. He is a man whose story grips from the beginning, and although the audience can only feel a sense of relief when he meets his inevitable end in *Act 5, Scene VIII*, we cannot help but feel a degree of sympathy for this potentially great man, whose ambition coursed through him like quicksilver, killing the hero and transforming him into *"This tyrant, whose sole name blisters our tongues"* (Malcolm, *Act 4, Scene III*).

Sympathy for Macbeth is rooted in Act 1. In *Act 1, Scene II*, the sergeant reports that a Scottish nobleman, Macdonwald, rebelled against the King, Duncan. At first, it seemed Macdonwald may be successful, but he was defeated and killed by Macbeth. Macbeth is described in glowing terms as a brave and merciless warrior. He is *"brave Macbeth"*, who, *"Disdaining Fortune, with his brandish'd steel, / Which smok'd with bloody execution, / ... carv'd out his passage / Till he fac'd the slave; / Which ne'er shook hands, nor bade farewell to him, / Till he unseam'd him from the nave to the chaps, / And fix'd his head upon our battlements."* However, this did not ensure the kingdom's safety, for as soon as Macdonwald was defeated, the king's armies were confronted by another enemy. This time the enemy was Sweno, the King of Norway, who led an invasion of Scotland. Neither Macbeth nor Banquo, his friend and fellow nobleman, were intimidated by these developments, and redoubled their efforts, defeating the invading Norwegian armies. Duncan praises Macbeth, calling him *"valiant cousin! worthy gentleman!"* There is no doubt that the audience's **sympathy** lies with this great warrior Thane, even before he has appeared on stage.

However, it does not take long before these feelings of **sympathy** begin to change. In *Act 1, Scene III*, the Witches' prophecy that he will be *"king hereafter"* leaves Macbeth *"rapt withal"*. The suggestion is clear. This loyal vassal has harboured dangerous ambitions for the crown. He hides his feelings from his comrade, Banquo, and his ambition is revealed in the aside, *"Two truths are told, / As happy prologues to the swelling act / Of the imperial theme... / If chance will have me King, why, chance / may crown me, / Without my stir."* He is an intriguing character, regarded as the epitome of nobility by others, but hiding shameful desires. This impression is reinforced in the next scene. Macbeth accepts Duncan's thanks and praise graciously, saying, *"our duties / Are to your throne and state, children and servants"*. He is clearly aware of his position in the feudal hierarchy and yet, seconds later, responds to Malcolm's appointment as Prince of Cumberland with *"That is a step, / On which I must fall down, or else o'er-leap."* It is clear that this man has the potential to betray his duty, and that is what makes him such an interesting character.

Later in Act 1, Macbeth's close relationship with his wife is revealed when he addresses her as *"my dearest partner of greatness"*. Lady Macbeth is clearly an intimidating character and her excoriating attack on her husband's masculinity *("I have given suck, and know / How tender 'tis to love the babe that milks me")* certainly elicits sympathy for her husband. However, the persuasive power of her speech must be judged in the context of Macbeth's soliloquy that precedes it. He eloquently describes his inner conflict, describing his duty as *"his kinsman and his subject"* and recognizes that Duncan's *"virtues / Will plead like angels trumpet-tongu'd against / The deep damnation of his taking-off"*. He recognizes that he has *"no spur / To prick the sides of my intent, but only / Vaulting ambition"*. The audience feels a deep sense of **sympathy** for a man torn between what he knows is his duty and his desire to be king. The sense remains, however, that the power of his ambition is overwhelming, and the audience is unsurprised when, in the next scene, his *"heat-oppressed brain"* leads to a fatal resolution – *"I go, and it is done; the bell invites me. / Hear it not, Duncan; for it is a knell / That summons thee to heaven or to hell."*

The **sympathy** felt for Macbeth is dissipated significantly, but elements remain, following the regicide in *Act 2, Scene II*. He is paralysed by this dreadful act, wondering if *"all great Neptune's ocean wash this blood / Clean from my hand?"* At least he feels guilt for his actions.

However, that guilt does not stop him from seizing the fruits of his crime. The suspicion remains that, while his guilt is real, it does not stop him from being, at his core, a horrid, selfish and hubristic villain. This suspicion is confirmed in *Act 3, Scene I*, when he worries, *"To be thus is nothing; / But to be safely thus... / Upon my head they plac'd a fruitless crown, / And put a barren sceptre in my gripe"*. It is clear that the fulfilment of his ambition is his driving force. He decides to kill Banquo, his best friend, who he now regards as a rival. This is a real turning point in our perception of Macbeth, as he decides *"Fleance his son... / Whose absence is no less material to me / Than is his father's, must embrace the fate / Of that dark hour."* Macbeth is now an amoral villain, capable of murdering a child to ensure his own safety. All **sympathy** for him evaporates at this point. He has been pressurized by the most extraordinary force of vaulting ambition and that has transformed him into an anti-hero.

The sense that Macbeth has reached a point of no return is confirmed when the murderers report to him in *Act 3, Scene IV*. He feels no guilt at the death of his erstwhile friend and the perversion of his morality is clear when he praises the murderer as *"the best o' cut-throats"* and comments that Banquo's blood is *"better thee without than he within."* Even his love for his wife, one of his redeeming features, is pushed aside in his obsession with the crown. He dismisses her, telling her to *"be innocent of the knowledge, dearest chuck"*. He then says, *"I am in blood / Stepp'd in so far, that should I wade no more, / Returning were as tedious as go o'er."* He is corrupt, amoral and determined to maintain his position through violence and mayhem. Any **sympathy** felt by the audience for this once great man is gone.

As Macbeth plunges into moral chaos and dissolution, Scotland is plunged into anarchy. Macduff's wife and children are slaughtered. In *Act 3, Scene VI*, a lord calls for Malcolm's return so that *"we may again / Give to our tables meat, sleep to our nights, / Free from our feasts and banquets bloody knives, / Do faithful homage and receive free honours"*. Macbeth's self-interest and egoism have led him to neglect the primary duty of any king – to ensure the security and well-being of his subjects. He is a tyrant, and in *Act 4, Scene III*, Malcolm and Macduff exchange condemnations of his reign:

> *Each new morn*
> *New widows howl, new orphans cry, new sorrows*
> *Strike heaven on the face. (Macduff)*
> *I think our country sinks beneath the yoke;*
> *It weeps, it bleeds, and each new day a gash*
> *Is added to her wounds (Malcolm)*

It is clear that Macbeth must be deposed. It is the wish of the people of Scotland, and the wish of the audience, that he be deposed. No **sympathy** can be felt for him. In Act 5, he rails against the betrayal of the Witches. He has desperately clung to their prophecies; *"none of woman born / Shall harm Macbeth"* and *"Macbeth shall never vanquish'd be until / Great*

Birnam wood to high Dunsinane Hill / Shall come against him." However, the Witches, while at all times duplicitous and equivocal, are not at fault for his downfall. He chose to believe them and to ignore those elements of the prophecy that did not suit him. He is a villain and our **sympathy** for him has evaporated.

And then, in the midst of breakdown and disaster, he produces the *"to-morrow, and to-morrow, and to-morrow"* soliloquy. Listening to that speech, which ends with the wonderful insight that life *"is a tale / Told by an idiot, full of sound and fury, / Signifying nothing"*, we are reminded of the greatness of Macbeth, of all of the reasons he was a character to admire in the first act of the play. He dies, and is remembered as *"this dead butcher",* and the audience is relieved at his death. And yet it is impossible not to be reminded of the great man, the heroic man, that was Macbeth before his fatal flaw of ambition enveloped him, overwhelmed him, and drove him to self-destruction. Despite ourselves, a sliver of **sympathy** remains.

"Lady Macbeth is a fascinating Character who inspires both loathing and sympathy in the audience."
Discuss this statement with reference to the play *Macbeth*.

Lady Macbeth is a fascinating character. She is a woman of extraordinary strength and power. At times she appears to personify evil and malicious self-interest. At times she utters words that are appalling and monstrous in tone. She is an enthusiastic participant in a plot to commit regicide and, at one stage in the play, even appears to countenance the infanticide of her own child. It would be very easy to look at this woman and to dismiss her as a mere villain, a wicked character representative of selfishness, greed and amorality. And yet, that would be to underestimate the complexity of her character, for there is so much more to Lady Macbeth. She is an incredibly driven and intelligent woman. Her love for her husband is intense and she is powerfully aware of the forces which forge his personality. Her sense of identity is bound up in being his partner, in being needed by this great man. That is why this formidable woman ends the play a broken figure and a shadow of her former self. She goaded and encouraged Macbeth to kill Duncan so that he could be king. However, she did not envisage the profound change the act would have on her husband. **Lady Macbeth is a fascinating character precisely because she inspires a sense of loathing in the audience. At the same time the audience finds itself compelled to feel sympathy for her when they learn of her death and witness her husband's nonchalant reaction to it.**

Lady Macbeth first appears on stage in *Act 1, Scene V*. She is reading a letter from her husband. The closeness of their relationship is clear from the fact that he addresses her as *"my dearest partner in greatness"*. The letter recounts Macbeth's meeting with the Witches and their prophecies. He also reveals that Duncan has appointed him Thane of Cawdor. She understands immediately that her husband's thoughts have turned to regicide and is greatly excited by the news. However, she fears her husband may be too weak to act to ensure the fulfilment of the prophecy, saying, *"yet I do fear thy nature; / It is too full o' the milk of human kindness"*. The implication is clear. Lady Macbeth wants her husband to seize the crown. This means she is contemplating regicide, the worst possible crime in the eyes of an Elizabethan audience. She appears to possess no moral qualms about this; *"The raven himself is hoarse / That croaks the fatal entrance of Duncan / Under my battlements."*

She appears to be a true villain and employs language and imagery in her speech that suggests that she is evil and is somehow connected to the supernatural world of the Witches; *"Hie thee hither, / That I may pour my spirits in thine ear"*. She is determined to encourage her husband to seize his opportunity, and is also determined to be cold and unemotional, ignoring the moral consequences of regicide. Lady Macbeth seems to be the epitome of immorality. She appears to have no conscience. She calls on the forces of evil to give her strength; *"Come, you spirits / That tend on mortal thoughts! / Unsex me here, / And fill me, from the crown to toe, top-full / Of direst cruelty."* Her speech is both spellbinding and appalling. And yet the fact remains that she has to ask for the *"access and passage to remorse"* to be blocked up. This shows that she **has** a conscience. She is aware that killing Duncan is an immoral act. She chooses to ignore the moral implications of the act in order to satisfy her husband's (and her own) ambitions. Later in the play, when we see her tortured by guilt in Act 5, we are reminded of our introduction to her in Act 1, and the sympathy we feel for her is diluted.

Lady Macbeth is an incredibly persuasive personality. When Macbeth wavers in *Act 1, Scene 7*, she provides him with strength and reassurance. When he informs her that he has decided not to go through with the plan, she is aghast, asking him *"Would'st thou have that / Which thou esteem'st the ornament of life, / And live a coward in thine own esteem."* She chides him and questions his manhood. Once again the language and imagery employed here is extraordinarily evocative and memorable. She knows her husband needs to be goaded to act. She tells him:

> I have given suck, and know
> How tender 'tis to love the babe that milks me:
> I would, while it was smiling in my face,
> Have pluck'd my nipple from his boneless gums,
> And dash'd the brains out, had I so sworn as you
> Have done to this.

These words are horrific. They represent a graphic description of infanticide. However, the lines should be read figuratively as she intends to shock Macbeth. She has perceived his moral weakness and is also aware that he will be driven mad by frustrated ambition if he does not act. It is at this point that she utters her most callous and sickening words of the play. She asks her husband, *"when in swinish sleep / Their drenched natures lie as in a death, / What cannot you and I perform upon / The unguarded Duncan?"* She is a villain and cannot be forgiven for the cold premeditation with which she approaches the regicide. However, it must not be said that Lady Macbeth forced her husband to commit the regicide. Rather, she offered the support he needed, at the moment he needed it, to have the fortitude to pursue his desires.

Lady Macbeth is an active participant in the murder of the king. She drugs the guards, coldly commenting in *Act 2, Scene II*, on how *"the surfeited grooms / Do mock their charge with snores: I have drugg'd their possets"*. She is excited by the night's events but significantly notes she could not kill Duncan herself; *"Had he not resembled / My father as he slept, I had done't."* Again, there is evidence of a conscience at work here. She has persuaded herself that the act of regicide is no big deal, that it can be forgotten after it is done. When Macbeth returns with the bloody daggers, he is distraught, asking, *"Will all great Neptune's ocean wash this blood / Clean from my hand?"* Her response, *"A little water clears us of this deed: / How easy is it then"*, is immediate. Again, she appals the audience, but these words must be examined in the context of the play as a whole. For although Lady Macbeth may be described as evil, she must also be recognized as naive and misguided. Unlike her husband, she refuses to face up to the fact that their crime is a crime against Duncan, against Scotland, and against God. It is this denial that creates a sense of reluctant sympathy for her character at the end of the play.

The really fascinating thing about Lady Macbeth is the speed of her decline. She hoped Macbeth would be content by becoming king, and yet, by *Act 3, Scene II*, she comments, *"Nought's had, all's spent, / Where our desire is got without content"*. Macbeth has embarked on his descent into odious tyranny and has become increasingly distant from his wife. He decides to kill Banquo and Fleance, yet tells her to *"Be innocent of the knowledge, dearest chuck"*. These patronising words must be like a dagger to her heart. She is excluded from her husband's thoughts from this point and, although she covers up for him one final time in the banquet scene, her importance to her husband, and therefore to the play, dissipates and finally disappears.

Lady Macbeth's final appearance on stage comes in *Act 5, Scene I*. She is a broken figure, all of her previous strength has evaporated. She is seen sleepwalking, and has *"light by her continually"*. When Macbeth voiced fears of the moral consequences of the regicide, she dismissed them as unmanly. Her attitude was simple – kill Duncan, seize the throne, and forget about it. However, her fervour to see her husband's ambition fulfilled blinded her to the realities of conscience. She erred and is here seen wracked by guilt, rubbing her hands, saying, *"Out, damned spot! out, I say!... I Yet who would have thought the old man to have so much blood in him."* She represents the truth of God's power. She tried to defy the natural order and has suffered the consequences.

While Lady Macbeth appeared monstrous, wicked and almost pathological in these early scenes, the first scene of Act 5 proves that she is not quite the amoral villain she appeared to be. She commits suicide off stage and news of her demise is met with apathy by her husband who comments, *"she should have died hereafter"*. The audience must feel that she is deserving of her fate, dying unmourned even by her *"dearest partner of greatness."* **She was loathsome, but the death of the "fiend-like queen" inspires sympathy in the audience. Lady Macbeth was a woman who was at once brilliant, persuasive and intelligent, and yet was also naive and blinded to reality and to the consequences of her immoral deeds.**

"Deception is a major theme in the play *Macbeth.*" Discuss.

A conspiratorial atmosphere pervades *Macbeth*. This is after all a play about **secrets** and about **deception**. The Witches personify malevolence and use **deceit** and **half-truths** to manipulate their prey and draw the Kingdom of Scotland into disaster. Duncan, the goodly, virtuous king, is aware of the potential **treachery** that surrounds him, and yet he is betrayed by a man he absolutely trusts. Malcolm, Duncan's son and heir, learns from his father's errors and instead of becoming a victim of **deceit**, uses **cunning** and **guile** to test the loyalty of Macduff in *Act 4, Scene III*.

Lady Macbeth realizes the need for **pretence** to ensure the crown is secured. She frames the chamberlains for Duncan's murder and constantly calls on darkness to mask her crimes. She also **deceives** herself into believing that she could participate in a regicide and yet avoid the moral and psychological backlash, and by the end of the play, she has become a victim of her own **duplicity**. Macbeth, the tragic hero, practices **deception** to achieve his goals, but increasingly discards the need for **deceit** and instead chooses brute force and violence to protect his position. Ultimately, he too falls because of the **trickery** of the Witches and his desperate determination to **delude** himself.

The Witches' appearance in *Act 1, Scene I*, sets the tone for the rest of the play. Their words *"fair is foul, and foul is fair"* establish a sense that **nothing in this play is what it seems to be**. Their sinister words echo throughout *Act 1, Scene II*, when it becomes clear to the audience that Duncan, King of Scotland, has been betrayed by two Scottish noblemen, the Macdonwald and the Thane of Cawdor. Duncan is appalled by Cawdor's betrayal – *"No more that thane of Cawdor shall deceive / Our bosom interest"* – and orders *"his present death"*. He then orders that *"brave"* and *"noble"* Macbeth should be rewarded for his valour with

Cawdor's land and estate. The King is unaware of Macbeth's own potential for **deception** and **betrayal**.

In *Act 1, Scene IV*, Duncan comments, *"There's no art / To find the mind's construction in the face"*. He is fully aware of the treachery that surrounds him, and yet at the same time rewards and trusts Macbeth, his *"worthiest cousin"*, who harbours a deep and secret desire to usurp the King and claim the throne for himself. In *Act 1, Scene III*, Macbeth meets the Witches on the heath and is astonished, terrified and thrilled by the prophecy that he would be *"king hereafter"*. He is immediately aware of the implications of the prophecies which *"doth unfix my hair / And make my seated heart knock at my ribs"*, and yet he chooses to ignore Banquo's warning against the **deceit** and **trickery** of the *"instruments of darkness"*, who *"tell us truths, / Win us with honest trifles, to betray's / In deepest consequence."* Macbeth ignores his friend's warning because he wants to believe the Witches. Their power to **deceive** is only as strong as his desire to believe. Macbeth **deceives** himself, and propels himself towards disaster.

Macbeth's ambition is what creates his **self-delusion**. His wife also **deludes** herself and suffers the consequences. On receipt of Macbeth's letter in *Act 1, Scene V*, Lady Macbeth realizes the need to hide their plans – *"Come, thick night, / And pall thee in the dunnest smoke of hell"*. She is a master of deception, understanding the need to *"look like the innocent flower, / But be the serpent under't."* She plans to place the blame for her husband's crime on Duncan's grooms, commenting in *Act 2, Scene II*, *"I'll gild the faces of the grooms withal; / For it must seem their guilt."* She **appears** to be the epitome of evil, and yet, even at this stage, close examination suggests that she is **lying to herself**. She calls on the *"spirits / That tend on mortal thoughts"* to fill her *"from the crown to the toe, top-full / Of direst cruelty!"* She wants to stop up the *"access and passage to remorse"*, to stymie her conscience. Later, in *Act 2, Scene II*, she assures her husband that the guilt implicit in the act of regicide can be washed away – *"A little water clears us of this deed: / How easy is it, then!"* These words reverberate through the play until, in *Act 5, Scene I*, we see a psychologically tortured Lady Macbeth wonder aloud *"all the perfumes of Arabia will not sweeten this little hand."* She **deceived** herself because she wanted to believe actions do not have moral consequences, and she is destroyed by that **pretence**.

Lady Macbeth uses **deceit** to achieve her goals and is ultimately destroyed by the moral forces of reality. Her husband's tragic fall is rooted in exactly the same circumstances. Macbeth places the blame for Duncan's murder on Malcolm and Donalbain, who sensibly fled Scotland following their father's death, Donalbain commenting in *Act 2, Scene III*, *"There's daggers in men's smiles: the near in blood, / The nearer bloody."* In *Act 2, Scene IV*, Macduff notes that *"the king's two sons, / Are stol'n away and fled, which puts upon them / Suspicion of the deed."* Macbeth **appears** to have seized the crown successfully. By Act 3, it